An Encounter with Evil:

The Abraham Zapruder Story

By Jacob G. Hornberger

ISBN print version: 978-1-890687-32-8
ISBN ebook version: 978-1-890687-31-1

The Future of Freedom Foundation
11350 Random Hills Road
Suite 800
Fairfax VA 22030

(703) 934-6101

An Encounter with Evil:

The Abraham Zapruder Story

THE FUTURE *of* FREEDOM FOUNDATION

"There is nothing so threatening to systemic evil as those willing to stand against it regardless of the consequences."

—James W. Douglass,
JFK and the Unspeakable:
Why He Died and Why It Matters (2008)

This book is dedicated to Douglas Horne
for his unwavering commitment to truth and accuracy,
no matter what the cost.

Contents

Introduction

In 1983, the late psychiatrist M. Scott Peck wrote a book entitled *People of the Lie.* It was a study of evil in human affairs. There is, in fact, evil in the world, Peck observed.There are evil institutions, and there are evil people. When a person encounters either one, it can be a deeply unsettling experience.

This book is also about evil, more specifically, one person's chance encounter with evil, an encounter that ended up destroying the rest of his life. The dark secret involved in that encounter also resulted in a decades-long family taboo, extending long after that person who had that encounter with evil had passed away.

That person was Abraham Zapruder, the man who filmed the famous "Zapruder film" that captured the assassination of President John F. Kennedy on November 22, 1963. Through sheer happenstance, Zapruder's life and the lives of his family were changed forever — for better and for worse — by his encounter with evil.

Revolving around a book entitled *Twenty-Six Seconds: A Personal History of the Zapruder Film,* which was written in 2016 by Abraham Zapruder's granddaughter, Alexandra Zapruder, this book is also about the avoidance of evil, specifically what some people will do to avoid identifying and confronting it.

I have studied the Kennedy assassination for some 30 years and have written four books prior to this one relating to the assassination: *The Kennedy Autopsy; The Kennedy Autopsy 2; Regime Change: The JFK Assassination;* and *The CIA, Terrorism, and the Cold War: The Evil of the National Security State,* all of which were published by The Future of Freedom Foundation, a non-profit libertarian educational foundation that I founded in 1989 and where I serve as president. FFF's mission is to present the principled, uncompromising case for free markets, private property, and limited government.

FFF previously published a book entitled *JFK's War with the National Security Establishment: Why Kennedy Was Assassinated* by Douglas P. Horne, who served on the Assassination Records Review Board in the 1990s and later authored a five-volume book entitled *Inside the Assassination Records Review Board: The U.S. Government's Final Attempt to Reconcile the Conflicting Medical Evidence in the Assassination of JFK.*

FFF has also published two books on the Kennedy assassination by Jefferson Morley, a former reporter for the *Washington Post,* entitled *CIA & JFK: The Secret Assassination Files* and *Morley v. CIA: My Unfinished JFK Investigation.*

FFF has hosted two conferences relating to the Kennedy administration and assassination: "The National Security State and JFK" (2017) and "The National Security State and the Kennedy Assassination" (2021). The video presentations from those two conferences are posted in the multimedia section of FFF's website (fff.org).

The multimedia section also includes a five-part video presentation by Douglas Horne entitled "Altered History: Exposing Deceit and Deception in the Medical Evidence" and a 29-part video presentation called "The JFK Assassination" by me.

Additionally, FFF's website contains countless articles on the JFK assassination.

Like most people who have taken an interest in the Kennedy assassination, I was acquainted with the Zapruder film when I discovered Alexandra Zapruder's book in 2021. I thought it would be an interesting account of the Zapruder family's experience with the film. As I began reading it, however, I quickly realized that it was much more than that. Although she does not realize it and although it was no part of her intention, Alexandra Zapruder's book provides a fascinating insight into evil, what happens to people when they encounter evil, and what people will do to avoid acknowledging and confronting evil.

In her book and in various oral presentations about the book, videos of which can be found online, Alexandra informed people that there was a taboo within the Zapruder family against discussing her grandfather's film. Mind you, she denies that it was an actual taboo because, she says, there was not an expressed prohibition against discussing the film within the family. It was just understood by everyone in the family that the film was not to be discussed.

But that's precisely what a family taboo is. It isn't based on a formally expressed prohibition but rather on an implicit understanding that develops within a family, one with which everyone is expected to abide. In a lecture at Stockton University, Alexandra stated, "There was sort of a code inside the family. The decision to violate that code — to completely go against the prevailing culture of the family — was a very, very difficult one." In a talk at Southern Methodist University, she stated, "One of the hardest things in writing this book was to go so much against the prevailing culture in our family."

Usually, everyone within a family is scared to death to openly violate the taboo. As Alexandra put it in her book, "But I knew — we all knew — that the grown-ups really didn't want to talk about it. Why was another story. I'm sure I never thought to ask. It simply existed somewhere offstage, there and not there, fascinating and a little bit scary." She relates in her book that when she was 11 years old, she didn't feel comfortable asking her parents about the film and so she went into her school library to read what William Manchester, the author of *The Death of a President,* had written about it. In her book, she describes it as a furtive and secretive "clandestine" endeavor.

Alexandra wrote, "Although in my growing-up years I did not experience our family's silence around the film as particularly unusual, I grew to wonder what it was all about. Why *didn't* we ever talk about it? Why *didn't* I know more about this when I was growing up? Was there something that I needed to understand in order to make sense of the film's place in our family's life? Was there a personal legacy of the Zapruder film and, if so, what was it?"

A family taboo is almost always based on a dark secret, one that family members who are privy to the secret keep under wraps at all costs, including to other members of the family. Alexandra herself alludes to the possibility of such a dark secret in describing her decision to write her book. She acknowledges that she embarked on this journey with much trepidation over what she might discover about her family and about the family culture against discussing her grandfather's film.

Alexandra wrote: "I had no idea what kind of book it would be or what I would find if I dug into this history; I just knew that there would be questions and that I would want to find answers. At the same time, the thought of publishing a book — that most public of actions — flew in the face of at least one central life principle about the Zapruder film, which was that we did not invite conversation about it. I could see the conflict looming from a hundred miles away.... I would run through all the reasons that this was a terrible idea. I would parse out all the ways that I didn't want to do this.... As I worked, I struggled to reconcile the personal and historical imperative I felt to write this book with the worry that it would bring unintended and unwelcome consequences. These were real fears and they made the early years of this work difficult.... I had to believe that challenging the prevailing culture of silence around the film was a reflection of our values, not a contradiction of them, and that we would be better for incorporating this part of our past into our understanding of our family legacy."

In deciding to write her book when she was about 40 years old, Alexandra was, in fact, displaying a remarkable degree of courage. When one decides to violate a decades-long family taboo and attempts to discover the reasons for it, it is entirely possible — even likely — that the person will find things that she might not want to discover — that is, the dark family secrets that lie behind the taboo. As she put it in her book, "Before learning the history of the film, without fully knowing the details of my grandfather's and father's handling of it, I knew there was a risk that I would run into facts, details, or decisions that might run counter to what I expected or undermine my fierce tendency to defend them against criticism." She added, "What if I stumble on something I don't want to write about?"

As we will see in this book, on a sunny day in late November of 1963, Alexandra's grandfather, Abraham Zapruder, through sheer happenstance, was sucked into a maelstrom of evil that ended up forcing him to choose between two alternative courses of action, each of which came with horrific consequences. It was the choice that Zapruder ultimately made that ended up destroying the rest of his life and ultimately led to the dark secret that underlay the long family taboo against discussing his film.

As I finished reading her book, I concluded that notwithstanding the courage that Alexandra Zapruder displayed in deciding to write it, acknowledging and directly confronting the evil that her grandfather encountered 58 years ago proved to be too much for her. In this book, we will do what she was unable to do. We will identify and confront the evil that destroyed the rest of her grandfather's life and uncover the dark secret that led to the Zapruder family taboo against discussing his film. We will also discuss what needs to be done to eradicate that evil, which is still among us. Our national well-being depends on it.

1

LIFE's Lie

Immediately after President John F. Kennedy was declared dead at Parkland Hospital in Dallas, where he had been treated for gunshot wounds suffered while riding in a motorcade in downtown Dallas, two of his treating physicians, Dr. Kemp Clark, chairman of neurosurgery at Parkland, and Dr. Malcolm Perry, assistant professor of surgery at Parkland, held a press conference. They stated that President Kennedy had suffered two gunshot wounds: one in the back of his head and one in the front of his neck, near his Adam's apple. Perry stated three times that the throat wound appeared to be a wound of entry, which implied a shot having been fired from Kennedy's front.

Perry's statement became problematic, however, because the official story of the assassination quickly became that Kennedy had been shot only from the rear, by a man named Lee Harvey Oswald, who, it was said, had fired from the president's rear from the sixth floor of a building called the Texas School Book Depository.

The Friday, December 6, 1963, issue of *LIFE* magazine, which was published precisely two weeks after Kennedy's assassination, included an article by an associate editor named Paul Mandel, who had joined *LIFE* in 1957. The article, entitled "End to Nagging Rumors: The Six Critical Seconds," stated that the 8mm film that Dallas businessman Abraham Zapruder had taken of the assassination "shows the President turning his body far around to the right as he waves to someone in the crowd. His throat is exposed — toward the sniper's nest — just before he clutches it."

But there is a big problem with Mandel's statement. It was a lie. Although most people didn't realize it at the time, Abraham Zapruder's film showed no such thing.

What does Abraham Zapruder's granddaughter Alexandra say in her book *Twenty-Six Seconds* about this knowing, deliberate, and intentional lie about the contents of her grandfather's film? Not very much, and what she does say reveals a lot about the lack of depth in her exploration into the family taboo against discussing the film.

Without even mentioning Mandel's false description of Kennedy turning around and facing the Texas School Book Depository, Alexandra simply pointed out that Mandel "went on to challenge the main arguments against the single shooter, though some of his facts are mistaken...."

Let's distinguish a mistake from a lie. They are two completely different things. A mistake is when a writer uses a comma when he intended to use a semi-colon, or when a driver turns left when he meant to turn right, or when someone addresses Mr. Smith as Mr. Jones.

A lie is completely different. It involves a specific intent to deceive. There are big lies and little lies, but they all have one thing in common: a mental state in which a person is knowingly stating a falsehood with an intent to deceive other people.

Contrary to Alexandra's assertion, Mandel's statement wasn't a "mistake." It couldn't be. It had to be a lie. How can we be so certain? Because *LIFE* magazine had ownership and possession of the Zapruder film at the time the Mandel article was published. When she wrote her book, Alexandra was well aware of that fact. Since she had seen the film a number of times, she also knew for certain that her grandfather's film does not show President Kennedy turning around and facing the building from which Oswald is said to have fired at the president.

That's not to say, however, that Mandel was aware that the information contained in his article was false. My hunch is that he never personally saw the film and instead was relying on false information that someone else had fed him. I say that because as a respected journalist who had been working at *LIFE* for six years, he would have known that if he got caught deliberately making up a false story, he'd be finished in journalism. Since *LIFE* magazine had possession of the film, its executives would have easily known that one of their writers had written a false story about what the film contained. Moreover, it is impossible to come up with a motive for Mandel making up such a story, especially since he would have quickly gotten caught in the act of lying about a critically important aspect of the Kennedy assassination.

Interestingly — and revealingly — when Alexandra was researching her book, she had the opportunity to talk to *LIFE* executives about her grandfather's film. Based on the account she gave in her book, she never asked any of them if there was an explanation for what she refers to as Mandel's "mistake," which *LIFE* never explained, corrected, or apologized for. Alexandra obviously did not want to go down that road, perhaps because she subconsciously knew that by doing so, she would be getting close to the outer edges of the centrum of evil that had enveloped her grandfather some 50 years before.

Please permit me a small digression that you might find interesting. The November 29 issue of *LIFE* magazine had already gone to press by November 22 but had not yet hit the newsstands. That issue contained an article detailing political corruption between Vice President Lyndon Johnson and his former Senate aide Bobby Baker. If the corruption charges were true — and there is every reason to believe that they were — it was a virtual certainty that Johnson would be facing a federal criminal indictment. Moreover, Kennedy would almost certainly have dropped Johnson from the ticket for the 1964 presidential race, which, according to some sources, he was looking for any excuse to do. It turns out that U.S. Attorney General Robert Kennedy, the president's brother, was secretly feeding information about LBJ's corruption to *LIFE* magazine. That's because he loathed Johnson, just as Johnson loathed him. Once the assassination occurred, the article about Johnson in the November 29 issue was squelched and replaced with black-and-white photographs from the Zapruder film. It's unfortunate that when Alexandra was talking to those *LIFE* executives, she apparently failed to ask them to comment about this matter and to explain why *LIFE* executives never went ahead and published the article about Johnson's corruption in a later issue of the magazine. It would be fascinating to know how they would have answered.

In any event, when that December 6, 1963, issue of *LIFE* magazine came out, it is a virtual certainty that Abraham Zapruder read the Mandel article. We can be virtually certain of this by reviewing how it was that Zapruder's film had come into the hands of *LIFE* magazine by the time it published Mandel's article.

We will begin, however, by reviewing Zapruder's personal background. As Alexandra describes in her book, her grandfather had come to America as a child of Russian immigrants. As a Russian Jew, he and his family had experienced extreme poverty as well as virulent anti-Semitism. That early life experience would play a critically important role in the choice that Zapruder would later be forced to make as a result of his encounter with evil in the aftermath of the Kennedy assassination.

Having little formal education, Abe Zapruder went into the New York garment business, where he worked for many years. While living in New York City, he met the woman who would become his wife, Lillian Shapovnick. While she too had little formal education, Alexandra describes her as being "street smart," a quality that would play an important role in the choice that her husband would make many years later in his encounter with evil.

In 1941, Abe and Lillian Zapruder left New York and moved to Dallas, where he accepted a job with a local sportswear company named Nardis. In the mid-1950s, he and a man named Abe Schwartz opened a dress store called Jennifer Juniors, located in the Dal-Tex Building, which was just across the street from the Texas School Book Depository. Schwartz later died, and his partnership interest was taken over by his son Erwin, who was in charge of the marketing end of the firm in November 1963.

As with any start-up business, the early years of the firm were difficult. Alexandra writes that her grandfather later prided himself on having cleaned the toilets and swept the floors. By the time the 1960s came around, however, the company was highly successful, generating some $2 million per year in sales. In today's dollars, that would be equivalent to $18 million. While the Zapruders had initially lived in the poorer Oak Cliff section of Dallas, by the 1960s, they were living in Highland Park, the most expensive and exclusive part of Dallas.

Alexandra describes what can only be called an idyllic marriage between her grandparents. Their lives were filled with love, joy, excitement, and fun. She writes that "theirs was a big love that endured for the 37 years of their marriage." Abraham loved playing the piano, which he had taught himself to do. But his favorite hobby was making home movies, which he had been doing for some 30 years, especially after his two children, Henry and Myrna, were born. While Zapruder wasn't a professional photographer, there is no doubt that he would have been considered a highly proficient amateur filmmaker.

Through a dark twist of fate, however, the happy life that Abraham and Lillian Zapruder had been living together for some 30 years in 1963 came to a screeching halt on November 22. It was on that day that Abraham Zapruder took his home movie camera — a high-end, expensive 8mm Bell and Howell Zoomatic Director Series 414 PD — to Dealey Plaza in downtown Dallas to film President Kennedy and his wife Jacqueline as they motorcaded on the way to the Dallas Trade Mart, where the president was scheduled to give a speech. Filming from atop a pedestal near what is now known as "the grassy knoll," Zapruder ended up capturing the Kennedy assassination on film.

On the night of the assassination, Zapruder was contacted by telephone by a man named Richard Stolley, who was *LIFE*'s Pacific Coast regional editor. Stolley told Zapruder that *LIFE* was interested in purchasing print-media rights to his film. The two men met the next morning — Saturday morning — at Zapruder's office to negotiate the purchase and sale of print-media rights to what would ultimately become known famously as the "Zapruder film." During their negotiation, Zapruder showed the film to Stolley on his personal 8mm movie projector, which he had brought from home.

Although there were other media outlets that wanted the film, Zapruder had little interest in selling it to anyone but *LIFE*. That's because he wanted to be certain that the film would be used in a responsible way, and he trusted *LIFE* magazine to do that. Relying primarily on the power of pictures to tell a story, *LIFE,* which had seven million subscribers in 1963, including Abraham and Lillian Zapruder, was the most popular and respected magazine in America in the 1950s and early 1960s.

On Saturday, November 23, Stolley and Zapruder struck a deal in which *LIFE* agreed to pay Zapruder the sum of $50,000 for worldwide print-media rights to his film. Zapruder retained the motion-picture rights but agreed that he would not permit the film to be shown as a motion picture until November 29, which was exactly one week after the assassination.

Under the terms of their agreement, *LIFE* was to borrow the original film for a week and then return it to Zapruder (presumably on November 29) in exchange for one of three copies that Zapruder had made on the day of the assassination. On Saturday afternoon, Stolley put the original film on an airplane from Dallas to Chicago, where *LIFE*'s national printing plant was located. Zapruder retained one of the three first-day copies. He had loaned the other two copies to the U.S. Secret Service in Dallas on Friday night, November 22.

It's important to keep in mind that in terms of actual purchasing power, the sale of the print rights of still images of the movie for $50,000 was in today's dollars about $454,000. (To calculate the value of money in previous years compared to today, Google "$50,000 in 1963 worth today" or go to https://www.usinflationcalculator.com.)

By Sunday night, November 24, however, something had caused *LIFE* magazine to change its mind. Stolley contacted Zapruder's attorney and told him that *LIFE* was now interested in purchasing the motion-picture rights in addition to the print-media rights to the film. It was an unusual decision, given that *LIFE* specialized in print media and had no means of exhibiting the film as a motion picture, like television did.

Zapruder and Stolley met again on Monday morning, this time at the office of Zapruder's attorney. Representatives of several other media outlets were also present attempting to buy the motion-picture rights to the film. Although Zapruder showed his copy of the film separately to every media representative who intended to bid on the motion-picture rights, he ultimately decided to go with Stolley's offer, not only because the amount *LIFE* was offering — $150,000 — was huge but also because he trusted *LIFE* to treat his film with decency and respect.

In return for *LIFE*'s promise to pay Zapruder $150,000 (instead of the initial $50,000 for the print rights only), Zapruder agreed to sell his film and all three copies to *LIFE*. (Zapruder would be obligated to deliver to *LIFE* the two copies that had been loaned to the Secret Service after receiving them back.) It should be noted that *LIFE* also agreed to pay Zapruder 50 percent of all receipts from motion-picture rights after *LIFE*'s $150,000 purchase price was recouped. Thus, *LIFE* clearly led Zapruder to believe that he would be making a lot more money than what they were paying him up front, at least with respect to motion-picture rights relating to the film.

What seemed odd is that instead of paying Zapruder a lump-sum payment up front, *LIFE* instead structured the payments in annual installments of $25,000. After all, it's not like $150,000 would have placed a financial strain on a huge magazine like *LIFE,* which was owned by Time Life. As it turned out, however, it was that structured payout that would be an important factor when Zapruder would later be faced with making the critically important choice that evil would force him to make and that would end up altering his life for the worse.

It was the receipt of that large sum of money — $150,000 (or the equivalent of about $1.3 million today) — that Alexandra Zapruder ends up citing as the one of the two reasons for the family taboo against discussing her grandfather's film. After embarking on her courageous journey to discover the truth about her family's experience with the film, she ends up concluding that her grandfather was so conflicted over receiving so much money that it led to deep inner turmoil and consternation, which ultimately resulted in the decades-long family taboo against discussing the film.

With all due respect, that is pure nonsense. If Abraham Zapruder was so guilt-ridden about receiving so much money for his film of the assassination, he had an easy remedy: inform *LIFE* magazine that he was waiving the balance of the yearly installments or simply give the money away. In fact, he actually did donate the first $25,000 installment to the family of J. D. Tippit, the Dallas policeman who was killed soon after Kennedy was assassinated. But that donation was not made because her grandfather was terribly guilt-ridden over having received so much money for his film but rather as a strategic way to avoid potential anti-Semitic accusations that he was profiting off the president's assassination.

From the time Abraham Zapruder returned to his office immediately after the assassination with his film, which he prudently locked in his office safe, he had one aim in mind: to sell the film for as much money as he could get. He openly and honestly acknowledged that to the Secret Service agent in charge of the Dallas field office, Forrest Sorrels, who helped Zapruder get his film developed on the afternoon of the assassination. In an affidavit written in January 1964, Sorrels wrote: "Mr. Zapruder agreed to furnish me with a copy of this film with the understanding that it was strictly for official use of the Secret Service and that it would not be shown or given to any newspapers or magazines as he expected to sell the film for as high a price as he could get for it."

Zapruder was a canny businessman, and he knew immediately after the assassination that he had something of value in his film. When he met with Richard Stolley on the Saturday morning after the assassination, he let Stolley do all the offering. Every time Stolley would make an offer, Zapruder would ignore the offer and just continue making small talk. He let Stolley continue bidding against himself until he reached Zapruder's price of $50,000 (which, again, was the equivalent of receiving $454,000 today). Just two days later, Zapruder was successful in getting that amount tripled. Clearly any internal conflict that Abraham Zapruder was having over receiving so much money for his 26-second film did not prevent him from seeking and getting top dollar for his film.

Alexandra concludes that the other reason for the family taboo was her grandfather's deep grief over President Kennedy's murder, which he had personally witnessed and filmed. In describing her stealthy search in her school library for William Manchester's book when she was 11 years old, Alexandra wrote: "I read that he was, in Manchester's words, 'a casualty, one of the weekend's walking wounded,' so traumatized that, unlike nearly everyone else, he shunned the TV news coverage of the assassination and the funeral. I remember reading these pages over and over again, drawn to and horrified by the idea of my grandfather so broken and filled with sorrow."

I couldn't help but smile when I read that passage because when the televised activities associated with the Kennedy funeral began to be shown on the Monday morning after the assassination, Zapruder was in his lawyer's office showing his film to all those media outlets that were interested in purchasing the motion-picture rights to the film. Thus, while it's certainly possible that Zapruder was too traumatized to watch the actual funeral on Monday afternoon, he certainly wasn't too traumatized to negotiate a contract on Monday morning that would ultimately bring him the equivalent of $1.3 million (in today's value) for the sale of his film.

It should also be noted that millions of people were grief-stricken over the murder of John F. Kennedy, including lots of other people in Dealey Plaza who personally witnessed the assassination. None of them ever reported that their grief led to a 50-year-long family taboo against discussing the Kennedy assassination.

Moreover, Zapruder died in 1970, only seven years after the assassination. Yet, the Zapruder family taboo against discussing the film continued for another 40 years. But why? If the taboo was based on Abraham Zapruder's grief over JFK's death or misgivings over receiving so much money for his film, why would the family taboo extend far beyond his death?

When the November 29 issue of *LIFE* came out, you can rest assured that Abraham Zapruder read every page of coverage of the Kennedy assassination, especially since that issue contained photographs of frames from his own film.

Like millions of other Americans, it is a virtual certainty that he also read the next issue — the December 6 issue — in which Paul

Mandel's article appeared, given the deep interest that most everyone, especially Abraham Zapruder, had in the assassination.

Readers of *LIFE* magazine would have had no reason to doubt Mandel's truthfulness and accuracy. That's because hardly anyone in the public had seen Zapruder's film.

In fact, if *LIFE* magazine had had its way, the public would never have seen the Zapruder film. That's because after *LIFE* purchased the film from Zapruder, *LIFE*'s publisher, a man named C. D. Jackson, locked it away in a vault and vowed to never let anyone see it.

In other words, while *LIFE* was interested in standard journalistic reporting and commercial use of print stills in its magazine when it purchased the print rights to Zapruder's film on Saturday, by the time Monday had rolled around, the situation had changed dramatically. Now the name of the game became suppressing the film as a motion picture (as well as using selected, controlled portions of the film as print stills in the magazine).

Jackson's desire to prevent people from seeing the Zapruder film as a motion picture was why *LIFE* now wanted to purchase all ownership rights to the film (as well to all three copies of the film) and why it wished to take physical possession of the original and all three copies of the film. It is also why *LIFE* offered an enormously large sum of money for the film (and the three copies) — $150,000 (the equivalent of $1.3 million today), or triple what *LIFE* had agreed on Saturday to pay Zapruder for just the print rights to the film.

In other words, by Monday, *LIFE* was willing to pay Zapruder an additional $100,000 (or the equivalent of $908,000 today) not for the purpose of making money off the film through licensing it as a motion picture but instead to prevent people from ever seeing the film.

As an aside, it's worth asking why the contract provided for Zapruder to receive additional revenue from commercial use of the film as a motion picture given that *LIFE* intended to simply lock away the film and never let anyone see it.

Alexandra explains in her book that the reason for Jackson's decision to suppress the film was that he had decided that he needed to protect the American people from seeing the violence depicted in the film. When I read that, I could not help but laugh. I asked myself: How can anyone actually believe such nonsense? It brought to mind the reason that Jack Ruby cited for having shot and killed Lee Harvey Oswald. Ruby, who had close ties to the Mafia, claimed that the reason he killed Oswald was to ensure that Jacqueline Kennedy would not have to return to Dallas to testify at a trial. That was absurd, and so was Jackson's rationale for suppressing the Zapruder film.

But Alexandra clearly buys into this paternalistic rationale for suppressing the most famous home movie in history. She says that this was before Americans had become accustomed to seeing violence, as with scenes from the Vietnam War and the 9/11 attacks. I guess the scenes from the massive death tolls totaling twenty million in World War I, seventy-five million in World War II, including the Nazi death camps and the atomic bombings of Hiroshima and Nagasaki, and five million in the Korean War don't count.

There is another possible reason, a much more likely reason, for Jackson's intentional suppression of the Zapruder film, one that we will explore later in this book. Suffice it to say for now that it revolves around the evil that ended up enveloping and destroying the life of Abraham Zapruder and that ultimately led to his family's taboo against discussing his film.

It is impossible to know what went through Abraham Zapruder's mind when he read Paul Mandel's article, but one thing is certain: No one knew the Zapruder film better than Abraham Zapruder. His partner Erwin Schwartz later told the author of a book entitled *Bloody Treason,* Noel Twyman, that he (Schwartz) viewed the film some 15 times during the weekend of the assassination. That means that Zapruder must have viewed it at least that many times and, almost certainly, several more times, given that he was showing it to so many people, including his family, local Kodak representatives, the Secret Service, and the various media representatives who were interested in purchasing it, both on the Saturday morning and Monday morning following the assassination. If there is anyone who knew the 26-second Zapruder film by heart, it was Abraham Zapruder.

Thus, Zapruder had to know that *LIFE* magazine was lying when Mandel claimed that Zapruder's film showed Kennedy turning around and facing his supposed assassin when he was shot in the throat. Zapruder would have immediately asked himself an important question: Why would *LIFE* magazine pay the equivalent of $1.3 million for his film, permanently sequester it (after leading Zapruder to believe that he was going to make more money from motion-picture rights), and then lie about its contents?

There is one thing that Zapruder almost certainly would have done to figure out the answer to his question. He would have gone to his trusted confidant — his wife Lillian. "They are lying about my film," we can imagine him saying to her. "My film shows no such thing."

And we can also imagine how the street-smart Lillian would have responded. "I have no doubts that you're right, Abe. But there are things that are much bigger than us that we simply cannot understand. We have to trust that *LIFE* magazine is lying for a reason. We need to keep our heads down and not rock the boat."

2

Skullduggery

In the 1990s — more than 30 years after the assassination of President Kennedy — an independent governmental agency named the Assassination Records Review Board discovered the existence of a man named Roger Boyajian, who told a remarkable story to the ARRB. As we will see later in this book, Boyajian's story leads inexorably to the Zapruder film, specifically frame 313, which depicts a fatal gunshot that hit Kennedy in the head.

On the day of the assassination, Boyajian was a U.S. Marine sergeant in charge of a Marine security detail at the Bethesda National Naval Medical Center morgue, where U.S. Navy personnel were conducting an autopsy on Kennedy's body. In a written after-action report submitted to his superiors dated November 26, 1963, Boyajian stated, "At approximately 1835 the casket was received at the morgue entrance and taken inside." Boyajian was referring to a casket containing Kennedy's body. He had actually kept an onion-skin copy of his report, a copy of which he sent to the ARRB.

Why was Boyajian's story so remarkable? Because the official entry time of President Kennedy's body into the Bethesda morgue was 8 p.m. ("2000 hours" in military time), almost an hour and a half after the 6:35 p.m. ("1835 hours") entry time stated in Boyajian's report. The 8 p.m. time is when Kennedy's body was carried into the morgue by a military color guard known as the Joint Service Casket Team, or "honor guard," which later filed its own report establishing the 8 p.m. entry time.

Questions naturally arise. Why would the U.S. military be sneaking the president's body into the morgue almost an hour-and-a-half before the official entry time of 8 p.m.? Why had the military never disclosed the early introduction of Kennedy's body into the morgue? How was the military able to introduce the body into the morgue at two separate times?

It is worth mentioning that Boyajian and his report were kept secret from the Warren Commission, the official governmental entity that ostensibly investigated the assassination of President Kennedy in 1964. Boyajian's report was also kept secret from the U.S. House Select Committee on Assassinations, which reopened the investigation into Kennedy's assassination in the mid-1970s.

No U.S. Navy official has ever challenged the veracity of Roger Boyajian or the authenticity of his report. It's also worth mentioning that the U.S. military never disclosed Boyajian's report to the ARRB, as it was required to do by the President John F. Kennedy Assassination Records Collection Act of 1992, which mandated that all federal agencies disclose their JFK assassination-related records to the public.

It would not be unreasonable to assume that the military was up to no good with its early secret introduction of President Kennedy's body into the Bethesda morgue and its deliberate effort to keep that fact secret from official investigators.

Let's review how the JFK Records Act and the ARRB came into existence.

In 1964, the Warren Commission issued its official conclusions regarding its investigation into the assassination. It concluded that the president had been shot by a communist former U.S. Marine named Lee Harvey Oswald, who purportedly had fired three rifle shots from the sixth floor of the Texas School Book Depository, with two of the bullets hitting the president as he motorcaded through Dealey Plaza.

Two days later, Oswald himself was assassinated by Jack Ruby. Federal officials quickly concluded that the Kennedy assassination case was now closed, and the Warren Report confirmed that conclusion.

Most Americans, however, didn't buy it. The whole scenario just seemed to be a bit too pat. Ruby's assassination of Oswald, who openly and publicly proclaimed his innocence and even claimed that he was being framed, had all the characteristics of an attempt to silence Oswald before he could be brought to trial. Moreover, if the assassination was really committed by a "lone nut" who just happened to be at the right place at the right time, why was the Warren Commission's investigation shrouded in secrecy?

Public doubts about the official scenario of the assassination led to the reopening of the assassination by the U.S. House Select Committee on Assassinations in the mid-1970s. After an extensive formal reinvestigation, the committee concluded that Oswald had, in fact, killed the president but had conspired with unknown other people to commit the assassination. At the conclusion of the hearings, the HSCA decided that its most sensitive staff files and official records relating to the Kennedy assassination would be kept secret from the American people for 50 years, until the year 2029. Other records classified by the Warren Commission also remained sequestered and unavailable to the public.

In 1991, Hollywood producer and director Oliver Stone came out with his movie *JFK,* which rejected the official version of the assassination and posited instead that the assassination was a highly sophisticated regime-change operation orchestrated and carried out by the U.S. national-security establishment, much like the U.S. regime-change operations that had taken place against political leaders in Iran in 1953, Guatemala in 1954, Indonesia in 1958, the Congo in 1961, and those attempted unsuccessfully against Cuba from 1961 to 1963.

At the end of *JFK,* Stone included a blurb that advised people that the HSCA was keeping its assassination-related records secret until 2029, which suggested that the government was continuing a cover-up of its regime-change operation in Dallas.

That blurb produced a public outcry that ended up pressuring Congress to enact the JFK Records Collection Act of 1992, which mandated that all federal agencies, including the CIA, Pentagon, Secret Service, and FBI, release their assassination-related records to the public. The JFK Records Act also mandated that Congress would have to release its own assassination-related records, including classified files from the Senate's "Church Committee" and the House of Representatives's HSCA.

To enforce the act, the ARRB was brought into existence. From September of 1994 until it went out of existence at the end of September 1998, the ARRB, an independent executive-branch agency, was successful in bringing about the release of tens of thousands of official assassination-related records that had been kept secret for more than 30 years.

However, there were two negative aspects of the JFK Records Act. One was that federal agencies were authorized, on grounds of protecting intelligence-gathering "sources" and "methods" or protecting "national security," to keep some of their assassination-related records secret until October of 2017, which would be long after the ARRB would go out of existence.

When that date came in 2017 under President Donald Trump, the CIA petitioned Trump for another four-year extension of time for secrecy, citing "national security" as its rationale. Although Trump had initially stated that he was going to order all the secret documents to be released to the public, he ended up granting the CIA's request for continued secrecy for the vast majority of the records (a few of the records were released). At the risk of belaboring the obvious, it was difficult to understand how "national security," whatever definition one places on that nebulous term, would be threatened by the release of 50-year-old records relating to the Kennedy assassination.

When that extension of time was up in October 2021, President Biden granted the CIA's request for yet another extension of time for secrecy, this time to December 2022, on grounds of "national security" and purported problems meeting the deadline arising from COVID-19.

The other negative aspect of the JFK Records Act was that it prohibited the ARRB from reinvestigating any aspect of the assassination. Thus, if the ARRB were to disclose records relating to the assassination that appeared incriminating or that challenged the conclusions of the Warren Commission or the HSCA, it would nonetheless be prohibited from investigating the matter. It's worth noting that the five board members of the ARRB strictly enforced the prohibition. Staff members were repeatedly warned that reinvestigating the JFK assassination was outside the ARRB's charter. Moreover, the culture and mores of the small agency made it clear that if any staff members openly advocated a reinvestigation or were caught reinvestigating, their employment would be endangered.

The staff of the ARRB was, however, permitted to engage in actions designed to "clarify the record," especially matters relating to the autopsy that the national-security establishment had conducted on the president's body on the evening of the assassination. Former Ohio Congressman Louis Stokes, who had chaired the HSCA during the 1970s, had encouraged the ARRB's five board members before they commenced their official duties in 1995 to do all they could to "clarify the record" relating to JFK's autopsy, since Stokes realized that almost no one had been satisfied with the HSCA's reexamination of the medical evidence.

That's how the ARRB came to discover the existence of Roger Boyajian. When ARRB staffers contacted him and secured his statement, they were ostensibly engaged in "clarifying the record" relating to President Kennedy's autopsy.

Boyajian was not the only person who witnessed the early secret entry of the president's body into the Bethesda morgue. His story was corroborated by Dennis David, a Navy hospital corpsman who was filling the role of "Chief of the Day" at Bethesda NNMC on the day of the assassination. David told the ARRB that he assembled and supervised the Navy working party that carried the president's casket into the morgue well before the official entry time of 8 p.m. David confirmed to the ARRB what had become public knowledge in 1981 after the HSCA shut down, which was that his working party of Navy personnel, acting on the orders of the Secret Service, met a black Cadillac hearse (a funeral vehicle common in the mortuary trade) containing men in suits outside the morgue loading dock at the rear of the hospital facility. The team then offloaded a lightweight, ordinary "shipping casket" made of aluminum (commonly used in transporting bodies on airplanes and trains) from the hearse and carried it into the morgue. The shipping casket was clearly not in any way similar to the heavy, ornate bronze casket into which Kennedy's body had been placed at Parkland Hospital in Dallas.

David was not the only person who witnessed the president's body being brought into the morgue in a shipping casket. Three other witnesses to the same event were Navy enlisted men Paul O'Connor, Donald Rebentisch, and Floyd Riebe.

The ARRB also uncovered a "First Call Sheet" report from Gawler's Funeral Home, the prestigious mortuary in Washington, D.C., that was in charge of embalming the president's body after the autopsy inside the morgue. The report, dated November 23, 1963, stated: "Body removed from metal shipping casket at USNH at Beth."

Moreover, hospital personnel at Parkland had wrapped the president's body in two white sheets. Yet, O'Connor, a hospital corpsman, told staff investigators for the HSCA that when JFK's body was taken out of the shipping casket at the Bethesda morgue, it was encased in a zippered body bag, with a sheet wrapped only around the head. John VanHoesen, a mortician with Gawler's Funeral Home, told the ARRB that he had seen Kennedy's body arrive at the Bethesda morgue in a "black, zippered plastic pouch."

Significantly, the secret entry of the president's body was also inadvertently confirmed by sworn testimony given by Army Col. Pierre Finck, one of the three military pathologists who conducted the official autopsy on the president's body. In 1969, in a state criminal prosecution in New Orleans of a man named Clay Shaw, Finck testified that he received a telephone call from Commander James Humes, a Navy pathologist who, along with another Navy pathologist named "J" Thornton Boswell, was ostensibly in charge of the autopsy that was conducted on the president's body. The purpose of Humes's call was to invite Finck to participate in the autopsy. Finck stated that Humes's call to him came in at 8 p.m. Finck testified that during that telephone call, Humes told Finck that they already had a fully developed set of x-rays of the president's head. Yet, 8 p.m. ("2000 hours") was precisely the time that the president's body was, according to the official report of the Joint Service Casket Team, being brought into the morgue for the first time.

The question naturally arises: How could Humes and Boswell already have a set of developed x-rays of the president's head by 8 p.m. if the body was being brought into the morgue for the first time at 8 p.m.? No x-rays had been conducted in Dallas. Moreover, the ARRB determined through its depositions of the x-ray technicians that it took about 30 minutes to fully develop the cranial x-rays. There is but one answer: The president's body was secretly brought into the morgue at 6:35 p.m., just as Boyajian's report said it was, and the president's cranium was x-rayed well before 8 p.m., when Humes called Finck at home.

After the cranial x-rays and an initial round of photographs were taken, JFK's body was then secretly placed back into the Dallas casket, reunited with the Joint Service Casket Team (which had lost track of where it was), and was then reintroduced by them into the morgue at 8 p.m., as noted in their after-action report. The reintroduction of the president's body into the Dallas casket was accomplished through a scheme orchestrated by a Secret Service agent named Roy Kellerman, who was in charge of physical security for JFK's trip to Texas. At about 7:17 p.m., the empty bronze Dallas casket was secretly carried into the morgue anteroom by Kellerman, Secret Service agent William Greer, and two FBI agents, Francis O'Neill and James Sibert. O'Neill and Sibert did not know that the heavy Dallas casket (over 400 pounds) was empty and did not contain JFK's body, whereas the two Secret Service agents — Kellerman and Greer — most certainly did know.

Subsequently (unknown to the two FBI agents, who were sequestered in another room outside the morgue proper), the president's body was placed back into the Dallas casket (after the cranial x-rays and an initial set of photographs had been taken). The bronze casket (with JFK's body now back inside it) was then placed back into a light gray Navy ambulance (there were two in use that night) and was then reunited with the Joint Service Casket Team, whose members then ceremonially carried it into the morgue at 8 p.m. Since the skullduggery had been done in secret, the Joint Service Casket Team naturally assumed that the 8 p.m. time was when the body was first introduced into the morgue. (They knew nothing about the earlier entry of JFK's body, inside the shipping casket, into the morgue at 6:35 p.m.) Each casket entry involved different participants, at distinctively different times, and they have conclusively been proven to be separate events. The entire episode was based on secrecy and deception, traits that characterize what psychiatrist M. Scott Peck, in his study of evil, termed "people of the lie."

We will conclude this chapter with an examination of how and why the autopsy on President Kennedy's body was conducted by the U.S. national-security establishment.

Immediately after President Kennedy was declared dead at Parkland Hospital, the Dallas County medical examiner, Dr. Earl Rose, declared his intention to conduct an autopsy on the president's body. This was not only normal procedure in a criminal case but was also procedure required by law. At that time, there was no federal law that criminalized the assassination of the president. Kennedy's assassination was an unambiguous murder case under state law, and Texas law required Rose to conduct an autopsy on the president's body.

At that point, a team of Secret Service agents went into action. Brandishing guns and implicitly threatening to shoot anyone who got in their way, the agents declared that Rose was not going to be permitted to conduct an autopsy on Kennedy's body. Declaring that they were acting on orders, emitting a stream of profanities, and physically picking up Rose and removing him as an obstacle, they forced their way out of Parkland Hospital, over Rose's vehement objections. Hospital personnel, some of whom had just tried to save the president's life, later said they were scared to death during the ordeal.

The head of that Secret Service team was none other than Roy Kellerman, the man who later that evening would be orchestrating the casket-switching event at the Bethesda morgue.

There is something else about Kellerman that is worth noting. He was the Secret Service agent in the passenger seat in the limousine in which President Kennedy was shot. After the first shot was fired, Kellerman never made a single effort to crawl over the seat and use his body to cover Kennedy, as he was supposed to do. Instead, he just sat there like a bump on a log, simply turning to view the president before he received the fatal gunshot (or gunshots) to the head.

After Kellerman and his team forcibly removed the heavy, ornate bronze casket containing the president's body from Parkland

Hospital, they transported it to Dallas's Love Field, where the new president, Lyndon Johnson, was waiting for it. It was then loaded onto Air Force One, on which Johnson was now traveling, and flown to Andrews Air Force Base in Maryland. At Andrews, the Dallas casket was then loaded onto a light gray Navy cardiac ambulance and driven to the front entrance of the Bethesda National Naval Medical Center. Among those inside the ambulance were the deceased president's wife, Jacqueline Kennedy, and his brother Bobby Kennedy. The ambulance arrived at the front of the Bethesda facility at 6:55 p.m., at which point Jacqueline and Bobby exited the vehicle, entered the facility, and went to an upper floor to await the finishing of the autopsy and the embalming of the president's body.

Two Navy enlisted x-ray technicians — Jerrol Custer and Edward Reed — stated that they were involved in taking x-rays of the president's body during the earlier 6:35 p.m. - 8:00 p.m. time period. When Custer was going from the morgue to the fourth-floor x-ray department after the early introduction of JFK's body into the morgue, he saw Jacqueline and Bobby entering the front door of the facility, which confirmed that the bronze ceremonial casket in the ambulance that was parked in front of the facility had to be empty.

After Jacqueline and Bobby exited the ambulance, it sat outside the front curb for 12 minutes before being driven around to the morgue loading dock at the rear of the building, where, as described above, the (empty) Dallas casket was then carted into the building by Kellerman, Greer, O'Neill, and Sibert. The president's body was then placed back into the Dallas casket and taken to the Navy ambulance and placed inside of it. The ambulance was then driven back to the front of the facility, where it was reunited with the Joint Service Casket Team, which then proceeded to carry the casket into the building at 8 p.m. The autopsy began at 8:15 p.m.

The evidence establishing the secret early entry of Kennedy's body into the morgue obviously has ominous implications. The evidence necessarily means that when the Dallas casket left Andrews Air Force Base and was driven to the front of the Bethesda facility in the Navy ambulance, it was, unbeknownst to Jacqueline Kennedy and Bobby Kennedy, empty. Somewhere between Dallas and Andrews Air Force Base, the president's body had been secretly removed from the Dallas casket, placed into a body bag and a shipping casket, and then secretly carried into the Bethesda morgue at 6:35 p.m. — almost one and a half hours before the 8 p.m. official entry time of the body into the morgue recorded in the official after-action report of the Joint Service Casket Team.

We will later examine a rather nasty attack that Alexandra Zapruder leveled against Douglas Horne, who served on the staff of the ARRB from 1995 until 1998 and is the author of a watershed five-volume book on the Kennedy assassination entitled *Inside the Assassination Records Review Board: The U.S. Government's Final Attempt to Reconcile the Conflicting Medical Evidence in the Assassination of JFK.* Horne published his book some 11 years after his service on the ARRB. It is not an easy read but it is, in my opinion, one of the two best books ever written on the Kennedy assassination. (The other is *JFK and the Unspeakable: Why He Died and Why It Matters* by James W. Douglass.) Horne's book had such a powerful impact on me that I dedicated my book *The Kennedy Autopsy* to him, and I have also decided to dedicate this book to him as well.

Although Horne's book focuses mostly on fraud in the Kennedy autopsy, including the early introduction of President Kennedy's body into the Bethesda morgue, volume IV of his book contains a detailed and extensive chapter on the Zapruder film. Therefore, in researching the Kennedy assassination, in general, and Horne's perspectives on the Zapruder film, in particular, it is a virtual certainty that Alexandra Zapruder became acquainted with what Horne had to say about the fraudulent autopsy, including the evidence establishing the secret introduction of the president's body into the morgue. Yet, she doesn't even mention any of this in her book.

Now, I'm sure she would say that the reason she didn't do so is because it didn't have anything to do with her grandfather's film. But how wrong she would be. In fact, the national-security establishment's fraudulent autopsy, including its secret early introduction of the president's body into the Bethesda morgue, has everything to do with the Zapruder film, as we will see later in this book. In my opinion, Alexandra Zapruder's failure to address these matters in her book demonstrates her subconscious desire to avoid acknowledging and confronting the evil that ended up consuming her grandfather and that ultimately led to her family's taboo against discussing his film.

3

Head Wound

In 1997, the ARRB discovered the existence of a woman named Saundra Spencer, who in November 1963 was serving as a U.S. Navy petty officer in charge of the White House Laboratory at the U.S. Navy Photographic Center in Washington, D.C. Spencer had a top-secret security clearance and developed social photography from the White House taken by White House photographer Navy Chief Robert Knudsen and others.

Testifying under oath, Spencer told the ARRB a remarkable story. She said that on the weekend of the assassination, she was asked to develop, on a classified basis, the photographs of President Kennedy's autopsy. Sworn to secrecy, Spencer had kept her story secret for more than 30 years, until the ARRB released her from her obligation of secrecy in 1997.

The ARRB showed Spencer the official autopsy photographs in the Kennedy autopsy. She carefully examined them and then, specifically referring to the autopsy photographs that showed the back of Kennedy's head to be intact, she unequivocally testified that those were not the autopsy photographs that she developed on the weekend of the assassination. The autopsy photographs she developed showed an exit-sized wound in the back of Kennedy's head.

It would be virtually impossible to find a more credible and competent witness than Saundra Spencer. As far as I know, no one has ever questioned her competency, professionalism, or integrity. Once her sworn testimony was released to the public, not one single Navy official accused her of inaccuracy or perjury or questioned her veracity or character in general. According to former ARRB staff member Douglas Horne, the ARRB's general counsel, Jeremy Gunn, considered Saundra Spencer to be the most credible of all the witnesses who gave statements to the ARRB.

If accurate and truthful, Spencer's testimony leads to but one conclusion — that the official autopsy photographs showing the back of President Kennedy's head to be intact are false and fraudulent. Of course, her testimony also provides a clue as to the shenanigans that were occurring when President Kennedy's body was sneaked into the Bethesda morgue at 6:35 p.m., almost one and a half hours before the official entry time of 8 p.m.

What does Alexandra Zapruder say about Saundra Spencer's testimony in her book *Twenty-Six Seconds*? Nothing! Absolutely nothing! While mocking and ridiculing "conspiracy theorists" in the Kennedy assassination, Alexandra carefully avoids addressing the virtual certainty of autopsy fraud raised by Spencer's testimony.

Now, I'm sure that Alexandra would, once again, respond that Spencer's testimony has nothing to do with the Zapruder film, which is the primary focus of her book. But how wrong she would be. Why? Because like those official autopsy photographs, the Zapruder film also shows the back of President Kennedy's head to be intact after he received at least one gunshot to it. If the autopsy photographs showing the back of President Kennedy's head to be intact are fraudulent, then the Zapruder film showing the same thing has to be fraudulent as well.

When I realized that Alexandra was not going to discuss this critically important aspect of the Kennedy assassination, I was not surprised. A fraudulent autopsy necessarily means criminal conduct on the part of the national-security establishment. As we will see as we progress through this book, a fraudulent autopsy leads inexorably to the centrum of evil that ended up not only assassinating President John F. Kennedy but also enveloping and destroying Dallas businessman Abraham Zapruder.

Therefore, an important question naturally arises: Was Spencer's testimony accurate and truthful? If yes, then that necessarily means that on the evening of November 22, 1963 — the same day that President Kennedy was assassinated — the U.S. national-security establishment conducted a fraudulent autopsy on the president's body. On the other hand, if her testimony is inaccurate or false, then the national-security establishment's autopsy photographs are genuine.

There is a big problem facing those who might be tempted to claim that Spencer's testimony was inaccurate or false. The problem is that she isn't the only one who saw the big exit-sized hole in the back of President Kennedy's head.

When the president was initially brought into Trauma Room One at Parkland Hospital, the treating physicians immediately spotted the small circular bullet-sized wound in Kennedy's throat. To assist Kennedy in breathing, the physicians performed a tracheostomy by using a scalpel to cut across the throat wound and insert a breathing tube.

While they were doing that, Dr. Robert McClelland, a Parkland surgeon, went to the end of the gurney where Kennedy's head was situated to assist with the tracheostomy. He immediately saw a massive exit-sized hole in the back of the president's head. He asked the other physicians whether they had seen the wound. They all said no, stating that they had just walked into the room before he did. He summoned the other treating physicians to the head of the gurney so that they could see the wound.

Why did McClelland deem it important to do that? Because he knew that the wound was fatal. In later testimony before the Warren Commission, he stated that after examining the wound, he estimated that at least one-third of President Kennedy's brain tissue was missing. No one could survive that type of wound. No matter that the president's heart was still beating. No matter that he still had a pulse. No matter that he was still breathing. Once they saw that big hole in the back of Kennedy's head, every physician in Trauma Room One knew that he was essentially "dead on arrival." It was just a matter of time before he officially expired.

As with Saundra Spencer, it would be virtually impossible to find a more genuine, honest, and competent witness than Dr. Robert McClelland. He graduated in 1954 from the University of Texas Medical Branch and then served in the U.S. Air Force for two years. After doing his residency at Parkland Hospital, he was hired as a faculty member at UT Southwestern Medical Center. He later became the founder and first editor of *Selected Readings in General Surgery*. He served at Southwestern for 45 years, and in 2007, he was appointed Professor Emeritus of Surgery at Southwestern.

Like with Saundra Spencer, as far as I know no one has ever questioned or challenged the veracity, competence, or professionalism of Dr. Robert McClelland.

In criminal cases, evidentiary rules preclude the use of hearsay, which is an out-of-court statement made by someone that another person is relating. One reason for this is that the law wants the jury to have the opportunity to see the person who made the statement and size him up to determine whether he should be believed.

Similarly, I want you, the reader, to watch Dr. McClelland himself describe exactly what he saw after he entered Trauma Room One at Parkland Hospital. I want you to size him up and decide for yourself whether he is credible and believable.

If you can go online, find the 1988 video series entitled "The Men Who Killed Kennedy." Go to 26:09 in Part 1 to view Dr. McClelland in his younger years. Or begin at 25:39 in order to first watch Dr. Paul Peters, another of the treating physicians at Parkland. Peters states: "I could see that he had a large — about 7 centimeters — opening in the right occipital-parietal area [gesturing with his right hand to the back of his head]. A considerable portion of the brain was missing there and the occipital cortex — the back portion of the brain was lying down near the opening of the wound. Blood was trickling out."

The occipital region of the skull is situated in the middle of the back part of a person's head. The parietal regions are situated on the right side and left side of the skull. Thus, a wound in the occipital-parietal region will be situated in the right or left rear of the back of the head.

In the video, Peters is followed by McClelland, who states: "Almost a fifth or perhaps even a quarter of the right back part of the head in this area here [gesturing with his right hand to the back of his head] had been blasted out along with probably most of the brain tissue in that area."

It is probably worth mentioning that the official autopsy report in the Kennedy autopsy states that the president's brain weighed 1,500 grams. An average-sized male brain weights 1,350 grams. No one has ever been able to explain how a brain that has lost a large portion of its mass could possibly weigh 1,500 grams.

If you are unable to find Part 1 of "The Men Who Killed Kennedy," then I refer you to an interview that was conducted of McClelland in 2013 on the 50th anniversary of the Kennedy assassination. The interviewer is Dr. Rod J. Rohrich, a clinical professor of plastic surgery at the Baylor College of Medicine and editor in chief of *Plastic and Reconstructive Surgery,* the official publication of the American Society of Plastic Surgeons. The interview is posted online in three parts. The entire interview is fascinating, and I highly recommend watching it in its entirety. The three-part interview can be viewed here:

Part 1: https://journals.lww.com/plasreconsurg/pages/videogallery.aspx?autoPlay=false&videoId=420

Part 2: https://journals.lww.com/plasreconsurg/pages/videogallery.aspx?autoPlay=false&videoId=419

Part 3: https://journals.lww.com/plasreconsurg/pages/videogallery.aspx?autoPlay=false&videoId=418

If you wish to go directly to his specific comments about the exit wound in the back of Kennedy's head, go to Part 1 at 5:55, where McClelland states: "I went to the head of the gurney and leaned over to put that retractor in the upper edge of that incision they were making and when I got there, I said, my God, I said, have you seen the back of his head? They said no, we just walked in here before you did, and we haven't seen anything but this hole in his neck. I said, well, there is a wound in the back of his head here in the right side that's at least five inches in diameter — a circular wound far in the back of his head. [Interviewer: Show us where that was.] It was back here [moving his right hand to the back of his head] and I could actually look down in the skull cavity and see that the whole right back half of the right cerebral hemisphere was gone."

McClelland also pointed out that the part of the brain known as the cerebellum was spilling out of the hole. The cerebellum is located in the lower back of the head.

Thus, we can see that McClelland's and Peters's statements about the exit-sized wound in the back of President Kennedy's head are consistent with the sworn testimony of Saundra Spencer before the ARRB.

If McClelland, Peters, and Spencer were correct and truthful, that can mean only one thing: The U.S. national-security establishment's official autopsy photographs depicting the back of Kennedy's head to be intact are false and fraudulent — that is, a lie.

In 2009, McClelland was interviewed by a Canadian broadcaster named Brent Holland. In that interview, McClelland stated that in 1988, he and four other treating physicians had been flown to Washington, D.C., to view the Kennedy autopsy photographs at the National Archives. McClelland described his reaction when he saw an autopsy photograph showing the back of Kennedy's head to be intact: "The only exception that I had was that they showed me one picture where apparently there was no wound in the right back part of his head, but I assumed it was because the anatomical prosector — the pathologist — had pulled a flap of scalp which had been loose up over that opening. And so I told them — I said that's, you know, I guess that's a flap of scalp up over the wound. Well, someone — I can't remember who — said no, that's not a flap of scalp — that's just where the scalp was. I said no that's not — that's where there was a massive hole in the back of his head that was at least five inches in diameter. And I looked into it from about 18 inches as I held that retractor over a period of about 10 or 12 or more minutes while the tracheostomy was completed. I had a vivid and a close look and still have in my memory what that wound in the right back, in the extreme back of his head, looked like."

Actually, McClelland, Peters, and Spencer are not the only witnesses to that large hole in the back of Kennedy's head. Let's review what some of the other witnesses who saw the same thing stated:

Dr. Kemp Clark, professor and director of neurological surgery at Parkland Hospital: "There was a large wound in the right occipital-parietal region."

Parkland Hospital physician Dr. Charles Carrico: "There was a large — quite a large — defect about here on his skull [pointing to the back of his head]."

Parkland Hospital physician Dr. Charles Crenshaw told the ARRB that there was a baseball-sized wound in the occipital-parietal region, in the right rear of the head.

Parkland Hospital physician Dr. Malcolm Perry: "I looked at the head wound briefly by leaning over the table and noticed that the occipital-parietal head wound was largely avulsive [meaning exploded outward]."

Parkland Hospital nurse Audrey Bell: "There was a massive wound in the back of his head."

Parkland Hospital nurse Diana Bowron: "At the back of his skull, an enormous hole."

Ft. Worth newsman Roy Stamps: "[At Parkland Hospital] I rushed up and saw Kennedy lying in the car on his side.... The back of his head was gone."

Dallas ambulance driver Aubrey Rike, who helped place JFK's sheet-shrouded body into the bronze Dallas casket at Parkland Hospital: "You could feel the sharp edges of the bone at the edge of the hole in the back of his head."

Secret Service agent Clint Hill: "The right rear portion of the head was missing."

Bethesda Naval Medical Center Dr. Robert Canada: There was a "very large, 3 to 5 cm wound in the right rear of the President's head, in the lower right occipital region ... clearly an exit wound" because it was "avulsed" (i.e., exploded outward).

Admiral George Burkley: Kennedy had a large wound "that had all the appearance of an exit wound" in the back of his head.

FBI agent James Sibert: Testifying before the ARRB and being shown an official autopsy photograph showing the back of Kennedy's head to be intact: "Well, I don't have a recollection of it being that intact.... I don't remember seeing anything like this."

FBI agent Francis O'Neill: Testifying before the ARRB and being shown an official autopsy photograph showing the back of Kennedy's head to be intact: "This looks like it's been doctored in some way.... Quite frankly, I thought there was a larger opening in the back ... opening in the back of the head."

What are the chances that all of these people are wrong? There is no reasonable possibility of that at all. That means either one of two things: All of them have gotten together in some sort of massive conspiracy against the national-security establishment, or the national-security establishment has created photographs that falsely and fraudulently depict the condition of the back of Kennedy's head. The notion of such a conspiracy on the part of all these witnesses is obviously ludicrous, which leaves but one reasonable conclusion: The U.S. national-security establishment's official autopsy photographs showing the back of President Kennedy's head to be intact are a lie, a deception, a fraud.

Autopsy photographs showing the back of Kennedy's head to be intact take us directly to the Zapruder film because it also shows the back of Kennedy's head to be intact after being hit by a gunshot to his head. Therefore, if the military's autopsy photographs falsely and fraudulently show the back of Kennedys head to be intact, then it naturally follows that the Zapruder film is equally false and fraudulent.

It therefore becomes clear why Alexandra Zapruder scrupulously avoided confronting, at least at a subconscious level, the national-security establishment's fraudulent autopsy in her book *Twenty-Six Seconds*. Doing so would have placed her in the position of challenging the veracity of Saundra Spencer, Dr. McClelland, Dr. Peters, Dr. Crenshaw, Dr. Clark, Dr. Carrico, Nurses Bell and Bowron, Secret Service agent Clint Hill, FBI agents Francis O'Neil and James Sibert, and all of the other witnesses whose direct and unequivocal statements about the large exit-sized wound in the back of President Kennedy's head established the fraudulent nature of the national-security establishment's official autopsy photographs that show the back of Kennedy's head to be intact.

Even more frightening, confronting the national-security establishment's fraudulent autopsy would have caused Alexandra Zapruder to get dangerously close to the centrum of evil that led not only to the destruction of her grandfather but also to her family's taboo against discussing his film.

4

Deferentials

When the team of Secret Service agents forced its way out of Parkland Hospital with the president's body, its actions were anything but normal. The normal routine is for law-enforcement agencies to work together in order to apprehend and bring criminals to justice. When the Dallas County medical examiner, Dr. Earl Rose, announced that he intended to conduct an autopsy on President Kennedy's body, the normal course of action would have been for the Secret Service to say, "We understand, Dr. Rose. State law requires you to do so. Please proceed, and we will stand by until you are finished."

After all, the autopsy is often a critical piece of evidence in a criminal prosecution. Its primary purpose is to determine the actual cause of death. By dissecting bullet wounds, the pathologist can determine the direction from which the bullets were fired. The entry wounds and exit wounds in a body together provide a "diagram of the shooting" and are, therefore, the best evidence of where the shots came from and where they did not come from.

Yet, here you had a Secret Service agent — Roy Kellerman — brandishing a Thompson submachine gun and informing Rose that under no circumstances would he be permitted to conduct an autopsy on the president's body. In the interview of Dr. McClelland with *Plastic and Reconstructive Surgery* that was described in chapter 3, McClelland said that Rose related to him that one very large Secret Service agent physically picked Rose up, carried him to a nearby wall, set him down, and wagged his finger in his face. Given the screaming and profanities emitted by the Secret Service agents, hospital personnel and ambulance driver Aubrey Rike later said that they were terrified, especially when the agents pulled back their coats and displayed their pistols.

The Secret Service agents said that they were operating on orders. The only person who could have issued those orders, either directly or indirectly, was Lyndon Johnson, who automatically became president when Kennedy expired. Who else would have dared to issue such an extraordinary order, one that called for a violation of Texas state criminal law?

In fact, we know it had to be Johnson who issued the order because after Kennedy was declared dead, Johnson headed to Dallas's Love Field, where he immediately ordered personnel to remove seats from the tail compartment of Air Force One to make room for Kennedy's casket.

Johnson did not end up departing Dallas until 2:47 p.m., more than an hour and a half after Kennedy was pronounced dead at 1:00 p.m. Dr. Rose would likely have been well on his way to wrapping up his autopsy in that period of time.

Some people would never consider questioning or challenging that Secret Service team's actions at Parkland Hospital. I term people who instinctively defer to the authority of the federal government — and especially the national-security establishment branch of the federal government — as "deferentials." Such people look upon the federal government as a parent or, even worse, as a god. The thought that their political parent or their god could be engaged in something dark, nefarious, and evil is not only inconceivable to them, it is also extremely frightening.

Imagine a small child who sees a parent murdering someone. What is the child to do? He depends on his parent for sustenance and support. If he reports the matter to the authorities, in his mind he might be left to starve to death. If he expresses objection or disapproval to his parent for what has happened, the parent might harm him as well. From the child's standpoint, it's better to remain silent and submissive and simply block out of his mind what he has seen.

That's the mindset of a deferential in America, especially when it comes to the national-security establishment. In large part, this mindset is inculcated in children who are educated in public (i.e., government) schools, whose primary mission is to produce "good citizens" — that is, those who defer to and do not question federal authority. Unfortunately though, the same thing happens in many private schools, at least those whose teaching methodology is largely modeled on that of the public-school system.

The conversion of America to a welfare state in the 1930s contributed to this phenomenon. People have come to look to the federal government for their sustenance and support, such as with Social Security, Medicare, Medicaid, education grants, farm subsidies, medical leave from work, minimum-wage laws, and the like. Challenging or questioning actions of this paternal entity could result in a termination of support, which is as frightening to many American adults as it is to a child who fears being cut off by his parents. Better to remain quiet and not make any waves.

As I was reading Alexandra Zapruder's book, it was not difficult to reach the opinion that she was a good example of a deferential. Her own mindset was undoubtedly reflected in what she wrote about her grandfather: "Abe's support for the Warren Commission is not at all surprising. Everything about his worldview and experience led him to have a basic faith in the American government.... Thinking back on the assassination from the vantage point of three years, he could grieve the murder of John Kennedy and at the same time reiterate his absolute faith in America. For him, the fact that America elected John Kennedy was the purest proof that its people possessed the values, courage, and strength to endure his assassination and prevail. I have to wonder if, somewhere in the back of his mind, he was thinking of the overthrow of Czar Nicholas II and how the Bolshevik Revolution had plunged Russia into chaos and violence. He was just twelve when he lived through those events. But America was not Russia. Even if he saw the fissures that Kennedy's assassination had caused, in his mind they could not threaten the basic foundation of American democracy. For him, and for many of his generation and background, the Warren Commission and its conclusions were part and parcel of that faith."

All too often in her book, whenever some action on the part of the federal government should have caused Alexandra to at least raise her eyebrows, she would defer to authority and come up with ways to rationalize the action so that it would appear innocent. For example, as we will see later, the CIA succeeded in keeping secret for some 30 to 40 years the complete role it played in the Zapruder film during the weekend after the assassination. That secrecy partly came to an end in 1978 with a Freedom of Information Act (FOIA) release of CIA document 450 to the United States President's Commission on CIA Activities, which came to be known as the Rockefeller Commission. Document 450 consisted of briefing notes made at the CIA's National Photographic Interpretation Center (NPIC) about CIA activity with the Zapruder film. The document established that the CIA played an important role in the handling of the Zapruder film. A more complete picture of the CIA role with the Zapruder film, however, wouldn't become clear until the 1990s and the late 2010s.

In her book, Alexandra never seems to question why the CIA was dealing with the Zapruder film at all and, equally important, why the CIA deemed it necessary to keep its involvement with the film secret from the American people. She apparently concluded that the CIA was simply helping to investigate the assassination. In the process, however, it apparently never occurred to her that the CIA had no legal jurisdiction to investigate anything within the United States. There is no indication in her book that she ever asked herself a simple question: Why was the CIA engaged in investigating the Kennedy assassination, when that job fell within the exclusive criminal jurisdiction of the Dallas County authorities? Moreover, she was apparently never aware that federal law prohibits the CIA from involving itself in domestic activity and that its central mission is to gather intelligence for the president, not investigate state murder cases. (At that time, it was not a federal offense to kill the president.)

But the problem goes deeper than that. What I found absolutely fascinating is that throughout her book, Alexandra Zapruder expressed no concerns or reservations about the CIA itself. On the contrary, it was clear to me that she has a deep and abiding faith in this federal governmental agency.

One of the characteristics of a deferential is that he or she can usually easily recognize evil within foreign regimes, at least when it is labeled as evil by federal officials. If we consider, say, the Nazi government, most every American would have no trouble labeling it as evil.

This would especially apply to Alexandra, given that she is Jewish. There is no question but that she would easily recognize the Nazi regime as evil, especially given that she wrote a book on the Holocaust and also worked in the Holocaust Museum in Washington.

But what if she were German? As a Jew, she would almost certainly have had the same mindset. But the fact is that many Germans who were not Jews did not believe that their government was evil and, once war broke out, considered it their duty to support their government and its troops. As good German citizens, they believed that patriotism dictated that they defer to authority and support their government and not question whether their government was in the right or the wrong.

Many years ago, I wrote an essay entitled "The White Rose: A Lesson in Dissent." Of all the essays I have written in the 32-year history of The Future of Freedom Foundation, this is my favorite. I was especially pleased when it got selected to appear in an anthology about the Holocaust for high-school students.

The White Rose was a group of college students in Munich, Germany, who were resisting the Nazi regime at the height of World War II. They were Christians, not Jews. The leaders of the group were a brother and sister named Hans and Sophie Scholl. What I found so inspiring about the White Rose was not just that they opposed an evil regime but that they were German citizens who were opposing their own government precisely because they recognized it as evil.

Many Germans were unable to do that. Like the judge who sentenced Hans and Sophie Scholl to death, such Germans considered the members of the White Rose to be bad citizens — traitors, especially given their refusal to support the troops during the middle of a war.

It's that mindset of deference to authority and false patriotism that unfortunately afflicts all too many Americans, at least with respect to actions taken by the U.S. national-security establishment — that is, the Pentagon, the CIA, the NSA, and, to a certain extent, the FBI.

In my opinion, Alexandra Zapruder is a prime example of this phenomenon. Consider her apparent allegiance to the CIA. This is an entity that secretly employed Nazis after World War II. Given the extreme evil nature of the Nazi regime, what does that say about a U.S. governmental entity that knowingly, intentionally, and deliberately hired people who willingly served that regime? As far as I'm concerned, when that came to light, the CIA should have been abolished immediately. One certainly does not find that suggestion in Alexandra Zapruder's book.

In the minds of deferentials, it is simply inconceivable that America's national-security establishment could engage in the evil and nefarious action of violently removing a U.S. president from office. Yet, everyone knows — or should know by now — that the CIA and the Pentagon do engage in evil and nefarious actions, and that they were engaged in evil and nefarious actions in the 1950s and 1960s. The problem is that owing to the indoctrination to which Americans are subjected as children, by the time many of them become adults, they have had their consciences so stultified that they don't consider such actions to be evil and nefarious. Instead, the actions are considered to be necessary to protect "national security," which has become the most important term in the American political lexicon, despite its obvious lack of objective meaning.

Consider, for example, the coup that the CIA initiated in Iran in 1953 — 10 years before the Kennedy assassination — when the CIA intentionally destroyed Iran's experiment with democracy by ousting the country's democratically elected prime minister, Mohammad Mossadegh, from power and replacing him with the brutal and tyrannical unelected Shah of Iran. How does one morally and legally justify such a thing, especially given that hundreds of innocent people were killed in the process? Why would the term "evil" not apply to that operation? Or should we just refer to that regime-change operation as a "conspiracy theory?"

What about the coup that the CIA initiated in Guatemala the very next year, in 1954? The CIA ousted the democratically elected president of the country, Jacobo Arbenz, and replaced him with a brutal right-wing military dictator whose goons proceeded to kill, torture, or injure multitudes of innocent people. The CIA even had an assassination list drawn up for that operation. The agency still will not let us see who was on its assassination list (on grounds of "national security"), but there can be no doubt that Arbenz was at the top of the list. Under what moral and legal authority did the CIA target the president of a foreign country with assassination, especially given that he had not committed any criminal act against the United States? How can that not be labeled as evil? Or should we also refer to this regime-change operation as a "conspiracy theory?"

In 1958, the CIA initiated a violent regime-change operation in Indonesia, with the aim of ousting the first president of Indonesia, President Sukarno, from office, which caused the deaths of many innocent people. How can such an operation not be considered evil? Should we refer to it as simply a "conspiracy theory?"

During the 1950s, the CIA was engaged in drug experiments against unsuspecting Americans and then intentionally destroyed its records relating to the program to prevent Americans from seeing the exact nature and extent of the program. The operation was called MKULTRA. How can such drug experiments not be considered evil? Or were they actually just a "conspiracy theory?"

In 1961, the CIA orchestrated the assassination of Patrice Lumumba, the leader of the Congo. Knowing that newly elected President Kennedy would never approve of Lumumba's assassination, the CIA made certain it happened before Kennedy took office. How can such a murder not be considered evil? Should we, again, simply refer to Lumumba's assassination as a "conspiracy theory?"

During the early 1960s, the CIA was hell-bent on assassinating the leader of Cuba, Fidel Castro, notwithstanding the fact that Cuba had never attacked the United States or even threatened to do so. Even worse, the CIA secretly partnered with the Mafia, the world's premier private criminal organization, to carry out the assassination. How can those repeated murder attempts not be considered evil? Should we simply refer to them as "conspiracy theories?"

In fact, the 60-year-long obsession with Cuba goes beyond the assassination attempts against Castro, who is now long dead. For some six decades, the U.S. government has targeted the Cuban people with a cruel and brutal economic embargo whose aim is to starve or impoverish the Cuban people until they oust their communist regime and replace it with another U.S.-controlled regime. Isn't the reason we condemn terrorism because terrorists target innocent people as a way to achieve a political end? Why shouldn't the Cuban embargo be labeled evil for the same reason? Or is it just a "conspiracy theory?"

In 1973 — 10 years after the Kennedy assassination — the CIA orchestrated the ouster of Salvador Allende, the democratically elected president of Chile. In order to do that, the CIA and the Pentagon had to convince their counterparts in the Chilean national-security establishment that they had a moral duty to remove their president from office, notwithstanding the fact that the Chilean constitution had no provision authorizing such action. That obviously provides us with powerful evidence of the U.S. national-security establishment's mindset with respect to matters here at home.

What was the reason that the U.S. national-security establishment gave to the Chilean national-security establishment as to why it needed to remove its democratically elected president from office? As president, the CIA said, Allende's policies posed a grave threat to Chilean "national security" because such policies would inevitably bring Chile under communist rule. Therefore, the Chilean national-security establishment had the moral duty, no matter how unsavory, to remove its president in order to save the nation.

When the head of the Chilean armed forces, Gen. Rene Schneider, refused to go along with the coup because it was unconstitutional and illegal, the CIA simply orchestrated his violent kidnapping, which left Schneider shot dead on the streets of Santiago. His widow and four children were left mourning their loss. How can Schneider's murder be considered anything but evil? Or should we simply refer to it as a "conspiracy theory?"

Moreover, how can such a coup, which left Allende dead and left the Chilean people to suffer for the next 17 years under a brutal military dictatorship, not be considered evil? Or should we just consider it to be a "conspiracy theory?"

In the 1970s, the CIA participated in an international kidnapping, torture, and assassination program called Operation Condor, which was orchestrated and carried out by right-wing, U.S.-aligned regimes in South America. How can such action not be considered evil? Or should we just refer to it as just another "conspiracy theory?"

I don't know where Alexandra Zapruder stands with respect to all those regime-change operations, but I do know that she did not criticize any of them in her book. I also know that those regime-change operations were not — and are not — considered evil and malevolent by many deferentials. In their minds, those actions on the part of the CIA were morally justified to protect us from the communists, who were supposedly coming to get us as part of an international conspiracy to take over the United States and the rest of the world, a conspiracy supposedly based in Moscow. That's what the Cold War was all about, along with ever-increasing budgets and power for the Pentagon, the CIA, and the NSA, the three principal components of the national-security establishment.

We will see later that in the months before he was assassinated, President Kennedy recognized the Cold War for the evil racket it was and decided to bring it to an end, a decision that ultimately led to his assassination.

5

The National-Security State

In December 2019, the *Washington Post* reported, "A confidential trove of government documents obtained by the *Washington Post* reveals that senior U.S. officials failed to tell the truth about the war in Afghanistan throughout the 18-year campaign, making rosy pronouncements they knew to be false and hiding unmistakable evidence the war had become unwinnable."

I don't know of anyone who was shocked by that disclosure. By now, most everyone has become aware that lying has been the foundation of the U.S. national-security establishment since its inception. In fact, it would be difficult to find a better example of psychiatrist M. Scott Peck's concept of "people of the lie" than the U.S. national-security establishment.

In 1973, the Senate Foreign Relations Committee asked former CIA director Richard Helms under oath whether the CIA had intervened in the 1970 Chilean presidential election while Helms had been serving as director of the CIA. That was the election that was won by socialist Salvador Allende, who the CIA deemed to be a threat to U.S.

national security and also to Chilean national security. Helms denied any CIA involvement. It was an intentional, knowing, deliberate lie.

Even though Helms had committed the felony offense of perjury, after he was caught, he was permitted to plead guilty to a misdemeanor and received a two-year suspended sentence and a $2,000 fine. When he returned to CIA headquarters, his CIA cohorts praised and honored him, even passing a hat around to raise the money to pay off his fine. Helms was considered heroic for intentionally, knowingly, and deliberately lying to Congress to protect CIA dark-side secrets.

In 2002, the George W. Bush administration scared Americans deeply by suggesting that Iraqi dictator Saddam Hussein was about to unleash "mushroom clouds" over American cities with his supposed stockpile of weapons of mass destruction. It was a lie. Bush figured that conjuring up the prospect of a nuclear attack on the United States was the best way to garner the support of the American people for a regime-change operation in Iraq.

Ironically, Saddam Hussein, who Bush and people within his administration were referring to as a "new Hitler," had been a partner and ally of the U.S. government during the 1980s, when Iraq was waging war against Iran. Why was the U.S. government helping Iraq in that war? Because in 1979, the Iranian people had violently revolted against the brutal and tyrannical dictatorship of the Shah, who, as I noted in chapter 4, had been installed into power in 1953 by a CIA-engineered coup. Adding insult to injury, after the coup the CIA helped organize and train the SAVAK, the Shah's brutal domestic police force, which was a combination of the Pentagon, CIA, NSA, and FBI.

The U.S. national-security establishment has never forgiven the Iranian people for ousting the Shah from power. That's why it was helping Saddam Hussein to kill Iranians in his war of aggression against Iran during the 1980s. That's also why it remains committed to regime change in Iran even today, as especially evidenced by its brutal system of economic sanctions that targets the Iranian people with death and impoverishment as a way to bring it about.

Nine months after President Kennedy was assassinated, the Pentagon claimed that North Vietnamese gunboats attacked U.S. Navy vessels in two separate incidents off North Vietnamese waters in the Gulf of Tonkin. The first attack took place, but the second one did not. The Pentagon's big press conference focusing on the second attack was based on a lie, one that was used to induce Congress to enact the Gulf of Tonkin Resolution, which authorized President Johnson to expand the war by initiating hostilities against North Vietnam. Moreover, the first attack (which did take place) was an appropriate defensive reaction by North Vietnam to a U.S. Navy destroyer engaged in Pentagon-conceived covert operations against North Vietnam's coastline, something that the Pentagon chose not to mention. Instead of violating our "freedom of the seas," North Vietnam was, instead, defending itself in the one minor attack that did take place.

In his book *People of the Lie,* Scott Peck cited the massacre at My Lai in South Vietnam of some 500 unarmed people at the hands of U.S. troops as an example of the evil to which he was referring. Little did Peck realize that what occurred at My Lai was just the tip of the iceberg. While the Pentagon claimed that the massacre was an isolated incident, investigative journalist Nick Turse, in his book *Kill Anything That Moves: The Real American War in Vietnam,* established that the Pentagon was knowingly, intentionally, and deliberately lying. In fact, there were many other My Lai–type massacres at the hands of the U.S. military in the Vietnam War.

That's not to say, of course, that everyone who works in or with the Pentagon, the CIA, and the NSA is a liar. We know that many are not. Saundra Spencer, the U.S Navy petty officer who developed post-mortem photos of President Kennedy, is a prime example. Later on, we will learn about three CIA officials who secretly had contact with the Zapruder film on the very weekend of the assassination and whose accounts come across as genuine, honest, and forthright. We also know that there are plenty of individual soldiers who honestly believed that they were doing the right thing when they invaded Afghanistan and Iraq.

But the fact is that all of these people are working for an institution — the national-security establishment — that is firmly based on lies and lying. When you have good people working in an evil system, the system is going to win out every time.

It's worth noting that in a national-security state, lying about its dark-side activities is considered to be a good, even honorable, thing, while telling the truth about such activities is considered to be a grave offense. That's why liars like Richard Helms and James R. Clapper, Jr., the director of the Defense Intelligence Agency who lied under oath to Congress about secret mass surveillance being carried out on the American people, are praised and glorified while people who tell the truth about the national-security establishment's dark-side activities, such as Edward Snowden and Julian Assange, are vilified, prosecuted, persecuted, and sometimes even assassinated.

It is important to point out something that some Americans are unaware of: America was not always a national-security state. Our nation's founding governmental system was a limited-government republic, a type of governmental structure that is entirely different from a national-security state. A limited-government republic served as America's system for more than 150 years, until the federal government was converted to a national-security state after World War II.

In her book, Alexandra Zapruder displays no awareness of this phenomenon. Like many other Americans, she most likely believes that the national-security state type of governmental system under which she has been born and raised is the same governmental system that has always existed in America.

What is a national-security state? It is a governmental structure that empowers certain federal officials to wield and exercise omnipotent, dark-side powers, including the powers of assassination, kidnapping, coups, torture, indefinite detention, secret surveillance of both citizens and foreigners, denial of due process of law, denial of trial by jury, and establishing partnerships and alliances with dictatorial regimes and criminal organizations.

To put the matter into context, North Korea is a national-security state. So are China, Pakistan, Egypt, Russia, Vietnam, and Cuba. And the post–World War II United States.

By contrast, under America's limited-government form of governmental structure, the powers of the federal government were few and limited, in nature and scope. The document that brought the federal government into existence, the Constitution, along with the Bill of Rights, expressly enumerated and restricted the powers of the federal government.

If the American people after the Constitutional Convention in Philadelphia had been told that the Constitution was bringing into existence a national-security state type of governmental system, they would have thought it was a joke. Once they realized that the proposal was serious, they would have summarily rejected it and chosen instead to continue operating under the Articles of Confederation, which was a third type of governmental structure. Under the Articles, which lasted about 10 years, the powers of the federal government were so weak that the federal government didn't even have the power to tax.

That's the way our American ancestors wanted it. They didn't trust government, including their very own democratically elected government. Unlike many Americans today, they never believed that the biggest threat to their freedom and well-being lay with foreign regimes or foreign criminals. Based on their study of history as well as their own personal experiences, they were convinced that the greatest threat to the citizenry of a country lay with their very own government.

Under America's limited-government republic, there was never a giant, permanent military establishment, CIA, NSA, or FBI. There was a relatively small, basic army that was never large enough to embroil the nation in European or Asian wars. Our American ancestors were fiercely opposed to "standing armies," the term they used to describe a national-security state.

There were also no powers to orchestrate or carry out assassinations, conduct secret surveillance of the citizenry, subject people to torture, and incarcerate people indefinitely without trial. The American people made certain of that with the enactment of the Bill of Rights, which expressly prohibited the federal government from depriving people of life, liberty, and property without due process of law, subjecting people to cruel and unusual punishments, denying people a speedy trial, and denying people the right of trial by jury.

America's founding foreign policy was also completely different from the interventionist foreign policy that has characterized our country for more than 100 years. Our nation's founding foreign policy was one of non-interventionism into the affairs of other nations. In his Fourth of July address to Congress in 1821, John Quincy Adams summarized America's foreign policy in a speech entitled "In Search of Monsters to Destroy." Adams pointed out that there were lots of bad things that happen in the world, including brutal dictatorships, famines, revolutions, and wars. America, he said, would not go abroad with troops and bombs to slay any of these monsters. If America were to do so, Adams said, the federal government would end up acquiring the traits of dictatorship.

Did that mean that Americans were indifferent to suffering in the world? On the contrary, it simply meant that the federal government would be prohibited from doing anything about that suffering. The American people, on the other hand, on a purely private basis, would be free to travel anywhere in the world and to donate money and other resources to help out whomever they wanted.

That wasn't all, however. Our American ancestors established a system of open immigration, which essentially sent the people of the world this message: We will not send our military forces to help you, but if you are able and willing to escape, know that there will always be at least one nation to which you can flee that will not forcibly return you to your homeland.

As an interesting aside, in her book Alexandra Zapruder writes about her grandfather Abraham's admiration for President Franklin D. Roosevelt. There is not even a hint of disapproval expressed by Alexandra of Roosevelt's role in the Holocaust, a role that she undoubtedly is aware of given her work at the U.S. Holocaust Museum, which has a huge exhibit describing Roosevelt's actions. In the 1930s — before the Holocaust — Hitler was willing to let Jews leave Germany, but no country was willing to take them. By that time, the United States had abandoned its founding system of open immigration and had instead followed the rest of the world by adopting a system of immigration controls. Pointing out that the United States now had "the quota system," Roosevelt refused to permit German Jews to come to the United States. The horrific story of German Jewish refugees seeking asylum in Cuba and the United States onboard the passenger liner S.S. *St. Louis,* which was made into a movie in 1976 entitled *Voyage of the Damned,* reflects Roosevelt's callous mindset, a mindset that Alexandra, when she mentioned her grandfather's admiration for FDR, could have condemned or even just mildly criticized in her book, but did not.

The winds of change began with the generations of Americans who were living at the end of the 1800s. The U.S. government intervened in the Spanish-American War, ostensibly to help Spanish colonies win their independence from the Spanish empire. It was a lie. Upon Spain's defeat, U.S. officials declared that the United States was stepping into the shoes of the Spanish empire and taking control over its colonies. When Filipinos objected, the U.S. government tortured and killed multitudes of them until they surrendered to U.S. rule.

The notion was that America could never be a great nation if it didn't become an empire, one with colonies just like the British, French, and Belgian empires. That's how the United States took control over Cuba and acquired its imperial base at Guantanamo Bay. It's how the United States also acquired Puerto Rico and Guam. In the excitement over empire building, the United States also annexed Hawaii in 1898, something that Congress had previously resisted doing.

Then came World War I. While 19th-century Americans were firmly opposed to intervening in Europe's forever wars, President Wilson felt differently. He was convinced that the United States, through force of arms, could finally bring an end to Europe's incessant conflicts. Securing a declaration of war from Congress, Wilson aimed to make this the war to end all future wars and to make the world safe for democracy.

Bringing about the total defeat and humiliation of Germany with the Treaty of Versailles, U.S. interventionism actually set the stage for the rise of Adolf Hitler and the Nazi regime in the 1930s. In the process, Wilson's government goons succeeded in destroying civil liberties here at home by prosecuting and punishing critics of the war, just as Nazi Germany would do to the members of the White Rose during the next world war.

It quickly became clear that Wilson's aims in World War I had not been achieved and that foreign interventionism had cost the United States tens of thousands of American lives and a very large amount of wasted taxpayer money. The fact that Wilson had forced American men, through conscription, to serve as fodder for his follies, only made his intervention that much worse.

Thus, by the time World War II rolled around, the American people were overwhelmingly opposed to entering the conflict. In his 1940 campaign for an unprecedented third term as president, Franklin Roosevelt told the American people that he was with them in their opposition to another foreign war. He said, "I have said it before but I will say it again, and again and again. Your boys are not going be sent into any foreign wars."

It was a lie. Actually, Roosevelt was secretly doing everything he could to embroil the United States in the conflict. He knew, however, that given the overwhelming sentiment against entry into the war, there was no way he would be able to secure a declaration of war from Congress, which the Constitution requires as a prerequisite to a president's waging war.

To circumvent the will of the American people, Roosevelt embarked on a course of conduct designed to provoke the Germans into attacking the United States. When Germany refused to take the bait, Roosevelt turned his focus to the Pacific, where he began provoking Japan into attacking the United States in the hope of getting a "back door" to entering the war against Germany. His efforts succeeded when Japanese forces attacked Pearl Harbor, which was quickly followed by Germany's declaration of war against the United States.

At the end of the war, Nazi Germany lay defeated. But the real winner of the war was the Soviet Union, which now controlled all of Eastern Europe and half of Germany.

When the Soviets refused to relinquish control over these lands, U.S. officials used this communist "aggression" as evidence of an international communist conspiracy to conquer the world, including the United States.

Never mind that the Soviet Union had been a partner and ally of the United States and Britain during the war. And never mind that President Roosevelt himself at the Big Three conference in Yalta in 1945 had acquiesced to the Soviet Union's control over Eastern Europe. And never mind that the Soviet Union had suffered massive death and destruction during the war.

Everything was now different. While the United States had just vanquished the Nazi regime, the American people could not rest, U.S. officials said, because they now faced an implacable foe that was arguably more dangerous than Hitler. That foe was "godless communism," which ruled the Soviet Union and the rest of the communist world. Americans were told that there was an international communist conspiracy to take over the world that was based in Moscow, Russia — yes, the same Russia with which so many U.S. national-security state officials are still so obsessed today.

The Cold War and the "anti-communist crusade" were used after 1947 to justify the conversion of the federal government from a limited-government republic to a national-security state. Given that the communist regimes were empowered to wield and exercise omnipotent, dark-side powers, U.S. officials maintained that it was necessary for them to be able to do the same in order to prevent America from going communist. The associated massive spending increases supporting a war economy, during peacetime, began in 1950 and continued on a permanent basis.

That's how we got the Pentagon, the vast military-industrial complex, the CIA, and the NSA, along with all their dark-side powers. It's how we got a veritable empire of military bases, both foreign and domestic. It's how we got ever-increasing budgets, power, and influence of the national-security establishment, which some people came to call the "Deep State." It's how we got an ever-growing army of well-heeled "defense" contractors and sub-contractors, many of whom were military and CIA veterans who were now getting rich from all the tax-funded largesse that was being poured into the "defense" industry. It's how we ended up with some 34,000 American men dead in the Korean War and another 58,000 dead in the Vietnam War. It's also how we got regime-change operations around the world, ostensibly intended to protect the United States from the communists.

The conversion to a national-security state would only be temporary, U.S. officials said. As soon as the Cold War against "godless communism" was over and the international communist conspiracy defeated, the American people could then have their limited-government republic back.

It was just another lie. When the Cold War suddenly and unexpectedly ended in 1989, the last thing the national-security state was going to do was permit itself to be dismantled in favor of restoring America's founding governmental system of a limited-government republic.

Every national-security state necessarily depends on official enemies that can be used to frighten the citizenry into supporting it. When the Pentagon and the CIA lost godless communism and the Soviet Union as their official enemies, that's when they went into the Middle East and embarked on a course of death, destruction, and humiliation that would ultimately produce a seemingly better and more long-lasting official enemy — terrorism — than godless communism and the Soviet Union. The war on communism was replaced by the "war on terrorism."

After the 9/11 attacks, U.S. officials, with straight faces, claimed that the attacks had been motivated by foreign hatred for America's "freedom and values." It was just another lie. In actuality, the attacks were motivated by the rage produced by the course of deadly and destructive interventionism on which the Pentagon and the CIA had embarked after the end of the Cold War.

The interventionism began with the Persian Gulf War, when U.S. officials turned against their former partner and ally Saddam Hussein. After U.S. forces killed thousands of Iraqis, U.S. officials imposed on the Iraqi people one of the most brutal systems of economic sanctions in history. The sanctions succeeded in killing hundreds of thousands of innocent Iraqi children, especially since the sanctions prevented Iraqi officials from repairing water-and-sewage treatment plants that the Pentagon had intentionally bombed during the Gulf War. It didn't help matters when the U.S. ambassador to the United Nations, Madeleine Albright, openly and publicly declared that the deaths of half-a-million Iraqi children from the sanctions were "worth it." It also didn't help when no one in the Clinton administration, including the president, condemned or criticized her statement.

Adding fuel to the deadly fire that U.S. officials had ignited in the Middle East was the stationing of U.S. troops near Mecca and Medina, the holiest lands in the Islamic religion. There was also the unconditional U.S. support of the Israeli government that added to this deadly and destructive mix.

It didn't take a rocket scientist to predict where all this was going to lead. At The Future of Freedom Foundation, prior to the 9/11 attacks we were publishing articles saying that the interventionism was going to inevitably result in a major terrorist attack on U.S. soil. We weren't the only ones. The noted analyst Chalmers Johnson said the same thing in his pre-9/11 book *Blowback: The Costs and Consequences of American Empire.*

No one should have been surprised about the consequences of all this deadly and destructive interventionism, especially given the 1993 terrorist attack on the World Trade Center, which was no different in principle from the one that followed eight years later, and the pre-9/11 attacks on the USS *Cole* and the U.S. embassies in East Africa.

The 9/11 attacks, of course, were used to justify even more interventionism, especially with the invasions of Afghanistan and Iraq. They were also used to justify the continuation of ever-growing budgets, power, and influence for the national-security establishment. They were also used to justify massive infringements on the rights and liberties of the American people.

What does all this have to do with the Kennedy assassination? When we approach the end of this book, we will see that there is a straight line from the assassination of John F. Kennedy to where we are today. That's one of the biggest reasons why the Kennedy assassination is still relevant today, almost 60 years later.

6

JFK's War

(Part 1)

In her book, Alexandra Zapruder ridicules the thesis of Oliver Stone's movie *JFK,* writing that "according to this scenario, killing Kennedy was necessary to prevent his gaining a second term and being able to pull out of Vietnam, which would in turn have hurt profits for the military-industrial complex in the United States."

While Alexandra is technically correct, she is, at the same time, so very wrong. What she obviously doesn't understand is that the vicious war that was waged between Kennedy and the U.S. national-security establishment from almost the start of his presidency went much deeper than Vietnam and the ever-burgeoning taxpayer-funded largesse that was being heaped on the military-industrial complex. This was a war that involved a fundamental conflict of visions, a war over the future direction of the United States.

The best book about that war is The Future of Freedom Foundation's *JFK's War with the National Security Establishment: Why Kennedy Was Assassinated* by Douglas P. Horne, who, as I previously noted, served on the staff of the Assassination Records Review Board.

The war actually began before Kennedy was sworn into office as president. As I pointed out in chapter 4, the CIA targeted Congo leader Patrice Lumumba with assassination because CIA officials deemed him to be a threat to U.S. national security. The CIA knew that if it waited until Kennedy assumed the presidency to murder Lumumba, Kennedy would have nixed the plan. That's because long before he came into office, Kennedy's view of third-world independence movements, like the one in the Congo, was different from that of the Pentagon and the CIA.

The Pentagon and the CIA were convinced that third-world independence movements were part of the supposed international communist conspiracy to take over the world that was supposedly based in Moscow. Since Lumumba was the leader of the movement in Congo seeking independence from Belgium, which, by definition in the minds of America's Cold Warriors, made him a communist or communist sympathizer, he was, therefore, deemed to be a threat to U.S national security. Thus, when President Eisenhower authorized Lumumba's assassination, the CIA was more than willing to carry out the task.

From the time he was a senator, Kennedy, on the other hand, sympathized with third-world independence movements. Recognizing that the imperialist powers had, more often than not, treated people who lived in their colonies with cruelty, brutality, humiliation, and economic exploitation, Kennedy openly advocated that the United States side with the independence movements.

Naturally, that made Kennedy suspect within the eyes of the national-security establishment even before he became president. For them, it was obvious that the new president was a naive neophyte who would have to be managed and handled if America was to win the Cold War and thereby prevent a communist takeover of the United States.

The CIA was right to assume that Kennedy would have nixed its plans to murder Lumumba. After Kennedy became president, he received word by telephone that Lumumba had been assassinated. His reaction to the news was caught by a photographer. That photograph appears on the cover of a book entitled *JFK: Ordeal in Africa* by Richard D. Mahoney. Please look up the book online. By seeing the expression of deep grief on Kennedy's face on receiving the news of Lumumba's death, you will know immediately that Kennedy would never have authorized the CIA to assassinate him.

Aside from his sympathy for third-world independence movements, Kennedy came into the presidency as pretty much a standard Cold Warrior. Like most other Americans, he had bought into the notion that the United States was in grave danger of falling victim to the supposed international communist conspiracy to conquer the world.

Thus, when the CIA presented Kennedy with a plan to invade Cuba soon after he took office, it didn't take a lot of persuading to get Kennedy to approve the plan. U.S. officials had determined that Cuba, which had been under communist rule since 1959, was a grave threat to the national security of the United States.

Since the time of the Spanish-American War in 1898, U.S. officials had controlled Cuba through a series of puppet regimes. But in 1959, the Cuban people, led by a woman named Celia Sanchez, revolted against the puppet regime of Cuban leader Fulgencio Batista, a crooked, corrupt, and brutal dictator who had partnered with the Mafia, the world's biggest criminal organization. In return for secret kickbacks, Batista had granted permission to the Mafia to operate casinos on the island.

As part of this cozy arrangement, Batista would send his goons into the Cuban countryside to kidnap underaged girls, who would then be delivered to high rollers in the Mafia's casinos who would proceed to rape them. One of the girls who fell victim to this evil scheme happened to be a good friend of Celia Sanchez, which motivated Sanchez to begin the Cuban revolution.

There is something important to know about Batista: The Pentagon and the CIA loved the guy. Like with other countries in which the national-security establishment had installed or aligned itself with dictators (e.g., Iran, Guatemala, and, later, Chile), U.S. officials couldn't care less how one of their puppets treated his citizenry. What mattered was that Batista was their man in Cuba.

The Cuban revolution succeeded in 1959, and Batista fled the island. Cuban revolutionary Fidel Castro became the political leader in Cuba. From the outset, Castro made it clear that under his leadership, Cuba was now going to be independent of the United States. That didn't sit well with U.S. officials. They had controlled Cuba for more than 50 years, and they were not about to surrender control now.

Tensions began ratcheting up, along with the adoption of measures and counter-measures by each side. Ultimately, Castro declared Cuba a communist nation. As a self-avowed socialist, he nationalized homes, businesses, and industries, including U.S. oil refineries. For its part, the U.S. government stopped the importation of sugar from Cuba and also placed an economic embargo on the island, which is still in place today and harshly enforced.

Most important, the U.S. government committed itself to regime change in Cuba. Remember: All this happened at the height of the Cold War, when the prevailing mindset was that the United States was in grave danger from the supposed international communist conspiracy. It was bad enough when a socialist who was friendly toward the Soviet Union was elected president of Guatemala, a country that was almost 2,700 miles away from the United States. Cuba was only 90 miles away, so it was clear that the Red Wave was getting closer. Unless Castro was removed from power and replaced by a pro-U.S. regime, it was believed, there was grave danger that the United States would end up losing the Cold War and falling to the communists.

Never mind that Cuba, like Guatemala, never attacked the United States or even threatened to do so. Never mind also that Cuba, like Guatemala, lacked the military capability, resources, and manpower to successfully invade, defeat, and occupy the United States.

What mattered was that "godless communism" and a regime that established friendly relations with the Soviet Union had come within 90 miles of American shores. Both the Pentagon and the CIA viewed the island as a communist dagger pointed at America's neck.

The CIA's plan to invade Cuba involved the use of Cuban exiles, who the CIA was secretly training in Guatemala, which, after the CIA's 1954 coup, was now being governed by a puppet U.S. military dictatorship. The U.S. role in the invasion was to be kept secret under the national-security doctrine of "plausible deniability." Thus, the CIA's plan entailed having the newly elected president immediately become a "liar-in-chief."

The CIA assured Kennedy that there was massive dissatisfaction among the Cuban populace for Castro's communist regime. The CIA told the president that once the Cuban exiles had landed, the populace would rise up in support of the invasion, head to Havana, oust Castro from power, and install another U.S. puppet regime into power.

For his part, Kennedy made it clear that he wanted the U.S. military to play no direct role in the invasion. The CIA assured Kennedy that no U.S. air support or troops would be needed, and Kennedy, for his part, told the CIA that no such support would be ordered.

The problem is that the CIA was lying. The agency was playing and manipulating the newly elected president. The CIA figured that once the invasion began faltering, there was no way that any U.S. president, including Kennedy, would permit brave Cuban exiles to be killed or captured by Castro's communist forces. The president would have no choice but to provide direct U.S. military air support and even bail out the invasion with U.S. troops, if necessary.

When Castro's forces began killing and capturing the invaders, the CIA asked Kennedy for the air support, fully believing that he would have to grant the request. But the CIA had misjudged the neophyte president it had been deceiving.

Kennedy said no, and much to the CIA's anger and rage, he let the invasion at Cuba's Bay of Pigs go down in defeat. More than a hundred men who were involved in the invasion were killed and over a thousand were captured. The communists had defeated the CIA's invaders and, at the end of the battle, were still in control of Cuba, where they would supposedly continue posing a grave threat to U.S. national security.

Even though the CIA had set up Kennedy as part of its plan, the agency was, nonetheless, livid. In his first confrontation as president with the communists, Kennedy had shown weakness at best and cowardice at worst. Having been given the opportunity to send U.S. bombers and U.S. troops into Cuba to save the United States from the grave threat to national security that Cuba supposedly posed, Kennedy had faltered. The communist dagger 90 miles from American shores remained pointed at America's neck.

For his part, Kennedy, too, was furious. He knew the CIA had lied to him and manipulated him. It became clear during the invasion — and subsequent declassified documents have confirmed — that the CIA knew as early as November of 1960 that there would be no internal uprising following the exile invasion of Cuba and had withheld this crucial information from both President Eisenhower and President Kennedy. In fact, the CIA knowingly perpetrated the lie of an internal uprising with JFK shortly after his election. The Cold Warriors in both the CIA and the Pentagon knew leading up to the invasion that the Bay of Pigs could only succeed as a joint CIA-Pentagon enterprise, including both covert operations and direct U.S. military intervention.

Kennedy could not believe that he had fallen for it. While he took public responsibility for the debacle, he embarked on a course of vicious retaliation against the CIA. He fired the much-revered director of the CIA, Allen Dulles, who, interestingly enough, would later be appointed by President Johnson to serve on the commission charged with investigating the president's murder. He also forced CIA Deputy

Director of Plans Richard Bissell and CIA Deputy Director Charles Cabell to resign. He began removing responsibilities for large paramilitary operations from the CIA and transferring them to the Pentagon. He also put his brother Bobby, who CIA officials loathed, in charge of monitoring the agency.

Reflecting the deep anger he had for the CIA, Kennedy is reputed to have said that he was going to "splinter the CIA into a thousand pieces and scatter it to the winds." While some have questioned the authenticity of the quote, it was reported by the *New York Times* in 1965, and there is no doubt that the words reflected Kennedy's mindset toward the CIA after the Bay of Pigs. Kennedy's relationship with the CIA never got better. It only got much worse.

For its part, the Pentagon had assured Kennedy that the Bay of Pigs invasion had a "fair" chance of success. That, too, was a lie. The Pentagon knew that the chances of success were minimal. It had estimated internally, prior to the invasion, that it had only a 20 percent chance of success and a 70 percent chance of failure. Yet, the Joint Chiefs chose to write in a formal assessment, prior to the invasion, that the Bay of Pigs had a "fair" chance of success. When this deception was revealed during the post-mortem assessments following the Bay of Pigs, it destroyed trust between Kennedy and the Pentagon.

Meanwhile, during 1961, the national-security establishment was pressuring Kennedy to send U.S. troops into Laos and, later, South Vietnam, to prevent communists from taking power in both countries. It alleged that if those two nations were to fall to the communists, other nations would begin falling like dominoes, which would mean that the Red Wave would get inexorably closer to the United States.

Kennedy resisted the pressure with respect to Laos and instead negotiated with the Soviet Union to establish a coalition government that included communists, who had been winning the guerrilla war in Laos and who demanded inclusion in the coalition government. Once again, that made the new president suspect in the eyes of the national-security establishment.

Kennedy had misgivings about sending troops to South Vietnam but finally did accede to the pressure that the Pentagon was putting on him. There was one important condition though: Kennedy made it clear that U.S. troops would serve only in an advisory role. To the day he died, he believed that this was South Vietnam's war — not America's war — to win or lose.

After the Bay of Pigs fiasco, the Pentagon kept up the pressure on Kennedy to invade Cuba, pressure that Kennedy continued to resist. As a compromise, Kennedy initiated Operation Mongoose, a plan to initiate economic chaos and political crisis in Cuba as a way to achieve regime change on the island.

As part of its regime-change operations, the CIA initiated secret measures to assassinate Fidel Castro. In the process, the agency entered into an assassination partnership with the Mafia, which was interested in getting back its casinos that Castro had nationalized.

After Kennedy and his brother Bobby were assassinated, the CIA maintained that both of them had approved the assassination plans against Castro, but that was just another of the CIA's many lies. President Kennedy made it clear to others that he steadfastly disapproved of state-sponsored assassinations as a foreign-policy tool. Moreover, the notion that Bobby Kennedy, who was fiercely prosecuting Mafia members in federal court, would approve of an assassination partnership between the CIA and the Mafia is patently ridiculous.

In 1962, the Joint Chiefs of Staff unanimously approved and forwarded to the Secretary of Defense a plan called Operation Northwoods, which was an extensive shopping list of elaborate pretexts for war with Cuba. Based entirely on lies, fraud, and deceit, it is one of the most extraordinary proposals in U.S. history. As far as I know, no one, including those who I label deferentials, has ever called Operation Northwoods a conspiracy theory.

Operation Northwoods called for real terrorist attacks inside the United States and simulated attacks on U.S. airliners as well as fake attacks on the American base at Guantanamo in Cuba and on U.S. ships in Guantanamo Bay. Innocent Americans or Cuban exiles or both were to be killed as part of the plan to launch terrorist attacks in Miami and Washington, D.C. The victims were considered expendable given the larger context of protecting America from a communist takeover.

Kennedy's job would clearly have been to go on national television after these "attacks" and say something like this: "My fellow Americans, today is another day that will live in infamy. Cuba's communist regime has attacked our nation by firing on American passenger planes, by initiating terrorist attacks here within the United States, and by attacking our forces at our Guantanamo Bay naval base. These attacks have cost the lives of American citizens and infringed our sovereignty. As your president, I have no choice but to defend our country. Today, I have ordered our military forces to bomb and invade Cuba, with the mission of defeating the communist regime responsible for these dastardly attacks. I assure you that we will avenge this communist aggression. God bless America."

To his everlasting credit, Kennedy rejected Operation Northwoods in a meeting held on March 16, 1962. Undoubtedly, he did so on moral grounds. But he also knew that if he invaded Cuba, it was a virtual certainty that the Soviets would invade West Berlin, which, given the overwhelming superiority of conventional weaponry of the Soviets in that part of the world, would have necessarily required U.S. retaliation with nuclear weapons.

It might also have occurred to Kennedy that Operation Northwoods presented the potential for blackmail on the part of the Pentagon and the CIA, similar to how FBI Director J. Edgar Hoover used secrets acquired about people's private lives to blackmail them into doing what he wanted. If Kennedy had approved the plan and if it had proved successful, for the rest of his presidency both the CIA and the Pentagon would have reminded him how they were protecting his secret whenever they walked into his office to make a request.

In October 1962, U.S. officials learned that the Soviet Union was in the process of installing strategic nuclear missiles — medium-range and intermediate-range nuclear surface-to-surface missiles — in Cuba. It is not difficult to imagine the reaction of the CIA and the Pentagon to that discovery. If the neophyte president had not shown weakness and cowardice at the Bay of Pigs or if he had approved Operation Northwoods, they undoubtedly reasoned, a U.S.-installed regime would have been in power in Cuba, and the nuclear crisis would never have arisen.

Whenever the mainstream media addresses the Cuban Missile Crisis, they refer to the Soviet missiles as "offensive" missiles. That's misleading. While the missiles could certainly reach the United States, their purpose was purely deterrence and defense. The Soviets and the Cubans knew full well that both the Pentagon and the CIA were determined to invade Cuba for the purpose of ousting Castro's regime from power and replacing it with a U.S.-installed regime. The purpose of the missiles was to deter U.S. officials from initiating such an invasion or, if that aim failed, to enable Cubans to defend themselves in the event of a war launched by the United States.

Informing the Soviet Union that the United States would never permit nuclear missiles to be installed in Cuba, Kennedy implemented a blockade, which he called a "quarantine." It prohibited any Soviet ship carrying offensive weapons (such as missiles and nuclear-capable bombers) from reaching Cuba. It was actually an act of war under international law. Fortunately for the world, however, Soviet Premier Nikita Khrushchev decided to comply with it.

Throughout the crisis, the Pentagon and the CIA were pressuring Kennedy to bomb and invade the island. In their minds, the crisis now provided the opportunity they had been waiting for since 1959 — an opportunity to invade Cuba and effect regime change.

It's a good thing that Kennedy resisted the pressure. What the CIA and the Pentagon did not know was that the Soviet commanders on the ground had fully armed tactical nuclear missiles, or "battlefield" nuclear weapons, designed for use on the beaches against any troops that might invade the island. While they technically were required to secure permission from Soviet officials before firing them, there is no telling whether all of the Soviet officers would have complied with that mandate while being bombed and attacked. Moreover, it is impossible to know how Khrushchev, who was under pressure from his own national-security establishment, would have responded if the Soviet commanders has requested permission to use their "battlefield nuclear weapons" to defend themselves from invading U.S. troops.

Knowing how close the two nations were to nuclear war, both leaders began searching for a way out of the crisis. In the end, Khrushchev and Kennedy struck a deal. In return for Kennedy's promise that the United States would not invade Cuba, Khrushchev agreed to withdraw the Soviet missiles from Cuba, which confirmed that the purpose of the missiles was always deterrence and defense. Additionally, as a secret unwritten codicil to the deal, Kennedy acceded to Khrushchev's demand to withdraw U.S. nuclear missiles from Turkey that were pointed at the Soviet Union. (Yes, that's right — the United States had nuclear missiles pointed at the Russians in a nation on the Soviet Union's border while, at the same time, it decried the authority of the Soviet Union to do the same in Cuba.) Six months after the Cuban Missile Crisis, President Kennedy quietly removed the U.S. government's 15 intermediate-range strategic nuclear missiles from Turkey.

With his deal with Khrushchev, Kennedy permanently squelched the hopes and dreams of the Pentagon, the CIA, and tens of thousands of Cuban exiles, who, until then, had continued hoping and dreaming of returning to a "free" Cuba.

The Joint Chiefs of Staff were enraged. One member, USAF Chief of Staff General Curtis LeMay, called JFK's peaceful resolution of the Cuban Missile Crisis "the biggest defeat in our nation's history" and compared Kennedy's actions during the crisis to British Prime Minister Neville Chamberlain's appeasement of Hitler at Munich.

The anger of the Joint Chiefs of Staff was understandable, given their fierce Cold War, anti-communist perspective. Rather than showing toughness in the face of communist "aggression" and using the Cuban Missile Crisis to free Cuba, they reasoned, Kennedy had surrendered Cuba permanently to the communists. Rather than bombing and invading to oust the communists from Cuba, they believed, Kennedy had chosen to let the communists keep their communist dagger permanently pointed at America's neck from only 90 miles away.

As much as the Pentagon and the CIA held Kennedy in extreme disdain for what they considered was his weakness, cowardice, and even treason when confronting the supposed communist threat to America, they hadn't seen anything yet. As we will see in the next chapter, Kennedy's war with the national-security establishment involved much more than just Vietnam and the loss of taxpayer-funded largesse to the military-industrial complex, as Alexandra Zapruder suggested when she ridiculed Oliver Stone's movie *JFK*.

7

JFK's War

(Part 2)

After the Cuban Missile Crisis, President Kennedy experienced one of the most monumental breakthroughs in history. Having come into the presidency as pretty much a standard Cold Warrior, Kennedy came to the realization that the Cold War was nothing but a great big deadly and destructive racket, one that was threatening mankind with extinction.

The catalyst for this breakthrough was the Cuban Missile Crisis. Kennedy knew how close the Soviet Union and the United States had come to nuclear war during the crisis. He also knew that in a nuclear exchange, his wife Jacqueline and his two young children, John and Caroline, would undoubtedly have been killed, given Jackie's refusal to leave Washington during the crisis. He also knew that millions of other people would have been killed or injured in a nuclear war.

Ironically, Soviet Premier Nikita Khrushchev achieved the same breakthrough. The two leaders embarked on a remarkable quest — to bring an end to the Cold War and have both nations co-exist in peace, harmony, and friendship, notwithstanding their different political and economic ideologies.

Kennedy had no illusions as to what the reaction would be within the U.S. national-security establishment. He knew that the Pentagon, the CIA, and the NSA would never countenance such a measure. They would look upon the neophyte president as hopelessly naive and incompetent. They would view his decision as the greatest threat to national security that could ever come from a U.S. president.

After all, what Kennedy was doing — reaching out to the Soviet Union in a spirit of peace and friendship — was what had caused President Arbenz to be regime-changed in Guatemala nine years before. It was also the reason why the U.S. national-security establishment would, several years later, prevail on the Chilean national-security establishment to oust their democratically elected president, Salvador Allende, from office.

In the eyes of the national-security establishment, the Cold War was a war to the finish, with a winner and a loser. Given the alleged communist conspiracy to take over the world, there was never any possibility, Pentagon and CIA officials believed, of establishing peaceful coexistence with the communist world. In the eyes of the Pentagon and the CIA, there could never be a negotiated peace between the United States and the Soviet Union. As the title of one right-wing book published in 1962 declared, you can always trust communists ... to be communists. In other words, trusting the communists could only result in defeat and a communist takeover of the United States.

It's worth mentioning, as an aside, that that is precisely what many Americans, especially conservatives, still believe today. In fact, if a poll were taken today, my hunch is that many Americans, especially conservatives, would say that the Cold War was absolutely necessary to protect America from a communist takeover. If told that Kennedy was negotiating with the communists to bring the Cold War to an end, many would consider him as hopelessly and dangerously naive as the national-security establishment did.

On June 10, 1963, President John F. Kennedy threw down the gauntlet by delivering what has gone down in history as his Peace Speech. Delivered at American University, it is a truly remarkable historical speech. You can view or listen to it online or just read the transcript of the speech. Just Google "JFK Peace Speech."

Kennedy did not consult either the Pentagon or the CIA as he was preparing his talk, with one exception: Joint Chiefs of Staff Chairman General Maxwell Taylor was shown a draft of the speech a few days prior to its delivery. His advice was: "Don't show this to the other Chiefs." Kennedy, therefore, did not advise the other JCS members what he was going to do. By this time, he held the national-security establishment in such disdain that he obviously decided to ambush them with his announcement, to avoid what would have inevitably been preemptive strikes by the Pentagon and its CIA allies against his grand policy initiative.

In his Peace Speech, Kennedy effectively declared an end to the Cold War. He said that there was no reason why the United States and the Soviet Union could not peacefully co-exist in the world. He pointed out that the two nations had worked together to win World War II. Sure, there were ideological differences between the two nations, but that was no reason for a hostile relationship. The two nations could compete ideologically in entirely peaceful ways.

Khrushchev, who was on the same page as Kennedy, found the speech so profound that he had it broadcast all across the Soviet Union and had its complete text printed, uncensored, in Soviet newspapers. That had never happened before.

It is not difficult to imagine the reaction within the national-security establishment. It was after JFK's Peace Speech that the covert decision to forcibly remove JFK from office, which likely was first arrived at immediately after the peaceful resolution of the Cuban Missile Crisis, surely hardened — and was finalized — within the national-security establishment. From the Cold War standpoint, America needed to be protected from what the national-security establishment was convinced was an incompetent, naive, and cowardly president whose policies were taking America to doom. After all, what Mossadegh,

Lumumba, Arbenz, and, later, Allende were doing to warrant forcible removal from office paled in significance compared to what President Kennedy was doing right here at home.

Kennedy didn't stop there. The very next night, June 11, he threw down another gauntlet before the national-security establishment, specifically the FBI, which, during the Cold War, became a de facto member of the national-security state. Kennedy went on national television and delivered a ringing endorsement of Martin Luther King and the civil-rights movement.

What was significant about that? The head of the FBI, J. Edgar Hoover, a serial blackmailer who loathed both Kennedy and his brother Bobby, had long been convinced that King was a communist and that the civil-rights movement was a communist front that received its orders from Moscow. Hoover believed that the communists were using the civil-rights movement to create strife, chaos, and conflict within America in order to pave the way for the communist takeover of the country.

So, here was John Kennedy, a president who, in the eyes of the national-security establishment, was already soft on communism, coming to the defense of what national-security officials were convinced was a communist front that was serving as a "Fifth Column" in the communist plan to take over America.

Kennedy didn't stop there. He announced that he would seek a limited nuclear-test ban treaty with the Soviets, which would end above-ground, atmospheric, and underwater testing of nuclear weapons. Both the United States and the USSR had been polluting the earth with radioactive fallout since the 1940s, and previous efforts by President Eisenhower to arrive at a test-ban treaty with the USSR had failed. Even though he knew that he had only a small chance of successfully getting such a treaty ratified by the U.S. Senate, given the predictable opposition of the Pentagon and the CIA and also given their tremendous influence over Congress, Kennedy nonetheless went forward with his plan.

When the predictable opposition arose from the national-security establishment as well as within Congress, Kennedy took his case directly to the American people by delivering speeches all across the country in favor of the treaty.

Kennedy struck a chord within the American populace. After almost 20 years of tension and fear arising from the Cold War, Americans clearly desired to move in a different direction — in the direction of peaceful and friendly relations with the Soviet Union and the communist world. So much public pressure was brought on the U.S. Senate that the treaty was ratified, which brought an end to the atmospheric nuclear pollution that came with above-ground nuclear testing.

Kennedy didn't stop there. At the United Nations in September of 1963, he proposed that the United States and the Soviet Union cooperate in a joint trip to the moon, which, needless to say, would have meant sharing U.S. rocket technology with the communists and abandoning the Cold War technological context known as the "Space Race."

But Kennedy went even further. In October 1963, in Top Secret National Security Action Memorandum (NSAM) 263, he ordered a partial pullout of 1,000 U.S. troops from Vietnam by the end of 1963 and a complete withdrawal of the remaining 15,000 advisors by the end of 1965. The order to withdraw 1,000 troops by the end of the year was severely resisted and watered down by the Joint Chiefs of Staff. Significantly, Kennedy confirmed to close aides that as soon as he won reelection in 1964, he would complete the pullout of all U.S. troops from Vietnam. The reason he wasn't willing to order a full pullout immediately was political. He knew that Barry Goldwater, who was likely to win the GOP presidential nomination, and American conservatives would accuse him of being soft on communism.

Although he was clearly ahead of public opinion, Kennedy was determined to move America in a completely different direction, one that was opposite from the direction in which the U.S. national-security establishment had been leading America since the start of the Cold War and in which it was determined to continue leading America. There was no way to reconcile those two conflicting visions.

Let's not forget something else of importance. The justification cited for the conversion of the federal government to a national-security state after World War II was the Cold War. No more Cold War meant no more justification for a national-security state. And there were plenty of Americans still alive at that time to be able to remember what it was like to live under a limited-government republic, our original system of government.

Thus, had Kennedy been successful in ending the Cold War in 1963, the American people at that time very likely would have demanded the dismantling of the national-security state and the restoration of the nation's founding system of government. Moreover, it would have been much more difficult under Kennedy for the Pentagon and the CIA to embark on a course of foreign interventionism in the Middle East, which would have meant no terrorist retaliation, no 9/11, no war on terrorism, no invasions of Afghanistan and Iraq, and no ever-increasing power, money, and influence for the military-industrial complex and its ever-expanding army of "defense" contractors.

Thus, Alexandra Zapruder is technically correct but, at the same time, wrong when she suggests that Kennedy's war with the national-security state involved only the Vietnam War and the ever-growing budgets for the "defense" industry. Kennedy's enemies within the national-security establishment weren't upset just because he was pulling out of Vietnam and threatening the ever-growing taxpayer-funded largess of the military-industrial complex. Kennedy was opposing the entire Cold War worldview of the national-security establishment and, in the process, threatening the continuation of the national-security state. Most important, in their eyes, he was leading America to doom — to a communist victory over the United States.

It's also worth mentioning that while Medicare and Medicaid were enacted during the Lyndon Johnson administration, both of those welfare-state programs, whose concept originated among socialists in Germany, were being proposed by President Kennedy. In principle, those two programs were every bit as socialist as the programs that were introduced by Jacobo Arbenz in Guatemala and Fidel Castro in Cuba as well as those that would be enacted by Salvador Allende's socialist administration in Chile.

Kennedy was not a dumb man. He clearly understood the extreme danger he was facing over the vision he had for the future direction of America. As a student of history, he was undoubtedly well-versed in the antipathy that our American ancestors had toward "standing armies" and their reasons for having such antipathy. Moreover, he had listened in 1961 as President Dwight D. Eisenhower delivered one of the most remarkable and shocking farewell addresses in U.S. history. Eisenhower, a West Point graduate who had made the military his career, had served as the overall commander of British and American allied forces in World War II after the invasion of France in June 1944. If there was anyone who understood the workings of the military establishment, it was Ike Eisenhower. In his speech, he warned the American people of the extreme danger posed by the national-security state, which he termed the "military-industrial complex." In an earlier draft of the speech, he used the term "military-industrial-congressional complex" to denote the extreme influence that the Pentagon, the CIA, and the NSA had over the members of Congress.

Eisenhower pointed out how the military-industrial complex had also expanded its influence all across the country, including in all 50 states. He was referring, of course, to the vast empire of domestic military bases, installations, and projects that were taking place in states and localities all across the country, all of which created a mind-set of dependency on the military-intelligence establishment.

Most important, Eisenhower warned Americans about the extreme danger to their liberties and democratic processes posed by the military-industrial complex. He was clearly alluding to the primary reason why our American ancestors, based on their study of history and their own personal experience with the English government and King George prior to July 4, 1776, fiercely opposed standing armies.

Eisenhower pointed out that while this new form of governmental structure was necessary because of the Cold War, Americans should, at the same time, be on their guard as to the dangers posed by this structure.

And now here was Kennedy, by effectively declaring an end to the Cold War, implicitly challenging the very necessity for a national-security state form of governmental structure.

Like Eisenhower, Kennedy was gravely concerned with the power of the generals and the intelligence officials within the military-industrial complex. He, too, issued the same grave warning to the American people, only he did it in the form of a movie.

But let's first back up a bit and provide some backstory.

Kennedy was once asked by a good friend of his named Red Fay whether Kennedy believed that the military-intelligence establishment posed a danger to a U.S. president. Fay had served with Kennedy in PT boats in the Pacific during World War II and was serving as undersecretary of the Navy in 1962 when he and Kennedy both read the thrilling bestseller *Seven Days in May,* about which they were both commenting. Kennedy responded that there was no question about it. Clearly alluding to himself, Kennedy said that if a young president came into office, he would be permitted a couple of major "mistakes," but with the third such mistake, the military-intelligence establishment would undoubtedly act to save the country from such an incompetent, neophyte president.

Kennedy's concern was reflected again during the Cuban Missile Crisis, when the Joint Chiefs of Staff were convinced that he was mishandling the crisis by not bombing and invading Cuba. During the crisis, Bobby Kennedy was negotiating with Soviet Ambassador Anatoly Dobrynin, with whom he had a friendly working relationship. At the height of the crisis, Bobby Kennedy told Dobrynin that he needed to inform Khrushchev that if they were going to strike a deal, they needed to do it now. The reason, Bobby said, was because his brother Jack was under severe pressure from the U.S. military establishment. According to what Khrushchev wrote in his memoirs, Bobby told Dobrynin that the possibility of a military takeover of the U.S. government could not be ruled out.

Dobrynin communicated that message to Khrushchev, who immediately understood that Kennedy was not bluffing. And he knew that a military takeover would inevitably mean war. Khrushchev quickly struck a deal with Kennedy that resolved the crisis.

Seven Days in May posited an attempted military takeover here in the United States owing to a president whose policies, U.S. military officials believed, posed a grave threat to national security. Kennedy, who, like Ike, wanted to send his own warning to the American people, persuaded a good friend of his in Hollywood, Director John Frankenheimer, to turn the novel into a movie. The movie turned out to be excellent. It starred Burt Lancaster, Ava Gardner, Kirk Douglas, and Fredric March. To watch a trailer for the movie, Google "Seven Days in May."

Thus, in a very real sense, President Eisenhower and President Kennedy were the earliest "conspiracy theorists" in the Kennedy assassination. So was President Harry Truman, the president who presided over the conversion of the federal government to a national-security state in 1947. On December 21, 1963, the *Washington Post* published an op-ed entitled "Limit CIA Role to Intelligence" by Truman describing how the CIA had become a sinister force in American life and stating that it needed to be strictly limited to an intelligence-gathering agency. It could not have been a coincidence that Truman wrote his op-ed less than 30 days after Kennedy was assassinated.

When Kennedy threw down the gauntlet with his Peace Speech at American University, the die was cast. In the war between Kennedy and the national-security establishment over their conflicting visions for the future direction of America, there was going to be a winner and there was going to be a loser.

It's also worth mentioning that on the very day of his assassination, a Kennedy emissary named Jean Daniel, a French journalist, was having lunch with Fidel Castro in a secret effort to normalize relations with Cuba, which of course would have meant a lifting of the brutal economic embargo against the Cuban people. That could not have sat well with the CIA, especially since the CIA at the very same time and unbeknownst to Kennedy was conspiring with a Cuban man named Rolando Cubela to attempt yet another assassination attempt against Castro, without Kennedy's authorization.

Moreover, it is not difficult to imagine what the reaction of the Pentagon and the CIA would have been to the following point that Kennedy wanted Jean Daniel to communicate to Castro: "I approved the proclamation which Fidel Castro made in the Sierra Maestra, when he justifiably called for justice and especially yearned to rid Cuba of corruption. I will go even further: to some extent it is as though Batista was the incarnation of a number of sins on the part of the United States. Now we shall have to pay for those sins. In the matter of the Batista regime, I am in agreement with the first Cuban revolutionaries. That is perfectly clear."

There was also Kennedy's extensive womanizing to consider in all this. While Americans were unaware of that part of the president's personal life, the Secret Service, which was charged with closely guarding the president, certainly was aware of it. There is every reason to believe that national-security state officials considered such womanizing to be a grave threat to national security, especially when one of the women with whom Kennedy was cavorting, Judith Campbell Exner, was purportedly also having affairs with Mafia leaders Sam Giancana and Johnny Roselli.

At the time of his assassination, Kennedy was having an affair with a woman named Mary Pinchot Meyer. A very intelligent woman, Meyer came from a prominent political family in Pennsylvania. Kennedy had known her when they were both in college and they had danced together at social functions, although they had never dated each other. She later married a man named Cord Meyer, a World War II hero who had lost an eye in battle.

After the war, the couple became leaders in a peace movement to end war forever, but Meyer's husband Cord became disillusioned as a peace activist and went to work for the CIA, where he became a high official. His decision to go to work for the CIA did not sit well with Mary, given her conviction that the CIA was actually a grave threat to world peace. That decision may well have contributed to the demise of their marriage, along with a much bigger reason, which was the loss of a young son in a tragic automobile accident.

Mary Meyer remained dedicated to peace for the rest of her life. At the time she was having the affair with Kennedy, she was living in the Georgetown section of Washington, D.C., where she was a prominent artist and a member of what was called the "beat" crowd, which was sort of a predecessor to the hippies. She was smoking dope and taking LSD.

As Peter Janney points out in his excellent book *Mary's Mosaic: The CIA Conspiracy to Murder John F. Kennedy, Mary Pinchot Meyer, and Their Vision for World Peace*, there is reason to believe that Meyer persuaded Kennedy to smoke marijuana with her. If true, and if the CIA or Secret Service became aware of it, it is not difficult to see how they would consider a doped-up president to be a grave threat to national security, especially during a nuclear crisis.

Janney writes that unlike his other affairs, Kennedy actually fell in love with Meyer. Given such, it is a virtual certainty that he would have discussed with her the breakthrough that he was experiencing after the Cuban Missile Crisis. In fact, there is a good chance that Meyer, who was still deeply committed to worldwide peace, may have played an instrumental role in bringing about Kennedy's breakthrough as well as the subsequent steps that Kennedy took to bring an end to the Cold War.

Immediately after the assassination, Meyer telephoned the famous LSD guru Timothy Leary, with whom she was friends, and in a clearly agitated voice said to him: "They couldn't control him anymore. He was changing too fast. They've covered everything up.... I'm afraid."

What was Mary Pinchot Meyer afraid of? Like other people whose lives became bound up with the Kennedy assassination, she feared the dark, omnipotent, evil power of the Deep State.

8

Avoiding Evil

In September 2004, Alexandra Zapruder's father Henry was diagnosed with terminal brain cancer. Knowing that he was going to die, he expressed a wish to be interviewed about the Zapruder film, a wish that he expressed to Alexandra. For the final 16 months of her father's life, however, Alexandra did not sit down with him and grant him his wish. In her book, she provided multiple reasons as to why she failed to do so: her father's rapidly declining health, her reluctance "to face the fact of his impending death," her first pregnancy and the birth of her daughter, and "trying to soak up every minute I could with him and eventually helping him to die with dignity."

I believe that there is another reason for Alexandra's reticence to interview her father about the Zapruder film: fear — deep fear, at least on a subconscious level. I think that subconsciously she knew that her father was going to unburden himself before dying and share with her the dark secret that had destroyed his father Abe and that had led to the decades-long family taboo against discussing the film. In my opinion, she could not muster the courage to listen to her father share that dark and foreboding secret with her. Her father undoubtedly understood that Alexandra did not want to hear the secret, and he obviously did not force it on her. He instead chose to take the secret to the grave with him.

After all, if Henry Zapruder had simply wanted to be interviewed about the family's general experiences with the film over the years, all that he would have had to do was get a tape recorder and record the salient facts and memories. Or he could have written down his recollections. Or typed them out on a computer. Or he could have dictated them to his legal secretary. In her book, Alexandra did not state that he did any of those things.

It's important to keep in mind that the family taboo against discussing the Zapruder film continued to exist long after Abe Zapruder died of stomach cancer in 1970, only seven years after the assassination, at the age of 65. When Abe died, Henry was in his late twenties, and Alexandra was just a baby. Yet, the family taboo against discussing the film lasted throughout the time she was growing up and all the way through 2006, when her father died at the age of 67. It wasn't until sometime around 2010 that she began contemplating her courageous journey to explore the roots of the family taboo.

Let's assume that Alexandra is correct in her conclusions as to the origin of the taboo. Let's assume that her grandfather's shock and grief over having witnessed the assassination and his internal conflict over having received $150,000 led to the family taboo. How would that explain why the taboo extended beyond the time that her grandfather died? What would her grandfather's grief about the assassination and his guilt over receiving so much money have to do with his son Henry? Why continue the taboo into Henry's life after Abe had passed away?

Remember that when she was 11 years old, Alexandra had to go her school's library to read what William Manchester had written about her grandfather's film. As she relates that story in her book, it is clear that she did not feel comfortable simply asking her father and mother about the film. In fact, her mindset clearly was that she was doing something secretive and forbidden when she went into that library and delved into Manchester's book. By that time, her grandfather Abe had been dead for about a decade.

According to her book, Alexandra's explanation as to why the taboo extended into her father's life was twofold. First, she says that her father didn't want the Zapruder family to be defined by the film. Second, she says that her father, like his father, was conflicted by the large amount of money that the Zapruder family received from the film.

Once again, however, those types of things do not lead to family taboos. It is dark, foreboding secrets that lead to family taboos. Neither of those two reasons is dark and foreboding.

After all, the fact is that the Zapruder family *was* defined by the Zapruder film, but that was largely a decision of their own making. Not only did the family receive a large amount of money when Abraham sold the film to *LIFE* magazine, Henry continued to receive money from licensing fees after reacquiring the film from *LIFE* in the mid-1970s. Then, in the late 1990s, when the government seized the film under the power of eminent domain, Henry Zapruder fought for and received an enormously large sum of money — $16 million (or the equivalent of $26.6 million in today's dollars). If the Zapruder family really was conflicted over the large amount of money they received from the film, there was an easy solution to that problem: waive receipt of the money or simply give it away. Neither Abe Zapruder nor his son Henry chose to take that course of action.

Let's review the major role that the Zapruder family played in having the film define the family, especially the large amount of money that they sought and received for it.

Immediately after the assassination, Abraham Zapruder returned to his office with his film. From that point on, it was clear that he had one goal in mind — to make as much money as he could from the film. When two Dallas policemen armed with shotguns arrived shortly after that demanding the film ostensibly as part of the investigation into the president's murder, Zapruder refused to let them have it.

It was a smart decision, given that other people who had taken videos or photographs of the assassination in Dealey Plaza had their films and photographs seized and never returned or simply destroyed on the spot by people purporting to be law-enforcement personnel. For example, a man wearing a police uniform confiscated the film of a U.S. soldier named Gordon Arnold, and he never saw it again. Another example was an eyewitness in Dealey Plaza named Beverly Oliver. In the video series "The Men Who Killed Kennedy," she said that the FBI took her film and promised to return it in 10 days but never did.

Shortly after those two policemen with shotguns demanded that Zapruder hand over his film, Secret Service agent William Sorrels entered Zapruder's office. Zapruder had a lot more faith in the Secret Service than he did in the Dallas police. He was willing to let Sorrels have a copy of his film.

As we saw in chapter 1, Sorrels later stated in an affidavit that Zapruder told him that he was determined to get as much money as he could for the film. In her book, Alexandra wondered whether Sorrels simply made that up. She wrote, "It seemed like an impossible thing for my grandfather to have said." In the process of questioning Sorrel's integrity, however, she obviously ignored something important: Her grandfather Abraham's actions were entirely consistent with his statement to Sorrels about hoping to get as much money as he could from the sale of his film.

First, when Zapruder took his film on the day of the assassination to the local Kodak facility to be developed and then later that day to the Jamieson Film Company to have copies made, he did everything he could to prevent any unauthorized copies of the film from being made. The reason he did so is obvious: Unauthorized copies that were being circulated and shown around would tend to reduce the value of his film.

Second, as Alexandra points out in her book, her grandfather had apparently taken the time to telephone his lawyer after the assassination to get advice on selling his film. Alexandra pointed out that his lawyer apparently advised him to secure affidavits from Kodak and Jamieson attesting to the fact that no unauthorized copies of the film were made. There can be only one explanation for these actions: Abraham Zapruder, the canny businessman that he was, immediately knew that he had a valuable asset and was doing everything he could to protect its value.

In her speculation as to whether Sorrels might have been lying about what Abraham Zapruder said to him, Alexandra pointed to the fact that her grandfather didn't initiate a bidding war among the media on Saturday morning, when he was meeting with *LIFE*'s representative Richard Stolley. His failure to do so purportedly showed, in her mind, that her grandfather wasn't really trying to get top dollar for his film after all and that Sorrels might have been just making it up.

In questioning Sorrels's veracity, however, she forgets that her grandfather was in his office early the very next morning after the assassination to discuss selling the film to *LIFE* magazine! In other words, he wasn't at home paralyzed with grief.

Alexandra ignores something else of importance. The night before (i.e., the night of the assassination), Zapruder took the time to talk on the telephone to Stolley and make an appointment to meet him at 9 a.m. the following morning. That's the reason why Zapruder was at his office on the morning after the assassination — to negotiate the sale of his film to *LIFE* magazine.

She also ignores another point. Stolley was willing to offer Abraham top dollar for the print-media rights to his film. Given Zapruder's deep respect for *LIFE* magazine and given the large amount of money that Stolley was offering, there was no reason for Zapruder to see if other media outlets would match or exceed what *LIFE* was offering.

On Monday morning, November 25 — the day of the Kennedy funeral — Zapruder was in his attorney's office, this time creating a bidding war among the media for the motion-picture rights to his film. As part of that war, Zapruder would invite each member of the media into a room where the media representative would view his remaining copy of the film (one of the three copies he had made on the day of the assassination) on Zapruder's 8mm projector, which he had brought from home. (He had relinquished the camera-original to *LIFE* on Saturday, when the magazine purchased still-picture or print-media rights for the home movie.)

It turned out to be not much of a war, however, given Zapruder's bias toward *LIFE* magazine and given the unbelievably generous offer that *LIFE* made for the motion-picture rights — an additional $100,000 on top of the $50,000 that *LIFE* had already agreed to pay for the print-media rights. As previously noted, that totals around $1.3 million in today's dollars. That's a lot of money for a 26-second film. Additionally, as previously noted, *LIFE* agreed to pay Zapruder 50 percent of all the revenue it received from the motion-picture rights to the film, after its $150,000 purchasing price was recouped, notwithstanding the fact that *LIFE* publisher C. D. Jackson, as we saw in chapter 1, actually intended to sequester the film and never let anyone see it.

Although low-quality bootleg copies of the film began popping up in various forums in the late 1960s and early 1970s, Jackson's decision to suppress the Zapruder film succeeded in preventing it from ever being viewed on television for some 12 years.

Then, on March 6, 1975, despite being threatened with a lawsuit by *LIFE,* the television journalist Geraldo Rivera showed a high-quality bootleg copy of the film on his nationally broadcast television show "Good Night America," which was broadcast on ABC. That showing had a monumental effect on what then happened to the film. Upon watching it, people were outraged and, needless to say, extremely suspicious about *LIFE*'s 12-year suppression of the film. Keep in mind, after all, that *LIFE* had originally intended to prevent anyone from ever seeing the film.

One result of Rivera's unauthorized showing of the film was that it caused the U.S. House of Representatives to reopen an official investigation into the Kennedy assassination. That investigation was carried out by the U.S. House Select Committee on Assassinations, which ended up concluding that Kennedy had been assassinated as a result of a conspiracy involving Oswald and unknown others.

The other result was that *LIFE* magazine decided that it no longer wanted to retain ownership of the Zapruder film.

At the time that Rivera showed the film, Abraham Zapruder was already dead. Matters relating to the film were being handled by his son Henry, Alexandra's father. Henry could have walked away from the film and simply let *LIFE* do whatever it wanted with it. Obviously, that would have been the easiest way to avoid having the film define his life or the lives of the Zapruder family. Instead, as Alexandra points out in her book, Henry offered to pay *LIFE* magazine the sum of $60,000 for the film.

LIFE magazine rejected Henry Zapruder's offer. Interestingly and somewhat shockingly, *LIFE* instead offered to sell the film back to the Zapruder family for only one dollar.

Yes, you read that right. After having paid the equivalent of $1.3 million (in today's dollars) to Abraham Zapruder, *LIFE* magazine left the equivalent (in today's dollars) of $309,000 on the table when it was negotiating with Henry Zapruder over the return of the film to the Zapruder family. *LIFE* instead decided to settle for receiving just one dollar, which is about $5 in today's money.

Having lost much of its popularity with the American people, *LIFE* magazine had ceased publication by 1972 — three years before it rejected Henry Zapruder's generous offer. No doubt the growing popularity of television was a large part of the reason for that, but I can't help but wonder whether it was also because people no longer trusted *LIFE* magazine, not only because of the still-unexplained lie in the Paul Mandel article back in 1963 but also owing to *LIFE*'s intention to prevent the American people from ever seeing the Zapruder film. What is befuddling is why Time, Inc., the owner of *LIFE* magazine, would reject Henry Zapruder's offer of $60,000 ($309,000 in today's dollars) and instead decide to effectively donate the film back to the Zapruder family. In her book, Alexandra surmised that the reason was that "Time Inc., which had taken plenty of beatings over the Zapruder film, hoped at least to get some positive media attention for giving up the film without making any profit." We will explore another possibility later on.

In her book, Alexandra observes that the final offer of $150,000 that Richard Stolley made to Zapruder for the purchase of all rights to the film was set by *LIFE* magazine publisher C. D. Jackson. As you will recall, Jackson's purported motive for suppressing the film after spending so much money was to protect the American people from seeing the violence depicted in the film.

Sometimes what a person doesn't mention is as significant as what he does mention. In describing C. D. Jackson as simply the publisher of *LIFE* magazine, Alexandra Zapruder failed to mention something of significance: Jackson had a long and close relationship with the Central Intelligence Agency.

In the 1950s, the CIA established a secret program called Operation Mockingbird, whose mission was to acquire CIA assets within the mainstream press. The idea was that since the Cold War involved a life-and-death struggle against godless communism and the Soviet Union, the U.S. government needed to mobilize all its forces to prevail in this war. Enlisting the support of the mainstream press was considered essential to this effort.

For their part, many mainstream journalists considered it their patriotic duty to become CIA assets by writing articles favorable to the CIA and to the viewpoints it advanced. They didn't see anything wrong with what they were doing. As far as they were concerned, they were simply doing their patriotic part to ensure that America didn't go Red.

According to the website of Spartacus Educational, "Jackson took an active role in Operation Mockingbird." Spartacus also points out that Jackson worked closely with John J. McCloy, who served as president of the World Bank and who, along with former CIA director Allen Dulles, would later be appointed by President Johnson to serve on the Warren Commission.

In World War II, Jackson served in the Office of Strategic Services (OSS), which was the predecessor of the CIA, in a psychological warfare role in London. He later served as special assistant to the president in the Eisenhower administration. From 1951 to 1952, he served as president of the anticommunist Free Europe Committee. After working in Eisenhower's 1952 campaign for president, Ike appointed him to serve as liaison between the CIA and the Pentagon. Spartacus Educational states, "According to the Eisenhower Presidential Library files in Abilene, Kansas, Jackson's 'area responsibility was loosely defined as international affairs, cold war planning, and psychological warfare. His main function was the coordination of activities aimed at interpreting world situations to the best advantage of the United States and her allies and exploiting incidents which reflected negatively on the Soviet Union, Communist China and other enemies in the Cold War.'"

According to Spartacus Educational, "Charles Douglas Jackson died on 18th September, 1964. On December 15, 1971, Jackson's widow gave his papers to the Eisenhower Presidential Library. These documents revealed that he had been working as a CIA agent since 1948."

Jackson wasn't the only one at *LIFE* magazine who was an ardent anti-communist and fierce proponent of the Cold War. Henry Luce, the magazine magnate who launched *LIFE* magazine, himself had a close relationship to the CIA and worked closely with the agency on various covert projects. Spartacus Educational's entry on Luce states, "According to Carl Bernstein, Luce's close friend Charles Douglas Jackson, the publisher of *Life Magazine,* was 'Henry Luce's personal emissary to the CIA.' He also claimed that in the 1950s Jackson had arranged for CIA employees to travel with Time-Life credentials as cover. [Nationally syndicated columnist] Drew Pearson supported this view: 'Life magazine is always pulling chestnuts out of the fire for the CIA; and I recall that C. D. Jackson of the Life-Time empire was the man who arranged for the CIA to finance the Freedom Balloons.... C. D. Jackson, Harold Stassen and the other boys who went with me to Germany spent money like water while I paid my own way. I always was suspicious that a lot of dough was coming from unexplained quarters and didn't learn until sometime later that the CIA was footing the bill.'"(Brackets added.)

Why would Alexandra Zapruder leave out any mention of C. D. Jackson's relationship to the CIA in her book? As we have seen and will continue to see, whenever she starts getting close to the centrum of evil that enveloped her grandfather and ended up destroying his life, she does whatever she can to avoid acknowledging and confronting it, even if it is on a subconscious level.

9

Confronting Reality

I grew up in Laredo, Texas, which, in the 1950s and 1960s, was a Democrat stronghold. My father was active in local Democrat Party politics. When I was in the fifth grade, I campaigned for John Kennedy and Lyndon Johnson for president and vice president by stuffing envelopes at night at local campaign headquarters. As part of a local delegation, my father and I traveled to the LBJ ranch in Johnson City for a campaign barbecue, where I shook hands with Johnson himself.

I was in the eighth grade when I learned that President Kennedy had been shot. I was as deeply affected as most other Americans were. Like most everyone else at that time, I remember where I was when I received the news: waiting to go into biology class when a fellow student came up and announced that the president had been shot.

Believe it or not, for most of my life, I knew only about the official version of the assassination — the one set forth by the Warren Commission. Until I was 41 years old, I had no idea that there were people who were questioning or challenging the official story. Like many others, I believed what I had been taught — that a lone-nut communist named Lee Harvey Oswald had assassinated the president and then, two days later, had himself been assassinated by a man named Jack Ruby.

In 1991, I walked into the theater to watch Oliver Stone's movie *JFK*. I had read no press accounts of the movie and I was totally unaware of the enormous controversy swirling around the movie. I thought I was going to be just watching a biographical account of the man for whom I had campaigned back when I was in grade school.

I was stunned when I walked out of that movie theater. The movie directly challenged the official story of the assassination. It contended that the assassination was actually a highly sophisticated regime-change operation on the part of the U.S. national-security establishment. I didn't know what to make of what I had just seen.

Cursed (or blessed, depending on one's perspective) with an inquisitive and analytical mind, I decided to seek out books on the assassination, especially those that challenged the official version of the assassination. The books I read made interesting points but there was always something that just didn't fit. What I mean by that is that I was trained as a lawyer, with a law degree from the University of Texas, and then I was a trial lawyer in Texas for 12 years. The way I figure out some unusual scenario is that I will compile all the available pieces to the puzzle and then overlay a particular hypothesis onto those pieces. If a piece doesn't fit, then I discard the hypothesis and try again with another hypothesis. I keep going until I finally find a hypothesis in which all of the available pieces to the puzzle fit in a logical, consistent, and coherent way. I might not have all the pieces to the puzzle, but once I have the correct hypothesis, the pieces I do have will fit together and oftentimes reveal what the overall puzzle shows.

What I found in my research into the Kennedy assassination was that when a particular piece of the puzzle didn't fit a particular hypothesis, some researchers would simply discard or ignore that puzzle piece rather than discard their hypothesis. Or they would cut and refine the puzzle piece to fit their hypothesis. It goes without saying that I found that approach to be inadequate.

Moreover, notice how the mainstream media always frames what is portrayed to be the pertinent issue in the Kennedy assassination: Did Oswald act alone, or was he part of a conspiracy? As I was delving into the assassination literature, I noticed that some assassination researchers were making the case for conspiracy, and yet, they never made a logical case with respect to the person or persons with whom Oswald was supposedly conspiring. The Soviets? The Cubans? The Mafia? His friends? Co-workers? Fellow communists? Fellow Marines? None of it made any sense to me. Regardless of whom one chose to have supposedly conspired with Oswald, that particular piece of the puzzle just didn't fit with any logical hypothesis of the case.

Consider, for example, the fact that U.S. officials immediately shut down any further investigation into the Kennedy assassination after Oswald himself was assassinated. Why would they do that? To protect the Soviet Union, Cuba, or the Mafia? That makes no sense. They hated the Soviet Union, Cuba, and the entire communist world. And even though the CIA was in partnership with the Mafia to assassinate Castro, would they really give a pass to the Mafia if it actually killed a president of the United States? And certainly U.S. officials would not let Oswald's friends, workers, or fellow communists off the hook even if Oswald himself was now dead.

As far as I was concerned, the only thing to do was to find a different hypothesis, one that made sense given the existing pieces of the Kennedy assassination puzzle.

The answer came in a telephone conversation I had with an assassination researcher named David Lifton, the author of a watershed book about the assassination titled *Best Evidence: Disguise and Deception in the Assassination of John F. Kennedy*. I mentioned the quandary I was in over who Oswald's possible confederates could have been if there was, in fact, a conspiracy to kill the president. I told Lifton that the quandary had led me to nothing but dead ends. He shattered my thinking by posing an entirely different hypothesis: that Oswald was an innocent man who was being framed by the national-security establishment as part of its highly sophisticated regime-change operation.

Wow! That was a stunner for me because I had been deeply indoctrinated into believing that at the very least, Oswald had to have participated in the assassination. As far as I was concerned, the only question was whether Oswald acted alone or in a conspiracy with others. It never occurred to me, just as it never occurs to many members of the mainstream press, that Oswald may have been exactly what he claimed to be — a "patsy" — that is, an innocent man who was being framed. Now that I had a new hypothesis to work with, I could now overlay it onto the available set of pieces to the puzzle. This time, all the pieces fit together.

It was not only that conversation but also Lifton's book that set me on the right course. As Douglas Horne points out in his book *Inside the Assassination Records Review Board,* Lifton's book was a paradigm shift in analyzing the assassination because it was the first book that set forth the hypothesis that the medical evidence surrounding the military's autopsy on President Kennedy's body was fraudulent.

That was a monumentally important insight, because if true, a fraudulent autopsy conclusively establishes that the Kennedy assassination was, in fact, a regime-change operation orchestrated and carried out by the U.S. national-security establishment. As I have emphasized time and again over the years, there is no innocent explanation for a fraudulent autopsy. It necessarily implies complicity and coverup in the Kennedy assassination on the part of the national-security establishment.

As much as Lifton's book influenced my thinking, it was Horne's book that ended up putting everything together for me in a logical, coherent whole.

In fact, I consider the following books the very best books on the Kennedy assassination: *JFK and the Unspeakable: Why He Died and Why It Matters* by James W. Douglass; *Inside the Assassination Records Review Board: The U.S. Government's Final Attempt to Reconcile the Conflicting Medical Evidence in the Assassination of JFK* by Douglas P. Horne; *JFK's War with the National Security Establishment: Why Kennedy Was Assassinated* by Douglas P. Horne; and *Best Evidence* by David Lifton. I would then add to the list David Talbot's two books, *Brothers: The Secret History of the Kennedy Years* and *The Devil's Chessboard: Allen Dulles, the CIA, and the Rise of America's Secret Government*. At the risk of being immodest, I would also add my books, *The Kennedy Autopsy, The Kennedy Autopsy 2, Regime Change: The JFK Assassination,* and *The CIA, Terrorism, and the Cold War: The Evil of the National Security State.* I have no doubts that anyone who reads those books will conclude beyond any reasonable doubt that what occurred on November 22, 1963, in Dealey Plaza was not a "conspiracy theory" but rather a highly sophisticated regime-change operation orchestrated and carried out by the U.S. national-security establishment. (See Appendix A for a larger list of recommended books and videos.)

Defenders of the official theory of the assassination have long maintained that people who don't accept the official story are psychologically incapable of accepting that the assassination was simply the work of some lone nut. I never looked on the matter like that. My quest was to seek the truth of the assassination. And at the time I saw the movie *JFK*, I knew that government officials were doing some bad things and, equally important, that they were lying about them. I knew, of course, about the lies and omissions regarding the supposed attacks by North Vietnamese forces against two U.S. Navy ships in the Gulf of Tonkin, which brought about the Gulf of Tonkin Resolution authorizing Johnson and the Pentagon to expand the war in Vietnam. I also knew from the Pentagon Papers about the many lies that the

Pentagon had told about the Vietnam War, a war that took the lives of 58,000 men of my generation, including schoolmates of mine at Virginia Military Institute, just as Pentagon officials would later lie about the progress they were supposedly making in their 2002 invasion and long-term occupation of Afghanistan.

To me, the psychological problem lies not with those of us who have inquisitive or analytical minds. Instead, the problem lies with people who are psychologically incapable of accepting the reality that the federal government, specifically the national-security establishment, does evil things and then lies about them. As I indicated in chapter 4, given that many Americans have come to view the federal government as a daddy (or a god) that provides their sustenance in the form of Social Security, Medicare, Medicaid, farm subsidies, education grants, food stamps, and various other forms of welfare, and that ostensibly protects them from communists, Muslims, drug dealers, illegal immigrants, terrorists, and other scary monsters in the world, the last thing that some Americans want to do is challenge or question what their daddy (or god) is doing. What if he were to get angry and suddenly cut them off or decline to keep them safe?

As we all know, defenders of the official lone-nut theory of the assassination deride those of us who have concluded that Kennedy was actually killed as part of a national-security regime-change operation as "conspiracy theorists." In fact, in her book, Alexandra Zapruder has a grand time mocking, ridiculing, and attacking "conspiracy theorists."

What Alexandra fails to inform her readers about, however, is that it was the CIA that promoted the use of that term — "conspiracy theorist" — to its assets in the mainstream press as a way to keep people from examining the assassination too closely. It has undoubtedly been the most successful propaganda campaign in CIA history. Today, there are countless Americans who will do everything they can to avoid being exposed to anything that questions or challenges the official version of the assassination. It's simply too scary to do so owing to the fear of being labeled a "conspiracy theorist."

I'm accustomed to being called a "conspiracy theorist," but it really doesn't matter to me. The reason is that I don't have a theory of the Kennedy assassination. My conclusion is based simply on the overwhelming mountain of clear and convincing evidence that establishes that a regime-change operation was carried out on November 22, 1963, for the same reason that regime-change operations were carried out against Iran, Guatemala, the Congo, Cuba (repeatedly), and Chile both before and after the Kennedy assassination. The evidence establishes beyond a reasonable doubt that U.S. officials felt duty-bound to protect America from political leaders, both here at home and abroad, whose policies were deemed to pose a grave threat to "national security."

Equally important, as we have seen so far and will see later in this book, the evidence also establishes beyond a reasonable doubt that the military-intelligence establishment carried out a fraudulent autopsy on the president's body a few hours after the assassination. Once one arrives at the conclusion that the autopsy was fraudulent, one also necessarily arrives at the conclusion that the military-intelligence establishment carried out the assassination, given that there is no innocent explanation for a fraudulent autopsy.

It's important to distinguish belief from knowledge. I don't *believe* that the Pentagon and the CIA assassinated President Kennedy and then covered it up. I *know* they did.

And actually, so might you, even if you don't yet realize it. Why do I say that? Because of Dr. Robert McClelland, Navy Petty Officer Saundra Spencer, Dr. Charles Crenshaw, Nurse Audrey Bell, FBI agents Francis O'Neill and James Sibert, Secret Service agent Clint Hill, and all the others who saw a large exit-sized wound in the back of President Kennedy's head.

There is no reasonable possibility that all those people could be lying. They are all too credible. There is also no reasonable possibility that they all entered into a conspiracy to pin the crime on the national-security establishment.

So, the question is: Could they all be independently mistaken? Could it actually be possible that they all imagined a wound that just wasn't there?

There is no reasonable possibility of that either. Go back and watch that video interview of Dr. McClelland. When you do so, keep in mind something important about Parkland Hospital. It was — and is — one of the finest trauma hospitals in the country. Treating gun-shot wounds was what Parkland specialized in.

Reflect on what McClelland stated during that interview. He walked into Trauma Room One and saw the doctors conducting a tracheostomy on President Kennedy to enable him to breathe more easily. McClelland went to the head of the gurney to assist with the tracheostomy and immediately saw an enormous exit-sized wound in the back of Kennedy's head. He asked the other physicians whether they had seen that wound. They said no — that they entered the room just before he had. McClelland told them they needed to see it.

There was one big reason that McClelland wanted them to see the wound. He knew that it was fatal. There was no way that anyone could survive that wound.

Now, what are the chances that McClelland, who was charged with treating and trying to save the life of the president of the United States, was simply imagining that wound? What are the chances that the other treating physicians — Dr. Crenshaw, Dr. Clark, Dr. Carrico, and the others also imagined that wound?

What are the chances that all those other people who witnessed that back-of-the-head wound independently imagined it: Nurse Audrey Bell, Nurse Diana Bowron, Secret Service agent Clint Hill, FBI agents O'Neill and Sibert, and all the rest?

Indeed, what are the chances that U.S Navy Petty Officer Saundra Spencer in Washington, D.C., imagined that big exit-sized wound when she saw it in the post-mortem photographs that she was asked to develop on the weekend of the assassination?

It's worth mentioning at this point that a medical student named Billy Harper found a piece of Kennedy's skull bone in Dealey Plaza the day after the assassination. He took it to his uncle, who was a pathologist at Methodist Hospital in Dallas. A team of pathologists at the hospital, which included his uncle, conducted a forensic study of the fragment and photographed it, concluding that it was occipital bone. Remember that the occipital region of the skull is in the back of the skull. Not surprisingly, after the bone fragment was sent to Washington, D.C., the military ended up "losing" it. Fortunately, the photographs of the bone still exist.

Defenders of the lone-nut theory of the assassination say: Trust the national-security establishment because it would never lie and it would never conduct a fraudulent autopsy. Conclude instead that all those witnesses just imagined that big exit-sized wound in the back of the president's head.

If you conclude that the national-security establishment does lie, and if you conclude that those witnesses who saw that large exit-sized wound in the back of Kennedy's head were telling the truth and accurately describing what they saw, then you have automatically concluded that the U.S. national-security establishment orchestrated and carried out the assassination of President John F. Kennedy.

You might respond, "Jacob, it can't be that easy. I know very little about the assassination and have done very little reading about it." But it is that easy, especially when one considers all the other evidence of fraud surrounding the autopsy, as we will see later in this book. And it doesn't matter how much reading one has done on the assassination.

You see, it works like this: If you believe that McClelland, Spencer, and the others are speaking truthfully and accurately, then that means that the military's official autopsy photographs depicting the back of Kennedy's head to be intact are fraudulent.

There is no other conclusion that can be drawn. There is no way to reconcile what all those witnesses say they saw with the military's autopsy photographs. It's one way or the other. If the photographs are authentic, then McClelland, Spencer, Hill, and other witnesses are either lying or speaking inaccurately. If they are speaking truthfully and accurately, then it is the national-security establishment that is doing the lying and committing the fraud.

That's where the power of Douglas Horne's five-volume book *Inside the Assassination Records Review Board* comes into play. Once a person concludes that the autopsy that the military conducted on President Kennedy's body was fraudulent, as Horne's book carefully and meticulously documents, it is "case closed" on who orchestrated and carried out the assassination. That's because, once again, there is no way to come up with an innocent explanation for a fraudulent autopsy. No one ever has, and no one ever will. The scheme to conduct a fraudulent autopsy was necessarily part of the overall plan of the assassination, which is why it was launched immediately after President Kennedy was declared dead, when that team of Secret Service agents, brandishing guns and screaming profanities, prevented Dr. Rose, the Dallas County medical examiner, from conducting the autopsy that was required under Texas law and instead forced its way out of Parkland Hospital with the president's body.

We will talk more about Douglas Horne when we delve into the CIA's secret role involving the Zapruder film. In the process, we will examine the nasty and overblown attack that Alexandra Zapruder leveled against Horne in her book.

Keep in mind something important, though: Once we accept that McClelland and the others who saw that wound in the back of Kennedy's head were speaking truthfully and accurately and that it is the government that is lying with respect to its fraudulent autopsy photographs, we run directly into the question of the authenticity of the Zapruder film, which, like those fraudulent autopsy photographs of the back of JFK's head, shows the back of Kennedy's head to be intact after the gunshot (or gunshots) hit him in the head.

10

The Film

On July 22, 1964, Abraham Zapruder entered the office of the U.S. Attorney in the Post Office building in Dallas to give sworn testimony to an attorney for the Warren Commission, the entity that President Johnson had appointed to ostensibly investigate the Kennedy assassination.

Zapruder was clearly nervous and disjointed. In her book, Alexandra Zapruder acknowledges this when she writes: "From the beginning of his testimony, Abe sounds a little nervous, explaining that he had been out of town when he was summoned and that his secretary had made the appointment for him."

Abe Zapruder had every reason to be nervous and disjointed, especially since it was a virtual certainty that he was going to be asked about his film.

It had been eight months since he would have read the Paul Mandel article in *LIFE* magazine — the article that falsely asserted that Zapruder's film showed that President Kennedy had been shot in the throat after he turned around and faced the Texas School Book Depository. Having seen his 26-second film at least 15 times (and, almost certainly, more times) on the weekend of the assassination, Zapruder had to have known that what Mandel wrote was a lie — a flagrant, out-and-out lie.

But why? Why would *LIFE* magazine pay Zapruder $150,000 — the equivalent in today's dollars of $1.3 million — to secure ownership and possession of Zapruder's film and then lie to the American people about its contents? Why would C. D. Jackson suppress the film after he had led Zapruder to believe that he would receive additional revenue from motion-picture rights to the film? What could possibly be going on? Those questions undoubtedly would have bedeviled Zapruder in the months following the assassination. They would have still been bedeviling him when he walked into that Dallas Post Office to give sworn testimony about his film. How could they not?

In fact, Alexandra states that in the months following the assassination, her grandfather spent considerable time carefully studying various aspects of the assassination that related to his film. She writes: "He knew the film well, and he understood about the camera speed, the critical frames, the time required to fire the rifle, and how all those elements related to the time clock of the assassination."

Equally important, Alexandra makes it clear that in those early months after the assassination, the decades-long family taboo against discussing the film had still not come into existence. She writes: "In fact, according to his daughter, Myrna, he talked so much about it in the months after the assassination that there was eventually a blowup at the dinner table, when she and her husband, Myron, told him he had to stop obsessing about it."

Does that sound like a man who was so grief-stricken or so conflicted over the large amount of money that he had received for his film that he was paralyzed from speaking about his film? Or does it sound like a man who is deeply troubled by a magazine that had paid him an enormous sum of money for his film and then, for some unknown reason, lied about its contents and then would not let the public see it?

Moreover, keep in mind that one of the two explanations that Alexandra gives for the family taboo against discussing the Zapruder film was the deep grief that her grandfather was experiencing as a result of having witnessed and filmed the assassination. But if that were the case, wouldn't you think that the taboo would have come into existence immediately after the assassination, when grief would ordinarily be more pronounced, rather than several months after the assassination, when grief would ordinarily have diminished?

In November 1966, Zapruder gave a rare television interview to a man named Marvin Scott. The transcript of that interview can be purchased from the Sixth Floor Museum in Dallas. Alexandra writes in her book: "Marvin Scott spent a considerable time in the interview asking Abe for his thoughts on the controversies around the assassination, such as the debate about the number, timing, and direction of the shots fired. From the interview, it seems that Abe was well versed in these issues, and he did not hesitate to contradict Scott when he thought he miscalculated the time elapsed between shots or other elements related to the time clock. He had apparently thought about the issues more than anyone in our family realized. He even mentioned that he had gone back to the site and looked at the stockade fence to the right of the wall on which he had been standing, to measure its distance from his position that day and to determine if the shots he heard might have come from that direction. In the end, he felt sure that — even though he heard only two shots and not three — the shots sounded consistent, leading him to conclude that they both came from the same direction."

That interview took place three years after the assassination. Again, does that sound like a man who was so grief-stricken or so conflicted over the large amount of money that he had received for his film that he was emotionally paralyzed by the assassination? Or does it sound like a man who is troubled by the official story and is trying to figure things out for himself?

When Zapruder sold the print-media rights to his film to *LIFE* on Saturday, November 23 — the day after the assassination — he handed the original film to the magazine's representative with whom he had been negotiating, Dick Stolley. You will recall that *LIFE* agreed to return the film to Zapruder in a week, after which he would then be free to sell the motion-picture rights to the film. At the time he delivered the original film to Stolley, Zapruder retained a copy of the film, one of three copies that had been made on the Friday afternoon of the assassination. Zapruder had handed over the other two copies to the Secret Service on Friday night, November 22.

When Stolley and Zapruder struck their deal for all rights to the film on the following Monday morning, Zapruder gave Stolley the copy of the film that he had retained. From that day forward until he walked into the Post Office building in Dallas to give sworn testimony, Zapruder had not seen his film.

As he took the oath to tell the truth, Zapruder had to realize that the primary reason he was there was to answer questions about his film. What was he going to do if asked about Mandel's assertion? Should he lie and confirm the accuracy and truthfulness of what Mandel had said about the contents of his film? Or should he instead tell the truth about the film and essentially accuse *LIFE* magazine of lying about the contents of his film?

Zapruder's questioner was a lawyer for the Warren Commission named Wesley J. Liebeler. The normal procedure would have been for Liebeler to show Zapruder the 26-second film (or a copy of it) and then ask him to identify and authenticate it. In fact, *LIFE* magazine had delivered a copy of the film to the commission several months prior to Zapruder's testimony.

Yet, that's not what Liebeler did. Instead of showing Zapruder a copy of his film, which was in color, Liebeler displayed the film to him by simply showing him printed images of individual frames from the film, which were dark, muddy, black-and-white, and difficult-to-decipher. Undoubtedly, Zapruder would have found that method of identifying his film as highly unusual and perhaps even a bit suspicious.

The initial black-and-white frames of what purported to be his film, which were later published in one of the Warren Report's 26 accompanying volumes of evidence and testimony, depict what the Zapruder film (i.e., the film in the Archives today that is purported to be the original) shows: motorcycle cops making the left-hand turn from Houston Street onto Elm Street, where the president would be shot and killed just a few minutes later. The film then suddenly jumps to show President and Mrs. Kennedy coming down Elm Street in the presidential limousine.

In other words, the black-and-white images that Liebeler showed to Zapruder do not show the president's limousine making the left turn from Houston Street onto Elm Street. For that matter, neither does the extant Zapruder film that so many of us have viewed today as a motion picture or movie. The Zapruder film that we know today completely omits that part of the motorcade — namely, the presidential limousine's left turn from Houston onto Elm.

There is something important to note about that extremely wide left-hand turn. According to researcher Fletcher Prouty, the turn violated the Secret Service's own protocols. The ARRB during the 1990s was unable to confirm Prouty's allegation because the U.S. Secret Service refused to share its formal motorcade protocols with the ARRB when asked to do so. In fact, the oblique left turn, which was well more than 90 degrees, was so wide that the president's large limousine was barely able to negotiate it. Witnesses say that the limousine almost went up onto the street curb in order to manage the turn. One thing is certain: The limousine had to slow to a virtual halt to make the turn. That's one of the reasons why the Secret Service protocols reportedly prohibited that type of wide turn. Slowing the speed of the limousine obviously makes it easier for someone to shoot the president.

Please permit me a relevant digression. After the JFK Records Act was enacted, the National Archives informed Secret Service officials that the law required them to preserve their assassination-related records. Nonetheless, as Douglas Horne details in volume 5, pages 1451–1458, of his book *Inside the Assassination Records Review Board,* Secret Service officials knowingly and deliberately destroyed "protective service reports" or "trip reports" for 23 of Kennedy's trips in the fall of 1963.

Chapter 6, part 1, of the *Final Report of the Assassination Records Review Board* states, "Whenever the President traveled outside of Washington, D.C., the Secret Service would generate a Protective Survey Report, or a 'trip report.' Trip reports, composed by Secret Service agents who conducted advance work for the President's trips, contained information ranging from logistical details about seating arrangements to details about individuals in the area known to have made threats against the President's life. Some of the survey reports document information Secret Service received from other agencies such as the FBI or the CIA. The survey reports detail President Kennedy's travel, whereabouts, associations, and activities for his entire administration. They also provide a complete picture of the Secret Service's protection of President Kennedy."

The Secret Service's intentional destruction of those records, after being told not to destroy such records, ensured that the American people would never get to see the information contained in them and that the ARRB would be unable to get a complete picture of the Secret Service's protection of President Kennedy. As Horne put it, "Their destruction occurred long after the Secret Service was initially briefed on the requirements of the JFK Records Act in December of 1992 by the NARA [National Archives] staff, and required willful action by officials within that agency; it was hardly an accident. The Secret Service clearly didn't want the ARRB poking into its past procedures and practices; the agency had been the recipient of severe criticism in the HSCA's 1979 Report, and apparently did not wish to repeat that experience, or to have its sealed records released to the Archives for placement in the JFK Records Collection, for all JFK researchers to peruse in the future."

In her book, Alexandra asserts that her grandfather stopped shooting his film when he first saw the motorcycle cops make the turn onto Elm Street and then resumed filming once the president's limousine was on Elm Street. The reason for this jump in the filming, she asserts, was that Abe Zapruder wanted to make sure that he didn't run out of film.

How does she arrive at that conclusion? Presumably from the film itself. She certainly didn't quote her grandfather saying that. Since the film doesn't show the president's limousine making the turn, she apparently automatically concluded that her grandfather didn't film the turn and then apparently assumed that the reason was that he wanted to make sure he didn't run out of film.

The problem is that in reaching that conclusion, she necessarily had to impugn the integrity and veracity of her very own grandfather as well as the integrity and veracity of his trusted, longtime assistant Marilyn Sitzman, both of whom related a completely different account of when he started filming.

After all, think about the situation. Abraham Zapruder had gone to Dealey Plaza to film the president of the United States, who he greatly admired. He obviously hoped to keep the film as a valued memento that he would share with friends and ultimately bequeath to his kids.

Zapruder clearly wouldn't have been interested in filming the president after the motorcade passed him, given that at that point, he would have been filming the president's back. He would only have been interested in filming President and Mrs. Kennedy from the front. Therefore, it stands to reason that he would have begun filming the president as soon as he appeared and was making the turn from Houston Street onto Elm Street. He would then have continued filming the motorcade as it approached him until he ran out of film. After all, since this was the end of the motorcade route and the crowds had significantly thinned out, it was entirely possible — even likely — that the motorcade would speed up after making the turn onto Elm and quickly depart Dealey Plaza in order to get the president to the Dallas Trade Mart, where he was scheduled to give his speech. In fact, in her book, Alexandra states that Erwin Schwartz had pointed out that morning that "when he comes around that corner, makes that run onto Elm off of Houston, they'll be going over a hundred miles an hour. You won't get to see anything. I mean, the parade's over."

In the interview that he gave on the day of the assassination to Jay Watson, the program director at Dallas television station WFAA, Zapruder stated, "As I was shooting, as the President *was coming down from Houston Street making his turn,* it was about a half-way down there, I heard a shot, and he slumped to the side, like this." (Emphasis added.)

In the 1966 interview that he gave to Marvin Scott, Zapruder stated: "And then I watched for the arrival of the, uh, cars, I saw the motorcycles, and then the car approached. *As they turned I started shooting the pictures, that turned from Houston Street to Elm Street,* and I was shooting as they were coming along, and Jacqueline and the president were waving, and as it came in line with my camera, I heard a shot." (Emphasis added.)

In his testimony at the Clay Shaw trial (the trial in New Orleans that we mentioned in chapter 2 and will discuss again later), Zapruder testified, "I started shooting — *when the motorcade started coming in, I believe I started and wanted to get it coming in from Houston Street.*" (Emphasis added.)

What does Alexandra say about these statements by her grandfather? Nothing! Although she writes about other aspects of these three episodes, she totally fails to mention those particular statements by her grandfather. Why?

Zapruder isn't the only one who stated that he had filmed the president's turn onto Elm Street. His assistant Marilyn Sitzman was there with him when he filmed the assassination. In 1993, she gave an interview to a man named Wes Wise, in which she corroborated what Zapruder had said in his interview in 1966: "I only remember when they started to make their first turn ... turning into the street, he said, 'OK, here we go....' or something to that effect. That's when I remember he started actually doing the filming."

Actually, that was not the only time that Sitzman related when Zapruder started filming. Back in November 1966 — the same year that Zapruder told Marvin Scott when he started filming — Sitzman gave an interview to assassination researcher Josiah Thompson, in which she stated, "Well, he stood up there, and he asked me to come up and stand behind him, cause when he takes the pictures looking through the telescopic lens, he might get dizzy, and he wanted me to stand behind him, so in case he got dizzy I could hold onto him. So I got up behind him, and we saw the motorcade turn the corner at Main onto Houston. He hadn't started taking the pictures there then, and we watched them as they came down Houston; and just as the motorcycles that were leading the parade came ... started ... came around the corner and started down the hill, he started taking the pictures then."

In Part 1 of the series, "The Men Who Killed Kennedy," Sitzman says, "And he started filming about, oh, just before they came around the corner and with filming they come around the corner and start coming down and, you know, waving at everybody."

What does Alexandra say about Sitzman's statements about when Zapruder started filming? Nothing! Like with her grandfather's statements about when he started filming, she doesn't mention Sitzman's statements in her book. Why not?

Alexandra's omission of these critically important statements, while at the same time maintaining that her grandfather did not film the turn onto Elm Street, is particularly ironic because throughout her book, she displays an extreme sensitivity to anyone who appears to question her grandfather's integrity or honor.

For example, you will recall that when Secret Service agent Forrest Sorrels stated in his affidavit that Zapruder had told him that he planned to get top dollar for his film, Alexandra took umbrage at that statement and even wondered whether Sorrels had made it up. Moreover, we will later examine the extremely overwrought attack that Alexandra leveled against Doug Horne, in which she wrote, "In other words, I don't believe that my grandfather was a liar."

As we will see later, there is a likely reason for this extreme sensitivity to anyone who suggests that Alexandra's grandfather was anything but a decent and honorable man. What's ironic, however, is that in doing whatever she can to avoid acknowledging and confronting the centrum of evil that ended up enveloping her grandfather and ultimately destroying his life, Alexandra Zapruder ends up questioning the integrity and veracity of both her grandfather and his longtime trusted assistant Marilyn Sitzman by implicitly challenging their veracity with respect to when he began filming.

In any event, the question naturally arises: What are we to make of all this? On the one hand, we have Zapruder and Sitzman stating that he filmed that extremely awkward turn onto Elm Street. On the other hand, we have his film that shows no such thing. How do we reconcile those two things?

We will examine those questions as we delve more deeply into the Zapruder film mystery. Suffice it to say for now, given that Zapruder himself was certain that he filmed the president's limousine turning onto Elm Street, it had to be deeply disconcerting for him to see that part of his film excluded from the black-and-white photographs of frames of the film that Liebeler was showing him in the summer of 1964. The fact that *LIFE* magazine had lied about the film's contents several months before in the Paul Mandel article would only have magnified Zapruder's discomfort.

Keep in mind, after all, that Liebeler was implicitly asking Zapruder to examine those black-and-white frames and to verify under oath that they were a true and accurate depiction of the film he took in Dealey Plaza on November 22. Should Zapruder point out that those black-and-white frames omitted the president's turn onto Elm Street? And should he point out that Paul Mandel had lied to the American people in his *LIFE* article when he falsely claimed that the president had turned around and faced the School Book Depository, when he was then shot in the throat?

Zapruder's discomfort would have only gotten worse when he reached frame 313, which is the only frame in the Zapruder film that shows the visible effects of the president being shot in the head.

Why would that have discomforted him even more? Because the wounds depicted in that frame would have been inconsistent with the wounds that he would have seen during the assassination. They also would have been inconsistent with the large exit-sized wound in the back of Kennedy's head that was seen by Dr. McClelland and the many other witnesses described in chapter 3. The obvious exit wound in the back of President Kennedy's head seen at Parkland Hospital was devoid of both scalp and bone, so there is no way that such a massive wound could avoid being depicted in Zapruder's film, as he shot it and as it was developed that day in Dallas.

Frame 313 and the frames following it, like the military's official autopsy photos of the back of JFK's head whose validity Navy Petty Officer Saundra Spencer challenged in her testimony before the ARRB, showed the back of Kennedy's head to be intact. Frame 313 also depicts blast damage (an explosion) on the right side of JFK's head. The Dallas physicians closest to President Kennedy in Trauma Room One at Parkland, however, all stated that they observed no obvious damage to the right side of his head.

What did Zapruder see? In the television interview with Jay Watson at WFAA just after the assassination, Zapruder stated, "Then I heard another shot or two, I couldn't say, it was one or two, and I saw his head practically open up, all blood and everything, and I kept on shooting. That's about all, I'm just sick, I can't."

Alexandra writes in her book that her grandfather telephoned his son Henry immediately after the assassination and exclaimed that he had seen the president's head "explode." In his sworn testimony in the Clay Shaw trial in New Orleans in 1969, Zapruder testified, "Then I heard another shot which hit him right in the head, over here, and *his head practically opened up and a lot of blood and many more things came out.*" A few minutes later in his testimony, he confirmed what he had just stated, by amplifying: "I saw the head practically open up and blood and *many more things, whatever, it was, brains, just come out of his head.*" (Emphases added.)

In her book, Alexandra relates a conversation between Abraham, his partner Erwin Schwartz, and Secret Service agent Sorrels in Abe's office immediately after the assassination. She quotes Sorrel's testimony before the Warren Commission about that conversation: "Mr. Zapruder was real shook up.... He said that he didn't know how in the world he had taken these pictures ... and he says, 'My God, I saw the whole thing. *I saw the man's brains come out of his head.*'"

Consider statements made by Phil Willis and his wife Marilyn, both of whom personally witnessed the assassination in Dealey Plaza. In the June 5, 1979, issue of the *Reading Eagle,* he is quoted as saying,"There's no doubt in our mind the final shot that blew his head off did not come from the depository (located to the rear of his motorcade). His head blew up like a halo. The brains and matter went to the left and the rear." In Part 1 of the series, "The Men Who Killed Kennedy," she stated, "The head shot seemed to come from the right front. It seemed to strike him here [pointing to her top forehead] and his head went back and all of the brain matter went out the back of the head [both hands raised upward and backward]. It was like a red halo, a red circle, with bright matter in the middle of it." Just after her statement, their daughter Rosemary stated, "The particular head shot must have come from another direction besides behind him because the back of his head blew off."

There was also Beverly Oliver, another witness to the assassination in Dealey Plaza. In a video interview she had with a man named Brent Holland, she stated, "When the ba-boom happened, it looked like the whole back of his head just blew off. It looked like a bucket of blood was thrown out the back of the car over the trunk."

The Willis and Oliver recollections, of course, are consistent with the statements of the many Parkland Hospital medical witnesses that established the massive exit-sized wound in the back of Kennedy's head. At the same time, however, they are inconsistent with the many frames immediately after frame 313 (the head explosion), namely frames 314-337 of the extant Zapruder film, which show the back of Kennedy's head to be very, very dark but intact and with an enormous wound on the top and side of his head that the Dallas doctors did not see.

You will recall from chapter 1 that Zapruder's partner Erwin Schwartz had watched the Zapruder film at least 15 times on the weekend of the assassination. In his book *Bloody Treason,* Noel Twyman wrote, "I also asked him if he saw the explosion of blood and brains out of the head. He replied that he did. I asked him if he noticed which direction the eruption went. He pointed back over his left shoulder. He said, 'It went this way.' I said, you mean it went to the left and rear? He said yes. Bartholomew [Schwartz's nephew, who was a researcher and writer on the Kennedy assassination] then asked him, 'Are you sure that you didn't see the blood and brains going up and to the front?' Schwartz said, 'No; it was to the left and rear.' We went over this several times with him to be certain that he was clear on this point. He was very clear." Twyman continued: "Of course,

Schwartz's statement that the blood and brains went back to the rear and left was completely consistent with all of the eyewitnesses who said they saw the rear of Kennedy's head blow out and brain and blood go to the rear. It was also consistent with Dallas motorcycle policeman Bobby Hargis's testimony that he was riding to the rear and left of the limousine and was splattered with blood and brains."

In his book, Twyman described an interview that he conducted with a Dr. Roderick Ryan. Twyman had Ryan study specific frames from the extant Zapruder film. Twyman wrote, "I then asked Dr. Ryan to inspect the mysterious blobs on JFK's face and in the successive frames after the fatal head shot.... *He said that it looked as if the blobs had been painted in.*" (Emphasis in original.)

Who was Dr. Roderick Ryan? Twyman detailed his credentials in a 2009 update in the Kindle version of his book: "Dr. Ryan has a Ph.D. from the University of Southern California, majoring in cinema/communications. He was with Eastman Kodak Company in Hollywood, California, from 1947 to 1986 where he held various engineering and executive positions, including regional director of engineering services — motion picture division. His entire career has been devoted to motion picture film technology. He has received numerous awards, honors, and commendations, including a Scientific and Engineering Award (1981) and a Medal of Commendation (1990) in appreciation for outstanding service from the Academy of Motion Picture Arts and Sciences. He is a Fellow of the British Kinematograph Sound and Television Society. A Life Fellow of the Society of Motion Picture and Television Engineers and a recipient of the prestigious Herbert T. Kalmus Gold Medal, for outstanding achievement in color motion pictures. Dr. Ryan's credentials include authorship of several books, technical papers, and articles on motion picture technology. Listed in 'Who's Who in Engineering' (1973); listed in 'Who's Who in Technology' (1986). At the time, he was retired from Eastman Kodak and was active as a consultant in his field. His advice to me was provided without charge."

There were few people, if any, who knew the contents of the 26-second Zapruder film that was developed on Friday, November 22, in Dallas better than Abraham Zapruder. Once he realized that the black-and-white photographs of his film that Warren Commission attorney Wesley Liebeler was showing him omitted the president's turn onto Elm Street and also misrepresented the head-shot sequence, Zapruder would have known that things were seriously amiss with his film, which, on top of the Paul Mandel lie that had been published in *LIFE* several months before, would have undoubtedly caused him extreme consternation, especially since he was now being implicitly asked to verify the authenticity of the film in his sworn testimony before the Warren Commission.

11

The Choice

After his testimony before the Warren Commission, during which he implicitly authenticated his film, Abraham Zapruder must have returned home in a state of deep distress. He had escaped having to answer any questions about *LIFE* magazine's false assertion about his film showing President Kennedy turning toward the Texas School Book Depository at the time he was shot in the throat. On the other hand, however, he had to have immediately wondered why he had been asked to authenticate his film by examining dark, black-and-white, difficult-to-decipher photographs of still frames rather than by examining the film itself.

More important, even though he was not seeing the 26-second film itself, Zapruder undoubtedly knew it by heart given the large number of times that he had watched it. When he saw that series of dark, hard-to-decipher, black-and-white photographs of frames that depicted his film, he would have known that the initial frames of the film — the ones showing the president's limousine attempting to navigate the wide turn onto Elm Street — were missing. Equally important, he would have known that frame 313 did not accurately depict the head explosion that he and others had seen. Furthermore, Zapruder would have known that subsequent frames immediately after the headshot (i.e., frames 314–337) did not accurately depict the large, posterior exit wound that President Kennedy suffered when he was shot in the head.

Yet, despite the misgivings he would have been experiencing, Zapruder ended up implicitly authenticating his film in his sworn testimony before the Warren Commission. What did he do afterward? There can be no doubt that when he returned home, he would have done the same thing he did after reading Paul Mandel's false statement in his December 6 *LIFE* magazine article. On returning home, he would have discussed what happened with his trusted, lifelong partner — his wife Lillian. He would have said something like this to her:

"Lillian, they didn't show me my film. I could have brought my 8mm projector with me if they had just asked. Instead, they showed me dark, black-and-white photos of frames from the film. That's how I was expected to confirm the validity of my film. I started filming as soon as the president's limousine began making the turn onto Elm. In the frames they showed me, that part of the film is now missing. It's just gone. Even worse, when the president was shot in the head, you could see some of his brain and blood erupt out of his head upward and backward. Those frames are also completely gone. The only frame showing the shot that hit the president in the head is frame 313, and it does not depict what actually happened when the president was shot in the head. I didn't know what to do, Lillian. I was nervous and afraid. I decided to go along and not object."

What would the street-smart Lillian have said, and undoubtedly did say? "Abe, I have no doubt that what you are saying is true and correct, just like when you told me about that *LIFE* magazine article last December by that man Paul Mandel. But we have to think very carefully about what we do at this point. It is obvious that we are dealing with something here that is much bigger than you and me. It is something that is impossible for us to understand, just as we were unable to understand why *LIFE* magazine would pay us a very large sum of money to purchase your film, lie to the American people about its contents, and then prevent people from ever seeing the film. The point is this, Abe: If you decide to go public with what they have done with your film, you know that I will stand by your side and support you, the way I always have. But before you do that, you just need to be aware that we are dealing with very powerful forces here. If you challenge them, we can be certain that they will come after you with everything in their power. They will do everything they can to destroy you."

The street-smart Lillian would have been absolutely right. For one thing, if Zapruder had questioned the authenticity of the film, *LIFE* magazine, led by its publisher, CIA loyal acolyte C. D. Jackson, would have immediately canceled any more payments on the purchase contract for the film. Remember that while *LIFE* magazine could have easily paid Zapruder up front for his film, that's not the way Jackson wanted the deal structured. He wanted the $150,000 paid out in annual installments of $25,000 (which, in today's dollars, equates to annual installments of $227,000).

At the time that Zapruder gave his testimony before the Warren Commission, he had received only $50,000 of the total purchase price. There was still another $100,000 to be paid, in $25,000 annual installments. That $100,000 is equivalent in today's dollars to $908,000. That is a lot of money.

It is not difficult to imagine what Jackson would have done if Zapruder had questioned the authenticity of the film that was now in *LIFE* magazine's possession. He would have told Zapruder in no uncertain terms that there would be no further payments made on the contract. Rather than continuing to receive his annual installments, Zapruder would have received none of the rest of the money that *LIFE* owed him. Jackson would have said to Zapruder, "You have devalued our asset with your false, scurrilous, and defamatory allegations. Not only will we not pay you another dime, if you sue us, we will countersue you for libel."

That would not have been the worst of it, however. The right-wing element in America would have gone into overdrive to destroy Zapruder. That would have been especially true in Dallas, which was undoubtedly the most right-wing city in America. Even though Kennedy had received a warm welcome in Dallas, the fact is that the city was dominated by people who had extreme right-wing mindsets. Alexandra herself acknowledged this phenomenon in her book, where she pointed out, "In fact, Dallas — more than any other American city — had become ground zero for a reactionary political movement that bitterly opposed President Kennedy.... Gripped by an ironclad conviction that the United States faced the threat of an imminent Communist takeover, they believed that Kennedy's international policies and his support of the United Nations amounted to a betrayal of the United States."

On the very day that Kennedy was assassinated, the conservative *Dallas Morning News* carried an advertisement entitled "Wanted for Treason," which detailed how Kennedy had betrayed and endangered the nation with his soft-on-communism policies. No wonder that Kennedy, upon seeing the advertisement, remarked to his wife Jackie, "We're headed into nut country today." On the same day, a flier containing similar material was being distributed by right-wing elements in Dallas. It is worth mentioning that the extreme right-wing viewpoints expressed in that advertisement and that flier expressed the sentiments of the U.S. national-security establishment.

That right-wing element would have come after Zapruder with all guns blazing. Given their fierce commitment to the anti-communist crusade that defined the Cold War, they would have immediately labeled him a communist sympathizer.

Here is where Abe's having grown up in Russia would have come into full prominence, something that Lillian would undoubtedly have pointed out to him. He would have been accused of being a communist plant — a mole sent by the Reds to foment lies about

America's trusted institutions, such as *LIFE* magazine and the U.S. national-security establishment.

And let's not forget that the accused assassin of President Kennedy was supposedly an ardent communist, one who had defected to the Soviet Union, America's avowed Cold War enemy. The right-wing element would have come up with ways to tie Zapruder and Oswald together, suggesting that they were both communist sympathizers who had conspired to kill the president.

You will recall that when Zapruder received the very first payment on the installment contract with *LIFE,* he decided to donate that $25,000 payment to the family of J. D. Tippit, the policeman who was murdered in Dallas soon after Kennedy was assassinated. Zapruder received accolades from all over the world for this generous act, especially since lots of people were under the impression that $25,000 was the full amount that Zapruder received from *LIFE,* an impression that Zapruder did nothing to correct. That good will and positive publicity arising from his generous gift was undoubtedly a tremendous boon to Zapruder's dress business. It would have evaporated the minute that the Dallas right-wing targeted Zapruder as a communist sympathizer.

The Dallas right-wing would have immediately announced a highly publicized campaign to boycott his business, with severe punishment being threatened against anyone caught violating the boycott. Sales would have plummeted. Zapruder might even have faced the prospect of bankruptcy. He would undoubtedly have dwelled on the possibility of returning to the extreme poverty of his youth in Russia, where, according to what Alexandra wrote in her book, he experienced "relentless hunger" — where he and his three siblings "had little to eat, sharing soup made from a single potato and fighting for the skin that rose to the top of a pot of boiled milk." Alexandra wrote in her book that "Abraham Zapruder had escaped the violence, discrimination, and limitations of Russia, although its imprint on his psyche would never entirely fade." His rumination undoubtedly would have also been reinforced by that of his wife Lillian. Alexandra wrote, "She had grown up in harsh poverty in a tenement in Brooklyn. She knew as well as anyone that money meant security and made important things — education, a home, contingencies for a sickness or a crisis — possible."

All of this adverse publicity would also have had an adverse effect on Zapruder's membership in his Dallas synagogue, where he was a prominent member. Social ostracism would have been the order of the day. After all, think about this: In 1964 Abraham Zapruder would have immediately been labeled a "conspiracy theorist" and an "alterationist," that is, a person who believes that the Zapruder film was altered, or at least labels to that effect. We all know what that would have meant, especially in 1964, when the Cold War was still going strong.

And after all, don't forget that Zapruder had already implicitly authenticated his film by expressing no objections to those dark, black-and-white photos of frames from his film that were shown to him during his Warren Commission testimony. Changing his position later would obviously have been problematic, opening him up to all sorts of accusations as to what was now motivating him to change his story, not to mention the possibility of a perjury indictment.

Alexandra Zapruder relates a fascinating exchange that took place between her grandfather and one of the first generation of assassination researchers who challenged the official lone-nut theory of the assassination, Mark Lane, a New York City lawyer who, in 1966, authored a *New York Times* best-selling book about the assassination entitled *Rush to Judgment*.

Lane had approached Zapruder about conducting an interview with him, and Zapruder had agreed. According to Alexandra, the meeting did not go well. Zapruder accused Lane of trying to make money off the assassination. Lane responded by suggesting that it was Zapruder who had made millions from his film. At that point,

Alexandra relates, Zapruder forcibly evicted Lane from his office premises.

That episode speaks volumes with respect to Alexandra Zapruder. She clearly is convinced that her grandfather was in the right and that Mark Lane was in the wrong with respect to their exchange. And it is also clear that her judgment is clouded by the fact that Lane was a "conspiracy theorist," a type of person who she ridicules, mocks, and criticizes throughout her book, always in very strong terms.

The fact is that Lane was never into the assassination for the money. From the very beginning, he was convinced that the government's lone-nut theory was just a bit too pat. As a practicing attorney, he was suspicious, especially given that Oswald, the accused assassin, was silenced two days after the assassination and also because the feds appeared much too hasty, in his opinion, to shut down the investigation immediately after Oswald was assassinated. Lane even offered to represent Oswald's interests before the Warren Commission, but they turned him down.

In those early days in the immediate aftermath of the assassination, Lane was holding a lonely position. Moreover, it was an extremely difficult position. Predictably, the U.S. national-security establishment labeled him a communist sympathizer, began secretly monitoring his activities, and did everything they could do smear and destroy him.

In other words, the way Lane was treated for questioning the official lone-nut theory of the assassination served as a model for what they would have done to Zapruder if he had decided to take the same course that Lane took.

While Lane was incorrect in the amount of money that Zapruder had made from his film, the mistake was understandable given that Zapruder had steadfastly kept secret how much money *LIFE* had agreed to pay him. He also had asked *LIFE* magazine to keep the matter secret.

My hunch is that the real reason that Zapruder took such umbrage over Lane is that he knew that Lane had made a different choice than Zapruder had made. Lane had chosen to adhere to his integrity even though the cost entailed being labeled a communist sympathizer and a conspiracy theorist. Given the choice that evil had forced him to make, Zapruder had chosen a different path.

But who can really blame Abe Zapruder? Here was a man who was in the prime of his life, enjoying happiness and success, when one day he decided to film a motorcade of the president of the United States. Little did he know that that one singular event would end up causing him to choose between two alternative courses of action, both of which came with horrific consequences. Should he tell the truth about what they did to his film and have him and his family destroyed? Or should he sacrifice his integrity and live the rest of his life with a lie in order to keep himself and his family from being destroyed? What would most people do when faced with that choice? What would you do? Abraham Zapruder was a prime example of what evil can do to a good person.

As I was reading her book, I couldn't help but wonder what Alexandra Zapruder would feel about her grandfather if she had gone all the way and acknowledged and confronted the true dark secret behind her family taboo, especially given her obviously deep antipathy toward people who don't buy the official lone-nut theory of the Kennedy assassination. How would she have reacted if her exploration into her decades-old family taboo against discussing the Zapruder film uncovered the dark secret that her grandfather was actually a "conspiracy theorist" or an "alterationist?" What would she have done if she had decided to grant her father Henry's wish to be interviewed before he died and he had disclosed this horrific dark secret to her?

I am convinced that Alexandra Zapruder would have ended up sympathizing with her grandfather and would have understood why he chose the way he did. The reason I say that is that despite her nasty attitude toward "conspiracy theorists" and "alterationists" in her book, she comes across as a very nice, sincere person in her in-person presentations, videos of which are online.

By the same token, if she had gone that far and discovered the dark truth about her family, I also am convinced that she never would have gone public with the secret. Moreover, I don't think that she would have ever published a book on the subject. She would have known that by disclosing the truth about her grandfather, she along with her grandfather would have been labeled "conspiracy theorists" and "alterationists," something that she does not seem to have the intestinal fortitude to handle.

If she had gone ahead and written a book that disclosed that dark secret responsible for the family taboo against discussing her grandfather's film, it is a virtual certainty that her book would never have received the many accolades from the mainstream press that it did, such as from the *Wall Street Journal,* the *New York Times,* the *Washington Post,* the *Boston Globe, USA Today,* and *Town and Country* magazine. Moreover, it is a virtual certainty that she never would have been invited to deliver oral presentations about her book to prominent, mainstream forums such as Politics and Prose in Washington, D.C., Southern Methodist University, the Sixth Floor Museum, and the San Antonio Book Festival.

How can I be so certain that she would never have received accolades and invitations from those types of prominent, mainstream groups? In 2016, a woman named Gayle Nix Jackson, like Alexandra Zapruder, wrote a book about her grandfather Orville Nix, who, like Abraham Zapruder, also filmed the Kennedy assassination in Dealey Plaza. When Nix took his film to be processed, he learned that the FBI had put out notices advising witnesses to deliver their photographs and films to the FBI. Nix complied and delivered his film to the FBI. Gayle Nix Jackson's book, entitled *The Missing JFK Assassination Film: The Mystery Surrounding the Orville Nix Home Movie of November 22, 1963,* details her grandfather's contention that when the film was returned to him, there were frames that had been removed.

Needless to say, unlike Alexandra Zapruder's book, as far as I know, there have been no mainstream accolades for Gayle Nix Jackson's book. There have also been, as far as I know, no speaking invitations at the mainstream forums at which Zapruder has been asked to speak. You see, Jackson is labeled a "conspiracy theorist" and an "alterationist." There can be little doubt that if Alexandra Zapruder had gone the same route as Jackson, she would have experienced the same ostracism that Jackson has experienced.

There is also no question but that the Zapruder film ended up destroying Abraham Zapruder's happy, joyful life. That point comes across loud and clear in both Alexandra's book and in-person presentations about her book. Home moviemaking had been Abe's lifelong hobby. After the assassination, Alexandra writes, her grandfather hardly ever made a home movie again. She writes that he also rarely gave out any interviews about his film.

In an interview with CBS broadcaster Anthony Mason, Alexandra stated, "I think he hated the film. I think he wished that he had never taken it. I think it was really devastating for him." In her talk at SMU, she stated, "He definitely said many times that he wished that he had not taken the film." A Mexican website called Quadratin Oaxaca quotes her as saying, "The only thing that tape left my grandfather was a broken heart and he was very sorry to be the one who filmed it." In an interview conducted by ArtsATL, she said, "He had nightmares and dreaded the anniversary of the assassination. He didn't really like to talk about it. He lost his passion for taking home movies."

But why would that be? Once again, Alexandra attributes it to the trauma and grief that Abe Zapruder had experienced over having witnessed such a brutal act, along with the misgivings associated with making a lot of money off the film. In an interview with *Smashing Interviews Magazine,* she stated, "Well, you know, my grandfather was certainly traumatized by what he witnessed. He was there because he loved the president and because he wanted to record this historic visit to Dallas for his family. So, to then end up recording this moment that was so tragic for the nation and for the Kennedy family, was just traumatic. I think it was something that pained him for the rest of his life. He said afterward that he had nightmares and that he dreaded the anniversary of the assassination. He really didn't want to take home movies very much after that, so I think he had a tremendous responsibility for the film and he wanted to do the right thing, but it also brought with it a lot of pain and sadness." In a rare 1964 interview with William Manchester for his book *The Death of a President,* Abraham Zapruder said, "I just happened to be in the wrong place at the wrong time."

But as I have noted, lots of people, including Orville Nix, experienced grief over the president's death. They didn't suffer chronic consternation for the rest of their lives and also never developed family taboos against discussing the assassination. Moreover, as I also noted, if Zapruder was suffering guilt over having made a large sum of money off the film, he could have waived the annual installments that *LIFE* was sending him.

Theoretically, there is no reason why, after a reasonable period of time, Zapruder could not have had the same lighthearted attitude toward the film that his granddaughter has. She travels around the county giving presentations about her book and about the film, bantering with audiences and cracking jokes about her grandfather and the film. (In one presentation, she good-naturedly described Zapruder's trusted assistant Marilyn Sitzman as "hot.")

For the rest of his life, Abraham Zapruder was unable to do that. I submit that the reason for that was the horrible secret that he carried with him, a secret that caused him to sacrifice his personal integrity for the sake of his family. That had to be an enormous source of internal consternation for a man who no doubt prided himself on being honest, honorable, religious, and moral. And every day, Abraham Zapruder would know that his beloved wife Lillian was aware of the fact that the man she had married was living a lie.

If internal stress and chronic anxiety can lead to cancer, as some people believe, it would not be surprising why Abraham Zapruder died from stomach cancer at the age of 65, only seven years after he filmed the Kennedy assassination.

Is it any wonder why Abe Zapruder was reluctant to do interviews? There was always the possibility that he could slip up during an interview and inadvertently reveal that his film had been altered. He couldn't afford to take that chance. He had to remain on his guard for the rest of his life.

I submit that it was that rational reluctance to talk about the film and the deeply seated fear that he would inadvertently reveal the dark secret surrounding the film that gave rise to the family taboo against discussing Abraham Zapruder's film of the Kennedy assassination.

12

Consternation

The question naturally arises: Why would the Zapruder family taboo against discussing the film extend beyond the life of Abraham Zapruder? Once he died in 1970, why wouldn't the family feel comfortable discussing the film? Why would Abraham's grief and misgivings over money extend to them? After all, don't forget the story Alexandra relates about going into her school library when she was 11 years old to sneak an account of her grandfather's film in William Manchester's book rather than simply ask her parents about it. By that time, her grandfather had been dead for some 10 years. And it was only when she was in her late 30s or early 40s that Alexandra, long after her father had died, finally felt comfortable embarking on her courageous journey to discover whatever dark family secrets lay behind the family taboo.

The answer lies in the virtual certainty that Abraham Zapruder shared his dark secret not only with his wife but also with his son Henry, a secret that I believe Henry Zapruder was going to share with his daughter Alexandra when he was facing terminal cancer and requested her to interview him about the film.

By the time of the assassination, Henry Zapruder was a Harvard-educated lawyer working in the Kennedy administration's Justice Department. He and his father had a very close relationship. It stands to reason that Abraham Zapruder would have sought his son's counsel after the Paul Mandel article came out in *LIFE* magazine that falsely depicted the contents of his film. He would have also sought his counsel after his July 1964 appearance before the Warren Commission, where he would have seen that his film had been altered.

It is a virtual certainty that Henry Zapruder's advice would have been the same as that of his mother Lillian. Henry would have told his father that if he publicly announced that his film had been altered after he sold it to *LIFE* for the equivalent in today's dollars of $1.3 million, he and the Zapruder family would not receive the rest of the money that *LIFE* had promised him and, even worse, his entire life would be destroyed. Henry Zapruder would also have been smart enough to realize that his legal career in Washington, D.C., would have been shattered. There was no way that his father Abraham was going to go down a road that would have destroyed not only his own life but also the lives of his wife and children.

In 1997, during the term of the ARRB, the federal government did a legal "taking" under its power of eminent domain and declared that it had assumed legal ownership of the Zapruder film as an "assassination record" under the JFK Records Act. (At the time, the film was in the National Archives in courtesy storage under climate-controlled conditions.) After a hard-fought arbitration battle in 1999, the Zapruder family was awarded $16 million for their film. That $16 million translates in today's dollars to $26.6 million. The copyright to the film remained with the Zapruder family, contrary to the expectations of ARRB chairman John Tunheim, who had assumed that once the U.S. government took the film, the government would henceforth hold the copyright. The Zapruder family then donated the copyright to the film to the Sixth Floor Museum in Dallas in December 1999. Alexandra did not disclose the tax benefits of that donation, but they had to be substantial.

Alexandra has convinced herself that her father Henry, like her grandfather Abe, suffered consternation over the fact that he brought the Zapruder family even more money for the Zapruder film than his father did. But as with his father, there was always an easy solution to that problem: just waive the money or give it away. Henry Zapruder did not do that. In fact, he sought even more money — $18 million — from the arbitration panel than the $16 million that it ultimately awarded. (Henry had made it clear, however, that if the government had been willing to accept his $18 million offer, he would have been willing to transfer ownership of both the film and the copyright to the government.)

I submit that the problem for Henry Zapruder, who ultimately became one of the most accomplished and prominent attorneys in Washington, D.C., was not that he was making money off the film. The problem for him was that he knew he was making money off a film that he knew was an altered version of the original film. That knowledge would obviously have had a deep, profound, and disconcerting effect on an attorney who prided himself on his commitment to ethical principles.

As I was reading Alexandra's book, I couldn't help but wonder whether Henry had shared his dark secret with his wife (Alexandra's mother), just as his father had done with his wife Lillian. I ultimately concluded that he didn't. There would have been no reason to burden her with carrying the dark secret that he and his parents carried. Moreover, the fact that he clearly wanted to talk to Alexandra about the film before he died indicated to me that he had not shared the secret with his wife. In fact, in her book, Alexandra writes about an interview she conducted of her mother about the film. Her mother stated, "Honestly, I was never interested in the film, so I'm not going to be much help. It's so sad you can't talk to Dad about all this, but I didn't want to have anything to do with it." Of course, as we saw in chapter 7, when her father wanted to talk about the film before he died, Alexandra failed to provide him with that opportunity.

In 1969, Abraham Zapruder was subpoenaed to testify in the criminal prosecution of Clay Shaw in New Orleans. The district attorney, Jim Garrison, was alleging that the assassination of President Kennedy was a highly sophisticated regime-change operation orchestrated and carried out by the U.S. national-security establishment, specifically the Pentagon and the CIA. Alexandra writes, "He clearly did not want to be there, and he seemed intimidated and uncomfortable about answering a rapid-fire set of questions in the crowded courtroom, thronged with reporters and spectators and under the unsympathetic eye of the judge."

Zapruder was asked under oath to identify and authenticate his film. Unlike his testimony before the Warren Commission in 1964, the prosecutor did not have Zapruder identify his film based on an examination of dark, black-and-white, hard-to-decipher still photographs of frames from the film. Instead, the prosecutor had Zapruder watch a copy of the film that had been subpoenaed from *LIFE* magazine.

It was the first time that Zapruder had seen his 26-second film since the weekend of the assassination. It had to have quickly become even clearer to Zapruder why he had been shown those black-and white-photographs of frames from his film back in 1964 rather than the motion picture itself.

A total of 59 witnesses to the assassination stated that after the first shot rang out, the president's limousine either stopped or slowed to a near stop. Drawing on an essay written by Vincent Palamara in a book entitled *Murder in Dealey Plaza,* Douglas Horne recaps statements made by some of these 59 witnesses in volume IV, page 1300, of his book *Inside the Assassination Records Review Board*:

"DPD motorcycle officer James W. Courson (one of two mid-motorcade motorcyclists): 'The limousine came to a stop and Mrs. Kennedy was on the back. I noticed that as I came around the corner of Elm. Then the Secret Service agent helped push her back in the car, and the motorcade took off at a high rate of speed.'

"Bobby Joe Dale (one of two rear mid-motorcade motorcyclists): 'After the shots were fired, the whole motorcade came to a stop. I stood and looked through the plaza [and] noticed that there was commotion, and saw people running around his (JFK's) car. It started to move and then it slowed again; that's when I saw Mrs. Kennedy coming back on the trunk and another guy pushing her back into the car.'

"Clemon Earl Johnson (standing on the triple overpass above Elm Street): 'You could see it speed up and then stop, then speed up, and you could see it stop while they threw Mrs. Kennedy back in the car.'

"DPD Patrolman Earle Brown (standing at the northern end of the triple underpass): 'The first I noticed the car was when it stopped ... after it made the turn and when the shots were fired, it stopped.'

"DPD motorcycle officer Bobby Hargis (riding inboard to the left rear of the presidential limo): 'At that time (immediately before the head shot) the Presidential car slowed down. I heard somebody say 'Get going' I felt blood hit me in the face and the Presidential car stopped almost immediately after that. [In another interview, Hargis said:] 'That guy (Greer) slowed down maybe his orders was to slow down, [he] slowed down almost to a stop.'

"DPD motorcycle officer James Chaney (riding inboard at the right rear of he Presidential limo): told DPD motorcycle officer Marion Baker [according to Baker]: '... at the time, after the shooting, from the time the first shot rang out, the car stopped completely, pulled to the left and stopped.... Now I have heard several of them say that Mr. Truly was standing there, he said it stopped. Several officers said it stopped completely.'

"DPD Patrolman J.W. Foster (standing on the triple underpass above Elm Street): '... immediately after President Kennedy was struck, the car in which he was riding pulled to the curb.'

"Phil Willis (the photographer standing near the corner of Elm and Houston): 'The party had come to a temporary halt before proceeding on to the underpass.'

"Mary Woodward (*Dallas Morning News* reporter): 'Instead of speeding up the car, the car came to a halt.'

"Alan Smith (standing near the pergola): 'The car was ten feet from me when a bullet hit the President in the forehead ... the car went about five feet and stopped.'

"Roy Truly (TSBD supervisor): 'I saw the President's car swerve to the left and stop somewheres down in this area.'

"Billy Lovelady (on the front steps of the Depository): 'I recall that following the shooting, I ran toward the spot where President Kennedy's car had stopped.'

"Bill Newman [who was standing with his wife and two sons abreast of the limousine on the north side of Elm Street during the head shot(s)]: '... the car momentarily stopped and the driver seemed to have a radio or phone up to his ear and he seemed to be waiting on some word. Secret Service men reached into their car and came up with some sort of machine gun [clearly, agent Hickey in the Queen Mary]. Then the cars roared off.' [In another interview]: 'I believe Kennedy's car came to a full stop after the final shot.'

"Charles Brehm (standing on the south side of Elm, opposite Zapruder): Brehm expressed his opinion that between the first shot and third shots, the President's car only seemed to move some ten or twelve feet. It seemed to him that the automobile almost came to a halt after the first shot."

CBS news anchor Walter Cronkite, reporting on television from New York, exclaimed, "Mrs. Kennedy screamed out, 'Oh, no!' The car stopped momentarily."

ABC news reporter Bob Clark, in the motorcade in an open camera car a short distance behind the presidential limousine and reporting via telephone on ABC television what he personally saw just after the shots rang out, stated: "We heard the shots very clearly ... about no more than two or three seconds before the car that the president was traveling in — this was an open limousine that had been sent out from the White House in Washington — this car came to an immediate stop."

Obviously, a film showing such a stop would not have looked good, especially for the Secret Service agent who was driving the presidential limousine, William Greer. And let's not forget three important things: First, the Secret Service agent in the passenger seat, Roy Kellerman, sat there and never moved after the first shot rang out instead of immediately jumping over the seat and using his body to cover President Kennedy. Second, Kellerman was the Secret Service agent who was in charge of the Secret Service team that launched the scheme for the fraudulent autopsy by forcibly preventing the Dallas County medical examiner, Dr. Earl Rose, from conducting an autopsy at Parkland Hospital — which was required by state law — and who then transported the body to Air Force One, where President Johnson was waiting for it at Love Field in Dallas. Third, as we saw in chapter 2, Kellerman and Greer both participated in the casket-switching operation at the Bethesda morgue, after Kennedy's body was sneaked into the morgue almost one and a half hours before the official entry time of 8 p.m.

Obviously, showing Abraham Zapruder those dark, black-and-white, difficult-to-decipher photographs of frames from his film during his Warren Commission testimony would not have shown that the car stopped or nearly stopped during the shooting, which might well have been another reason why Zapruder was not shown his film when he gave his testimony to the Warren Commission. But as soon as Zapruder saw the film in New Orleans, it would have become crystal clear to him that the frames from the car stop or near-stop were missing from the film, just like the initial frames showing the presidential limousine making the extremely wide turn from Houston Street onto Elm Street.

When Zapruder saw a copy of his color film at the Clay Shaw trial for the first time in six years, he would have noticed that frames had been deleted from his film in three critical places: (1) the awkward left turn onto Elm Street, which would have drawn attention to the fact that the turn reportedly violated Secret Service protocols and would have made it easier to shoot the president shortly thereafter; (2) the stopping or near-stopping of the limousine, which would have looked even more incriminating than the wide turn onto Elm Street; and (3) the head explosion, which had consisted of more than one frame and would have shown brain matter and blood blowing high into the air in large quantities. He would have also noticed that the frames immediately after frame 313 (which depicted the head explosion), had been altered by painting a black patch over the rear of the president's head (where Dr. McClelland and other witnesses said the large exit wound was) and by falsely depicting a large wound on the top and right side of the president's head (which the treating physicians at Parkland never saw).

After viewing the film, Abraham Zapruder was asked under oath to authenticate it. He knew he was about to commit perjury. And he knew that his wife, who was in the audience weeping, knew that her husband was about to commit perjury, but he had gone too far to now turn back. He had authenticated the film back in 1964 when he examined it through those dark black-and-white photographs in his testimony before the Warren Commission. He had publicly endorsed the lone-nut theory of the assassination since then. He also was still fully aware of what the consequences would be for him and his family if he were to tell the truth about the film now, especially given the long lapse of time and the fact that he had previously already authenticated his film under oath.

When asked to authenticate a copy of his film that *LIFE* magazine had delivered to the prosecution, Zapruder's answer was fascinating. The following is an excerpt of his testimony:

"**Q:** Is the copy you have here today identical to the original or are there any plates missing out of this copy?

"**A:** That would be hard for me to tell, sir.

"**The COURT:** I cannot hear the witness. What is it?

"**The WITNESS:** That would be hard for me to say. He asked me if any frames were missing.

"**THE COURT:** What is your answer?

"**THE WITNESS:** I couldn't say.

"**BY MR. DYMOND:**

"**Q:** So you don't know whether it is a complete copy of the film you took on the 22nd of November?

"**A:** Not if there are one or two frames missing. I couldn't tell you."

One possibility was that Zapruder was referring to six frames in the purported original that were now missing because the film had been damaged by *LIFE* — broken in two places by *LIFE* during handling. But he likely was not referring to that damage because it was still unknown to the public. It occurred only to the purported "original" film and has apparently never been imaged in any copies of the film. If Zapruder was somehow, inexplicably, referring to that damage (which he should not have known about), it would seem that he would simply have said that. Another possibility is that Zapruder's answer reflected a deeply troubled man who was threading the needle in the hope that he wasn't technically committing perjury.

Given Zapruder's conditional answer, the judge in the Clay Shaw trial should never have allowed the copy of the film to be admitted into evidence. He should instead have required *LIFE* to produce the original film for Zapruder to authenticate. But the judge obviously considered Zapruder's qualification to be a "technicality," and he admitted the film into evidence.

13

Alteration

(Part 1)

For more than 45 years, until 2009, it was impossible to figure out how the Zapruder film came to be altered. That's because the CIA kept secret its complete role in the Zapruder film mystery for all those years.

To understand the role that the CIA played with respect to the film, it is necessary to go back to the weekend of the assassination, when Abraham Zapruder struck his deal with *LIFE* magazine for the purchase of his film.

Recall that Zapruder initially sold *LIFE* only the print-media rights to the film. That took place on Saturday, November 23, the day following the assassination, when Zapruder delivered the original film to *LIFE*'s representative, Richard Stolley. At 3 p.m. on Saturday, the film was placed on a plane to Chicago, the city in which *LIFE* was printed.

By that time, *LIFE* had stopped the presses on its November 29 issue in order to include pictures of frames from the film in that issue. By the following Tuesday, the first copies of the Friday, November 29, issue were hitting the newsstands.

That necessarily meant that if the film was altered, it would almost certainly had to have been done under *LIFE* magazine's auspices (or by someone else with *LIFE* magazine's willing cooperation) sometime between Saturday, November 23, and Tuesday, November 26. Yet for decades there was no evidence that surfaced to establish that *LIFE* had altered the film.

Moreover, let's assume that the alteration entailed simply the optical removal of certain frames and the alteration of the head wound. Those alterations would have nonetheless required extremely sophisticated equipment and, more important, people who were experts in the art of film modification. Those type of experts were located in Hollywood, but no evidence ever surfaced that any of them were ever brought to Chicago on the weekend of the assassination.

Although they couldn't explain how it was done, some assassination researchers remained convinced that the film had to have been altered. Why is that so? Because of all those witnesses who stated that the back of President Kennedy's head had a large exit-sized wound. Recall Parkland Hospital treating physician Dr. Robert McClelland's statement about summoning the other treating physicians to the head of the gurney to show them that fatal wound. Recall all the other witnesses who stated that they saw that massive hole in the back of Kennedy's head, including Dr. Carrico, Dr. Clark, Dr. Crenshaw, Secret Service agent Clint Hill, FBI agents Francis O'Neill and James Sibert, Parkland nurses Audrey Bell and Diana Bowron, and all the rest. Recall U.S. Navy Petty Officer Saundra Spencer telling the ARRB that the set of photographs she was asked to develop, on a top-secret basis, on the weekend of the assassination, showed a large exit-sized wound in the back of Kennedy's head. (That wound, she recalled to the ARRB, was two to two-and-one-half inches wide — which was inconsistent with a small wound of entry — and had obviously, based on the appearance of the body, been photographed *following* the reconstruction of the head and embalming of the body — that is, after the conclusion of the autopsy. She told the ARRB that the hole she remembered in the photograph she developed constituted what she called "a blown-out chunk.")

Anyone who concluded that those witnesses were speaking truthfully and accurately and that it was the military establishment that was engaging in deceit with fraudulent autopsy photographs that showed the back of President Kennedy's head to be intact would confront the reality of what the Zapruder film showed. Like the military's autopsy photographs of the back of JFK's head, the film shows the back of his head to be intact after the gunshot wounds to his head — that is, with no big exit-sized hole in the occipital region of the skull.

Moreover, frame 313 of the extant Zapruder film shows a head explosion on the forward, right side of Kennedy's head. Yet, the treating physicians saw no damage on the right side of the head. Moreover, no damage consistent with either an entrance wound or an exit wound at that location was noted at Parkland Hospital by the Trauma Room One treatment staff in their written treatment notes.

The fact that all those witnesses contradicted what the Zapruder film showed is the reason that some assassination researchers remained convinced that the film had to have been altered, even if they couldn't explain how it was possible to do so within that short time frame between when the film was developed on November 22 and the time when the first frames appeared in the November 29 issue of *LIFE*. They simply believed what those witnesses were saying about the large exit-sized hole in the back of Kennedy's head, and once they had reached that conclusion, that necessarily meant that the autopsy photographs and the Zapruder film, both of which showed the back of the head to be intact, had to be false and fraudulent.

As we have seen throughout this book, whenever Alexandra Zapruder appears to be getting close to the centrum of evil that enveloped her grandfather, she does everything to avoid acknowledging and directly confronting it. As I have repeatedly emphasized, however, I am convinced that this is not a conscious decision on her part, especially because she comes across as an honest person in her speeches and in her book. I'm convinced that her desire to avoid acknowledging and confronting the evil is a subconscious reaction on her part, one that involves a deep-seated, subconscious fear of the truth.

Consider, for example, the fact that nowhere in her book does Alexandra even mention all of the evidence establishing that massive exit-sized hole in the back of Kennedy's head. As I indicated earlier, I'm sure that she would say that her book was about the Zapruder film, not the Kennedy autopsy or his wounds. But the fact is that the president's head wound bears a direct relationship to her grandfather's film, because the extant Zapruder film, like the official autopsy photos, does not show the massive exit-sized wound in the back of President Kennedy's head.

I believe that one would have an extremely difficult time finding a more credible group of witnesses than Dr. Robert McClelland, Dr. Charles Crenshaw, Dr. Kemp Clark, Navy Petty Officer Saundra Spencer, Secret Service agent Clint Hill, FBI agent Francis O'Neill, FBI agent James Sibert, nurse Diana Bowron, nurse Audrey Bell, and all the others whose statements established that big wound in the back of President Kennedy's head.

Moreover, don't forget the Harper Fragment, which a team of three Dallas pathologists at Methodist Hospital in Dallas examined and concluded was occipital bone, which means that it came from the back of Kennedy's skull. That is powerful physical evidence that corroborates the statements of all those witnesses.

It's also worth noting that the U.S. national-security establishment is known for its lies and deceptions, especially when it comes to matters relating to "national security." The most recent example, of course, is the revelation of 20 years of lies and deception relating to the war in Afghanistan. But we can go all the way back to the Gulf of Tonkin Resolution several months after Kennedy was assassinated to see that lying has long been an integral part of the national-security establishment.

By not directly confronting all those witnesses who established the large exit-sized wound in the back of the president's head, Alexandra Zapruder was subconsciously avoiding having to accuse them of speaking falsely or incorrectly. Thus, she simply omitted that part of the analysis from her book even while mocking and ridiculing people who reject the lone-nut theory of the assassination, as well as those people who contend that her grandfather's film was altered.

Yet, it is a virtual certainty that Alexandra was aware of the evidence establishing the fraudulent autopsy. That's because she obviously did extensive research into what Douglas Horne had to say about the Zapruder film. In her book, she cites Horne's article "The Two NPIC Zapruder Film Events: Signposts Pointing to the Film's Alteration," which is posted at LewRockwell.com. That article refers to Horne's book *Inside the Assassination Records Review Board: The U.S. Government's Final Attempt to Reconcile the Conflicting Medical Evidence in the Assassination of JFK,* which is primarily about the fraudulent autopsy that the national-security establishment conducted on President Kennedy's body. Moreover, volume IV of Horne's book has a very lengthy and detailed analysis of the Zapruder film controversy, which Alexandra undoubtedly read as part of her research into Horne. If she did read it, it would stand to reason that she would peruse the rest of that volume, which focuses on the fraudulent autopsy.

In 1997, during the term of the ARRB, part of the Zapruder film mystery came to light. Then some 10 years later — in 2009 — another piece of the puzzle fell into place. Both pieces to the puzzle revealed how the U.S. national-security establishment succeeded in secretly altering the Zapruder film on the weekend of the assassination. Let's examine what happened.

At around 10 p.m. on Saturday, November 23, 1963 — the day after President Kennedy was assassinated — two Secret Service agents arrived at the CIA's National Photographic Interpretation Center (NPIC) in Washington, D.C. The two agents handed what later became known as the "Zapruder film" to CIA imagery intelligence analyst Dino Brugioni, who had served as NPIC's chief information officer since NPIC was founded in the mid-1950s and who Wikipedia describes as "the world's foremost imagery intelligence analyst."

On that particular weekend, Brugioni was serving as the duty officer at NPIC, meaning he was responsible for performing after-hours work of an urgent nature. That also meant that he would ordinarily know whatever was transpiring at the center during the entire weekend, even though he was not required to actually be on site.

The reason Brugioni was at NPIC on that Saturday night was because Arthur Lundahl, the CIA's NPIC director, had informed him that the Secret Service would be bringing a particular film to him that evening. Brugioni's job was to photograph whatever individual frames from the film the Secret Service agents wanted displayed, enlarge the photographs, and then mount them on what were called "briefing boards."

Once Brugioni received the film from the two agents, he knew immediately that he had a problem. Zapruder's film was an 8mm film, and NPIC didn't have an 8mm projector. So, members of the NPIC staff were sent out late at night to procure one.

Once NPIC had purchased an 8mm projector, Brugioni, his team, and the two Secret Service agents carefully watched the film several times as a motion picture and then began examining individual frames. The agents selected certain frames from the film that they wanted photographed and enlarged, and Brugioni's team then made internegatives of the desired frames that were about 40 times larger than the originals. They next made two color prints on photographic paper from each of the internegatives and posted them on "briefing-board" panels. They prepared two duplicate briefing-board sets, with each set consisting of two briefing-board panels that were connected by a hinge in the middle, thereby enabling the two panels to close in on themselves.

Brugioni returned the film to the two Secret Service agents after the internegatives and a few test prints were developed. The two agents left Washington, D.C., with the 8mm film in the middle of the night early on Sunday, November 24, before the color prints were all developed and before they were mounted on the two briefing boards. The two sets of briefing boards that Brugioni prepared were delivered some time Sunday morning, November 24, to CIA Director John McCone by Brugioni's boss, NPIC Director Lundahl, who arrived at NPIC about 8 a.m. to pick up the completed briefing boards and accompanying notes from Brugioni. One set of briefing boards was for the Secret Service, the "customer" who had provided the film and requested the work. The other set was an informational copy for Director McCone.

The preparation of briefing boards was not new to Brugioni. His job responsibilities at NPIC often included making photo enlargements and posting them on briefing boards. In his article "'The Two NPIC Zapruder Film Events: Signposts Pointing to the Film's Alteration," Horne wrote that Brugioni was known as the "briefing-board czar" at NPIC.

Keep in mind that Brugioni and his team created the photo enlargements and briefing boards commencing on Saturday night, November 23. The very next night, Sunday, November 24, a different team was summoned to NPIC by NPIC's deputy director, Navy Captain Pierre Sands. That team was headed by an NPIC official named Homer McMahon, who was the head of NPIC's color lab. He was assisted that night by a young employee and recent NPIC hire named Ben Hunter.

A Secret Service agent who identified himself as "Bill Smith" arrived well after dark and handed McMahon and Hunter what was purported to be the Zapruder film. The agent told them that a citizen from Dallas had shot the film and had donated it to the government, free of charge. Smith also stated that he had brought the film from "Hawkeyeworks," the top-secret codeword for a highly classified CIA photographic facility within the Eastman Kodak headquarters research-and-development building, which was known informally within Kodak as the "Hawkeye Plant," in Rochester, New York. "Hawkeyeworks," Smith said, had developed the film that he was giving McMahon and his team. Smith asked McMahon and Hunter to make three enlargements of photographs of selected frames from the film, which would then be placed on briefing boards.

In other words, Smith was requesting that the Sunday-night team do exactly what Brugioni's team had done the night before — make enlargements of selected frames from the film for the purpose of making briefing boards on which the enlargements would be posted. The Sunday-night team made the requested enlargements, using the same state-of-the-art enlarger that Brugioni's team had used the night before. The person identifying himself as Bill Smith stayed all night while the three prints — all enlargements — were made of the 28 frames selected. The three sets of briefing boards requested by "Bill Smith" were later prepared by other people at NPIC, whose identities are still secret.

However, we do know that it wasn't Brugioni and his Saturday-night team who prepared the briefing boards for those Sunday-night enlargements. More than 45 years after the assassination, in 2011, Brugioni was shown high-resolution photos of the briefing-board panels that contained the Sunday-night enlargements, and he specifically denied that they were the briefing boards that he and his team prepared beginning on Saturday night. Unlike Brugioni's Saturday-night sets, which consisted of two panels that were connected to each other by a hinge, the Sunday-night sets consisted of four panels that were not connected to each other in any way.

Brugioni was not made aware of the Sunday-night operation at all, notwithstanding the fact that he was both the chief information officer at NPIC and the duty officer at NPIC that particular weekend. The first time Brugioni discovered that there was a Sunday-night operation was in 2009 — more than 45 years later.

Moreover, the Sunday-night team of Homer McMahon and Ben Hunter did not know about Brugioni's Saturday-night operation. The two events were tightly compartmentalized to ensure that each team did not learn about the other team's operation. Both were sworn to secrecy, which ensured that they didn't discover each other. Everyone understood that what he was doing was highly classified. The two operations were so tightly compartmentalized that McMahon and Hunter were instructed to not answer any questions about their overtime that weekend and to direct all such questions to Captain Sands, the NPIC deputy director and second in command at NPIC.

There was one distinguishing feature pertaining to the Sunday-night version of the Zapruder film, however, a feature that is critically important. The film on Sunday night was in a 16mm-wide, "double 8" format. To understand why that is so important, we need to go back to Friday afternoon in Dallas.

Zapruder's camera used what was called "double 8" home-movie film. That meant that the spool of film that was inserted into the camera was actually a 16mm-wide film with sprockets on each side. The supply reel full of unexposed film was inserted at the top of the camera, and as the operator pressed the "run" button, the 16mm-wide film would move past the operating shutter in an 8mm-wide "gate." Thus, only an 8mm-wide image exposure would be made. Once "side A" was fully exposed and collected on the take-up reel inside the camera, the operator would open the camera, take out the now-full take-up reel, turn it upside down, and place it at the top of the camera again, where it would now become the new supply reel. This time, as the partially exposed reel of film was moving past the 8mm-wide "gate," another 8mm-wide image exposure would be made on "side B." Thus, a fully exposed home movie would contain a 25-foot long piece of exposed film that was 16mm wide, with upside down and opposing image strips (8mm-wide each) on the 16mm-wide reel of film.

After the film was developed, the company doing the developing (it was always Kodak in 1963; there were only four developing plants that could process the Kodachrome II movie film that Zapruder used, and they were all run by Kodak) would then "split" or "slit" the film vertically down the middle. This would result in two strips of film, each one 25 feet long, with sprockets on only one side. These two strips (side A and side B) would then be spliced together end-to-end, creating a film that was now 50 feet long. The film would now be an 8mm-wide film and could only be watched in an 8mm projector, which propelled the film through the projector by a set of sprocket wheels that engaged only one side of the film — the side with the sprocket holes in it.

There is something extremely important to note about this process: Once the developed 16mm-wide, camera-original film was slit down the middle at the processing plant, thereby converting it to an 8mm film, the two slit 8mm films, side A and side B, could not ordinarily be physically reunited to become a 16mm-wide film again. This could only be done optically, or photographically, using sophisticated equipment in a film lab — more on this later. Once it was slit, what had begun as a camera-original 16mm-wide "double 8" film permanently remained an 8mm film and could only be viewed using an 8mm movie projector.

Thus, when Abraham Zapruder took his film to the Kodak facility in Dallas to be developed, it was developed as a 25-foot long, 16mm-wide film. The developed 16mm-wide film would have shown opposing image strips, upside down and backwards from each other.

After a quick, cursory viewing in a 16mm projector for quality-control purposes, the film would ordinarily then have been slit or split vertically down the middle and converted into a 50-foot long, 8mm film.

However, in this case, after developing Zapruder's 16mm-wide "double 8" film, Kodak did not slit the film down the middle, at least not right away. The reason for that decision was that Zapruder wanted to have three copies made of his film. While the Kodak facility in Dallas could develop Zapruder's camera-original 16mm-wide "double 8" Kodachrome II film, it lacked the necessary equipment to create a copy of that film (or any other motion picture). All the Kodak processing plant in Dallas could do was develop "double 8" movie film, view it while it was still 16mm wide, and slit it afterwards.

That's where the Jamieson Film Company in Dallas came into the picture. The Jamieson lab had a 16mm-format contact printer, but not an 8mm-format contact printer. Thus, it had the equipment to copy Zapruder's film, but only in a 16mm-wide format. If Kodak had slit the film, thereby converting it to an 8mm format, the Jamieson Film Company would have been unable to make copies of it.

Therefore, after Kodak developed his camera-original film, Zapruder took the film in its unslit 16mm format to the Jamieson Film Company, along with three rolls of unexposed Kodachrome IIA film provided to him by Kodak. The Jamieson lab then proceeded to make three identical *undeveloped* copies of his camera-original film, all in a 16mm format, using its 16mm-format contact printer.

Zapruder then returned to Kodak, where he had the three first-day copies developed by the Kodak plant (since they were all exposed on proprietary Kodachrome IIA film). The Kodak personnel then proceeded to slit the original film and all three first-day copies of the film down the middle — converting all of them to an 8mm format. When he returned home late that evening, he and family members watched the film on his 8mm film projector. On Saturday morning, he brought his 8mm projector from his home to his office, which he used to show the original film to *LIFE* magazine's Dick Stolley. (Incidentally, side A of Zapruder's movie recorded family scenes, and side B recorded the assassination of President Kennedy.)

Zapruder loaned two copies of the film to the Secret Service in Dallas on Friday night. Max Phillips, the Dallas Secret Service official to whom Zapruder loaned the two first-day copies, put one of them on an airplane bound for Secret Service headquarters in Washington, D.C., and it arrived in Washington a few hours before dawn on Saturday, November 23. By the early morning hours on Saturday, this copy would have been available for viewing by the Secret Service in Washington and anyone they chose to share it with. The Dallas Secret Service loaned the other copy to the FBI in Dallas on Saturday morning. The FBI shipped its copy to Washington, D.C., specifically, BWI airport, late on Saturday night, which meant it would have arrived at FBI Headquarters very early Sunday morning, November 24.

Keep in mind, for now, three things: (1) In Dallas, the camera-original Zapruder film, as well as all three first-day copies, were slit down the middle, thereby converting them to 8mm films; (2) The Zapruder film that Secret Service agent Bill Smith brought to NPIC on Sunday night was a 16mm-wide "double 8" film that appeared to Homer McMahon to be a camera-original film; and (3) Once a 16mm film has been slit down the middle, thereby converting it to an 8mm film, it cannot be reconstituted into a 16mm film by any normally employed mechanical means. (Again, this could only be done optically by a sophisticated piece of photographic machinery called an optical printer.) We will return to this issue in chapter 15.

Returning now to the operations at NPIC, there is something important to note about those two Saturday-night and Sunday-night events: the CIA kept the Sunday-night event partially secret for 12 years and the remainder of that event secret for more than 33 years after Kennedy was assassinated; and it kept the Saturday-night event secret for more than 45 years after Kennedy was assassinated.

You will recall from chapter 4 that in 1975, the CIA delivered to the Rockefeller Commission a set of NPIC working notes that indicated that CIA personnel had played some sort of role with the Zapruder film — namely, that it (1) had made photographs of individual frames that were mounted on four briefing-board panels and (2) had done some analysis of what the film depicted, coming up with three different shot scenarios in its analysis notes.

On May 14, 1975, the CIA delivered to the Rockefeller Commission, by letter, a photocopied set of NPIC working notes. On that same day, NPIC Director John Hicks gave an oral briefing to Robert Olsen, the senior counsel for the Rockefeller Commission, regarding the "domestic activity" that the CIA had conducted with the Zapruder film — namely, that CIA personnel had made briefing boards and that they had conducted, based on how they interpreted the film, a "shot and timing" analysis of the shots that struck President Kennedy and Texas governor John Connally. The six photocopied pages of NPIC notes that Hicks handed Olsen in person at that briefing mentioned the creation of four briefing-board panels (panels I, II, III, and IV). Hicks's own handwritten memo of May 13, 1975, which was also transferred to the Rockefeller Commission in that letter, mentioned the physical discovery of the four briefing-board panels (for the Sunday-night McMahon / Hunter event).

Hicks, however, had a big problem — Dino Brugioni. Hicks knew that if he delivered the Sunday-night briefing boards to the commission, there was a possibility that the commission could release them to the public. Alternatively, they could get released as a result of a Freedom of Information Act request, which is what ultimately happened with the NPIC working notes.

Either way, if Brugioni were to see the Sunday-night briefing-board panels, he would undoubtedly begin asking questions. Who prepared those briefing boards? When were they prepared? Why were they prepared, given that he had already prepared a set of briefing boards on Saturday night? Why had the Sunday-night event been kept secret from him, both in his role as NPIC's chief information officer and as the duty officer at NPIC that weekend?

Moreover, recall from chapter 8 the public furor that developed after Geraldo Rivera showed a bootleg copy of the Zapruder film on his national television show the previous March. That was only two months before Hicks was having to deal with Olsen and the Rockefeller Commission. Given the heightened interest in the film because of Geraldo's showing, there would clearly have been an intense interest in the briefing boards. The last thing the CIA would have wanted was a public discussion of frame-by-frame *image content* of the film — or of the six small colored triangles that appear on the briefing boards, which are very suggestive of a six-shot scenario.

Therefore, Hicks had to figure out a way in which he would appear forthcoming to Olsen and also in which he would make it look like there had been only one briefing-board event. At the same time, he had to figure out a way to make certain that the CIA retained possession of the Sunday-night briefing-board set rather than turn it over to Olsen and the commission.

It is a virtual certainty that Hicks showed Olsen the four briefing-board panels (constituting one of the three sets of the Sunday-night briefing boards) when he handed him the letter containing the NPIC notes on May 14. This would have been the whole purpose of the oral briefing — to "finesse" the briefing-board issue by only letting Olsen view the briefing-board set on a one-time basis, in person; otherwise, the May 14, 1975, cover letter, along with the NPIC notes, could simply have been transmitted by mail or courier. By giving Olsen the NPIC notes in a formal letter and by only *showing* Olsen the four briefing-board panels, Hicks and the CIA deftly avoided having to relinquish custody of the briefing boards.

Although the discovery in 1975 of one set of the four-panel briefing boards that had been made using Homer McMahon's

Sunday-night prints and the six pages of NPIC notes made it clear that the CIA had engaged in some analytic activity with respect to the Zapruder film, the agency's full role remained unclear and was hidden from Olsen and the Rockefeller Commission by NPIC Director Hicks. More about this will be revealed in chapter 15, specifically the full extent of what Hicks knew and what he withheld from Olsen and the Rockefeller Commission.

For now, it goes without saying that if the CIA's activities with the Zapruder film on the weekend of the assassination had been legitimate — that is, if they had been part of an investigation into the assassination, as Alexandra Zapruder seems to believe — Hicks would have openly and forthrightly disclosed both the Saturday-night event and the Sunday-night event to Olsen and the Rockefeller Commission. He also would have given the commission the briefing boards from both events. The fact that he intentionally misled the commission by knowingly creating the false impression that there had been only one event — the Sunday-night event — constitutes powerful evidence that the CIA was up to no good in its dealings with the Zapruder film on the weekend of the assassination.

In 1997 — more than 33 years after the assassination — the ARRB uncovered the Sunday-night operation through interviews conducted with NPIC personnel Homer McMahon and Ben Hunter. At the time of their 1997 ARRB interviews, the only thing clear was that McMahon and Hunter had not duplicated the film as a motion picture — they only made three copies of selected still-image "blow-ups" of individual frames for use in three sets of briefing boards.

At that time, the ARRB had no knowledge of the Saturday-night Dino Brugioni briefing-board event, and the CIA never informed the ARRB of that event. Furthermore, the ARRB had no evidence that the CIA had duplicated the film as a motion picture at NPIC. (NPIC did not have that capability, as the ARRB learned from McMahon and Hunter in 1997.) Bill Smith's story about the film being developed in

Rochester, New York, at "Hawkeyeworks" — at Kodak headquarters — was very troubling because it conflicted dramatically with the known events in Dallas, where Zapruder's film was actually developed. The implications of what Bill Smith told Homer McMahon about the film's provenance were potentially devastating to the film's authenticity because Smith's story clearly implied that the film may have been altered or edited by the CIA's classified "Hawkeyeworks" lab at Kodak headquarters in Rochester.

How was the Saturday-night event at NPIC ultimately uncovered? In chapter 7, I mentioned Peter Janney, the author of *Mary's Mosaic: The CIA Conspiracy to Murder John F. Kennedy, Mary Pinchot Meyer, and Their Vision for World Peace.* In 2009, Janney made a remarkable discovery. He discovered the existence of Dino Brugioni who, by that time, was long retired from NPIC. Brugioni, along with his boss Arthur Lundahl, had helped to create NPIC in the mid-1950s to support the U-2 spy plane program. It just so happened that Janney's father had been a high official in the CIA. Janney contacted Brugioni and introduced himself. It turned out that Brugioni, a genial man, had known Janney's father and thus was happy to talk to Janney. Their conversations included Brugioni's account of his activity with the Zapruder film on Saturday night (and the wee hours of Sunday morning), November 23, the day after the assassination. That was when the Saturday-night piece of the puzzle was uncovered — a piece that the CIA had succeeded in keeping secret for more than 45 years after the assassination.

Janney, along with Doug Horne, who became good friends with Janney during 2009, ended up conducting several interviews with Brugioni. Janney conducted numerous recorded telephone interviews with him in 2009. He interviewed him again in person at his home in April of 2011, which he again recorded.

Janney then asked Horne to conduct a major video interview of Brugioni in the summer of 2011. In July 2011, during that interview,

Horne showed Brugioni a copy of the extant Zapruder film. It was the first time that Brugioni had seen as a motion picture what purports to be the original film since that Saturday-night operation at NPIC on November 23, 1963, when he and his team made internegatives and photographs of individual frames from the film and posted them on briefing boards. What Brugioni recounted to Horne in that interview in 2011 on HD video will be recounted in chapter 17.

Let's return briefly to chapter 10. You will recall that there were several witnesses to the assassination in Dealey Plaza who stated that when President Kennedy got shot in the head, a large quantity of brain tissue and blood shot up in the air. Recall, for instance, what the Willis family said: "His head blew up like a halo. The brains and matter went to the left and the rear." "His head went back and all of the brain matter went out the back of the head (both hands raised upward and backward). It was like a red halo, a red circle, with bright matter in the middle of it." Abraham Zapruder's partner Erwin Schwartz, you will recall, stated that he viewed the Zapruder film at least 15 times that weekend. He said that he saw an eruption of brains and blood to Kennedy's left and rear. Recall also Dr. Roderick Ryan, the Kodak film expert we mentioned in chapter 10, who stated that in his opinion the mysterious red blob on the side of Kennedy's head and in front of his face in the extant Zapruder film appeared to be painted in.

In an April 2011 interview at Brugioni's home, Janney showed Brugioni the extant Zapruder film's frame 313, which supposedly depicts the head explosion from the fatal bullet(s) that hit Kennedy in the head. The following is their conversation (based on the audio recording made by Peter Janney):

Janney: [displaying frame 313, the head explosion] This is the only frame where you had any indication of, you know, his brains exploding.

Brugioni: No, it went into the air, I remember, it went into the air.

Janney: Was it more than one frame? It would have to have been, wouldn't it?

Brugioni: Oh yeah, oh yeah.

Janney: Yeah, see, there's only one frame on the entire Zapruder film, frame 313, that gives any indication—

Brugioni: No, it was in the air — I remember it was in the — in the sky!

Janney: Yeah, but you see that's the only frame, it's just one frame....

Brugioni: There's no 314?

Janney: Yeah, there is a 314, but it has none of this, ah, you know, pink haze, blood water.

Brugioni: No, I remember all of us being shocked.

Janney: And was it going out the back when you saw it?

Brugioni: No, it was going out the front — up, going up —

Janney: OK, but was it leaving a trail in the rear?

Brugioni: No, no, it was straight up, I remember.

Janney: But if that event took place, wouldn't you suspect [sic] to see it on more than one frame?

Brugioni: Oh yeah, yeah.

Janney: Because you're shooting with, 18 frames per second, isn't that what that camera did?

Brugioni: There should have been more than one frame.

Janney: Yeah, right, there should have been....

Brugioni: No doubt in my mind, and I remember all of us being shocked, because I thought the spray was, you know, three or four feet from his head.

Janney: Uh huh, up in the air?

Brugioni: Yeah.

Janney: Uh huh ... I want to just have you look at this one more time [displaying frame 313 again]. So —

Brugioni: What I saw was more than that.

Janney: This is frame 313. So you saw more pink mist going straight up?

Brugioni: Going — what I remember it was, like right here, but high, it wasn't low, it was high.

Janney: Now, OK, so there, this [displaying frame 313] is the only frame on the Zapruder film [where] you get to see —

Brugioni: No, there was more than that.

Janney: You're saying there was more than one frame for sure. How many frames do you think there would be?

Brugioni: I don't know. All I know is we were shocked when we saw it.

Janney: Right. Right.

Brugioni: Well, now, do they claim, if you go down to the Archives and ask for the Zapruder film, they claim that that's the true one?

Janney: That's the true one, right. The frames we just looked at. No? You're shaking your head. That's not the true one, is it? Is that what you mean?

Brugioni: I'm saying that the one I saw, man, his head was — it was way high off of his head.

Janney: The debris?

Brugioni: And I can't imagine that there would only be one frame.

Janney: Right. That's it, right there.

Brugioni: Because that film — I remember looking at the film and ah, I remember how shocked we were. All of us that were there were shocked.

Janney: And you wouldn't have, I mean, there couldn't have been that much of a shock if there was just one frame, right? That would have gone by pretty quickly.

Brugioni: No, no, that's right.

Janney: This was a pretty dramatic event, that lasted probably 2 or 3 seconds at least, right?

Brugioni: Yeah. It was — what I saw was more than what you have there.

Thus, what Brugioni saw on the original Zapruder film on Saturday night, November 23, 1963, matched in its basic essentials the statements of the witnesses to the assassination who stated that brain tissue and blood shot up into the air when the fatal shot (or shots) hit Kennedy in the head. To be sure, most of the Dealey Plaza eyewitnesses, and, indeed, even Erwin Schwartz (when viewing Zapruder's film), recalled seeing exit debris in the air that traveled to the left and rear of President Kennedy, whereas Brugioni recalled in his conversations with Janney and Horne that the debris from the head explosion he remembered seeing in the film with which he worked on Saturday night went straight up into the air (instead of to the left rear). What those two differing accounts have in common, however, is seeing a large amount of exit debris traveling high into the air at the time of the fatal shot(s).

The problem, of course, is that the extant Zapruder film shows no such thing. It only shows a low head explosion (not a high one) and does not show a lot of exit debris traveling through the air.

14

Alteration

(Part 2)

Let's now put all of the known pieces of the Zapruder puzzle together to understand what was taking place on the weekend of the Kennedy assassination.

After Abraham Zapruder filmed the assassination, he returned to his office. Soon afterwards, two police officers with shotguns arrived and demanded that Zapruder turn over his film to them. Having placed his film in his office safe, Zapruder refused their demand. As I previously noted, it was a prudent decision on his part. There were people in Dealey Plaza such as Gordon Arnold and Beverly Oliver, who were mentioned in chapter 8, who later said that people dressed as law-enforcement officers forced them to hand over their films and photographs and then either took them away from them and never returned them or destroyed them on the spot.

As an aside, it is worth mentioning that immediately after the assassination, there were men on the "grassy knoll" (which was located to Kennedy's right front) at the time of the assassination who identified themselves as Secret Service agents. The Secret Service later said that there were no Secret Service agents in that area. At the risk of belaboring the obvious, it is virtually impossible to reconcile a lone-nut theory of the assassination with the fact that there were men in Dealey Plaza falsely identifying themselves as Secret Service agents immediately after the assassination.

From the very beginning, Zapruder was certain that he had a valuable asset in his film of the assassination. In her book, Alexandra Zapruder wrote that he "apparently" telephoned his lawyer to get advice about selling the film. Presumably, his lawyer advised him to secure affidavits that would establish the provenance of the film for prospective buyers. After Zapruder appeared in an interview at a local television station — WFAA — that was broadcast live, the television station personnel advised him that they could not develop his film because they could only develop 16mm black-and-white newsreel footage (Zapruder's film was in color). They told him that he would have to go to the local Kodak plant in Dallas to develop his film, so the station called the Eastman Kodak plant and alerted them that Zapruder would be bringing his assassination film to Kodak for developing.

Accompanied by Secret Service agent Forrest Sorrels and the two police officers, Zapruder headed to the local Kodak facility in Dallas to get his film developed. After Kodak developed it, he then took the 16mm-wide developed but unslit "double 8" film to the Jamieson Film Company, which created three undeveloped copies of it on the Kodachrome IIA movie film that the Kodak plant had supplied him. Zapruder then returned to Kodak, where the three copies were developed. Once the copies were viewed and determined to be satisfactory, Kodak then slit all four films — the camera-original film and all three copies — down the middle, converting them all into 8mm films.

Well before this happened, Sorrels had departed for Dallas police headquarters to participate in the questioning of Oswald. With all four films in hand, Zapruder went to Dallas police headquarters to talk to Sorrels about giving him copies of the film. Since Sorrels was busy, he told Zapruder to take the copies to the Secret Service office downtown. Zapruder did so, transferring two of his three "first-day copies" to Secret Service agent Max Phillips. That night Phillips put one of the two copies Zapruder had given him on an airplane and sent it to the Secret Service in Washington, D.C., where it arrived a few hours before dawn on Saturday morning. The Secret Service in Dallas loaned the other copy to the local Dallas FBI on Saturday morning, which viewed its copy of the film several times at the Eastman Kodak plant using an 8mm movie projector at the facility. The Dallas FBI then put its copy of the Zapruder film on an airplane to FBI headquarters in Washington, D.C., where it arrived at BWI airport late Saturday night. Zapruder retained one of the three "first-day copies" of his film all weekend and into Monday, November 25.

On Friday night, *LIFE* magazine's Richard Stolley telephoned Zapruder at home. They agreed to meet the following morning — Saturday — at Zapruder's office to discuss the purchase and sale of the film. On Saturday morning, Zapruder showed him the film on his 8mm home projector. They struck a deal for $50,000, which is the equivalent in today's dollars to $454,000. It was only for print-media rights, however. Zapruder retained the option to sell the motion-picture rights to the film. They agreed that Zapruder would wait a week before selling the motion-picture rights.

As part of the deal, Zapruder relinquished possession of his original film to *LIFE* magazine, which planned to publish photographs from selected frames in its Friday, November 29, issue. *LIFE* agreed to return the original film in a week, so that Zapruder could then license the motion-picture rights to the film to others, at which point Zapruder, in exchange, would give *LIFE* his first-day copy of the film. (Recall that Zapruder gave the other two first-day copies to the Secret Service on Friday night.)

At 3 p.m. on Saturday, Stolley put the Zapruder film on a plane to Chicago, where *LIFE* magazine was printed. The official story was that after the film arrived at the airport in Chicago, it went directly to *LIFE*'s printing facilities.

The November 29 issue of *LIFE* began to hit the newsstands, in Chicago, on Tuesday, November 26, but it displayed 31 dark, black-and-white, difficult-to-decipher photographs of selected frames from the Zapruder film, not color photographs as one might have expected. Most of them were very small, which made any details even more difficult to see.

What we now know, based on the statements that Dino Brugioni made to Peter Janney and Douglas Horne in 2009, is that the Zapruder film was actually diverted to Washington, D.C., most likely immediately upon arriving at the Chicago airport. It was then taken by two men identifying themselves as Secret Service agents to the CIA's National Photographic Interpretation Center (NPIC) in Washington, where it arrived at about 10 p.m.

How did this diversion get arranged? It would not have been difficult. The CIA would have made the arrangements through its trusted longtime acolyte C. D. Jackson, the publisher of *LIFE* magazine, who, given his longstanding ties to the CIA, would have been more than willing to do whatever the CIA requested him to do, especially if he had been told that national security was at stake. You will recall that Jackson's longstanding ties to the CIA were detailed in chapter 8, something that, you will also recall, Alexandra Zapruder, for some reason, failed to mention in her book.

By this time, the CIA would have known how dangerous the Zapruder film was, in three major respects.

First, the original film contained the presidential limousine's wide, oblique turn onto Elm Street, which, as we saw in chapter 10, may have violated Secret Service protocols. You will also recall from chapter 10 that the left turn from Houston to Elm was when both Abraham Zapruder and his assistant Marilyn Sitzman said he started filming. The original film would have shown how the limousine practically went up onto the sidewalk while making the turn. More significant, it would have shown that the limousine was proceeding at an extremely slow speed after negotiating that very wide turn, which would obviously have made it easier to shoot the president.

Second, the original film would have shown that after the first shots rang out, instead of speeding up to escape Dealey Plaza, the presidential limousine either completely stopped or almost stopped, which enabled a shooter or shooters to more easily hit Kennedy with a fatal gunshot or gunshots to the head. We quoted some of the 59 witnesses to that event in chapter 12.

Third, the film would have contained frames showing brain debris shooting high into the air, some of it straight up in a huge cloud of white mist, and other debris (brain tissue and blood) traveling backward and to the left, as it exited the back of Kennedy's head.

Why didn't the CIA simply destroy or lose the Zapruder film? I believe there are two reasons.

First, Zapruder still had a copy of the film in his possession.

Second, and more important, altering the film was actually an absolutely ingenious strategy on the part of the CIA. Remember that the fraudulent autopsy had already been conducted on Friday night, and many of the autopsy photos were developed on Saturday, November 23. A film of the assassination that showed the back of Kennedy's head to be intact would be powerful — almost dispositive — evidence that all those witnesses in Dallas were simply mistaken — that, in fact, the official autopsy photographs placed in the record showing the back of Kennedy's head to be intact were genuine and authentic.

After all, who in the world is going to believe that anyone could and would alter a film of the assassination, especially in a very short period of time? The very idea would seem so outlandish that no one would ever reasonably believe that it could happen or did happen. Anyone who suggested that the film was altered could be derogatorily labeled as an "alterationist."

Keep in mind, after all, that no one knew about "Hawkeye-works," the CIA's top-secret facility that was located in Eastman Kodak's research-and-development facility at its corporate headquarters in Rochester. The CIA kept that information secret for more than 33 years, until the ARRB discovered it in 1997 through Homer McMahon. By keeping "Hawkeyeworks" secret, as well as its compartmentalized Saturday-night and Sunday-night operations at NPIC on the weekend of the assassination, the CIA succeeded for almost three-and-a-half decades in diverting the focus of assassination researchers in a false direction — toward how *LIFE* magazine could possibly have altered the film in the days following the assassination.

The success of the CIA's strategy is perfectly reflected by the mindset of Alexandra Zapruder. For her, the notion that the CIA altered her grandfather's film is simply inconceivable. In fact, her mindset — and the obvious success of the CIA's strategy — was perfectly captured in a somewhat acerbic statement that Alexandra made in her book: "There is a still fringier lunatic element who believe that the film was fabricated by cutting and pasting frames, and that it is a hoax and a fraud."

Never mind that no credible JFK film researcher has ever claimed that the Zapruder film was altered by physically cutting out frames and then pasting the remaining frames together. That's just a "straw-man" argument that Alexandra is making. Any alteration of the film, including removal of frames, would have occurred optically, or *photographically*, in an optical printer at a lab.

Let me give you another example of how the CIA's ingenious strategy played out. In December 2016, Alexandra appeared at a popular bookstore named Politics and Prose in Washington, D.C., to discuss her book. (The program can be found on YouTube at https://www.youtube.com/watch?v=wFil6WPcAo8.) A woman named Susan Shreve was interviewing Alexandra. At 44:10 in the video, Alexandra answered a question from the audience, where she stated in no uncertain terms that she considered the possibility that the CIA altered her grandfather's film to be outlandish. That, of course, is not surprising. But notice Shreve's facial expression as Alexandra is addressing the issue. You can tell from her expression that she too considers the possibility of alteration to be absolutely ludicrous. After all, as the interviewer, Shreve could have asked some interesting, probing questions, such as: "Why do some people believe that your grandfather's film was altered? How do they propose that the alteration was done?" She didn't ask any such follow-up questions, and her facial expression tells why. To her, the possibility that the film has been altered was so outlandish and inconceivable that it wasn't even worth addressing.

It's that type of reaction to the possibility that the film was altered that demonstrates the sheer brilliance of the CIA to keep and alter the film. The CIA knew that no one would ever believe that such a thing could actually have taken place.

Let me give you another example of how ingenious this strategy was. Recall Parkland Hospital treating physician Dr. Robert McClelland, who never deviated for the rest of his life from stating that Kennedy had that massive defect or hole in the back of his head that was in every way consistent with an exit wound. In an interview, even he stated that he didn't think that the Zapruder film had been altered, no doubt because he considered the possibility of alteration so outlandish and inconceivable. He obviously didn't realize that taking that position negated his statement about that massive exit wound in the back of Kennedy's head, given that the Zapruder film, like the official autopsy photos, shows the back of Kennedy's head to be intact.

There was one small problem and one big problem, however, with altering the original film. The small problem was that the Secret Service and the FBI had two of the three first-day copies of the film. Substituting altered copies of the film for the copies held by the Secret Service and the FBI, however, would not have been difficult to accomplish, especially since the switch would have been engineered by the CIA under the guise of "national security."

The big problem was that Abraham Zapruder still had a copy of the original film in his possession. That's where C. D. Jackson, the publisher of *LIFE* magazine, would have come into play. The CIA's decision to alter the film was obviously the real reason why Jackson suddenly changed his mind and decided to purchase the Zapruder film itself. That's undoubtedly also why Jackson tripled the amount of the original $50,000 offer, even though *LIFE* magazine had no means by which to show the film as a motion picture, as television or Hollywood did.

After all, *LIFE* magazine could have made lots of money by simply licensing the film as a motion picture to be shown in movie theaters (like a newsreel) or on television. But as *LIFE*'s publisher, Jackson clearly had no intention of doing that. The name of the game was now suppression of the film. Thus, Jackson decided to spend that extremely large sum of additional money ($900,000 in today's money) to ensure, he said, that sensitive Americans would never have to see the violence depicted in the film.

In her book, Alexandra wrote, "Also on Sunday afternoon, senior staff at *LIFE,* including Dick Pollard and publisher C. D. Jackson, had gathered in New York to screen a copy of the film that had been made in Chicago and sent to their office." Presumably, that was when Jackson decided to protect the American people from seeing the violence depicted in the film. But we now know that given the chain of custody of the original and the three copies, it would have been impossible for Jackson to have viewed a copy of the film on Sunday afternoon. Recall, again, that the original of the film was diverted from the Chicago airport to Washington, D.C., on Saturday, where it was delivered to Dino Brugioni at NPIC on Saturday night and then taken to "Hawkeyeworks" in Rochester early Sunday morning. Recall also that Zapruder retained one copy of the film in Dallas. He gave the other two copies to the Dallas Secret Service, which sent one copy on Friday night to Secret Service headquarters in Washington, D.C., and loaned the other copy on Saturday to the Dallas FBI, which shipped it on Saturday evening to FBI headquarters in Washington, D.C. Thus, given what we now know about the chain of custody of the original of the film and the three copies of the film, it is impossible for Jackson to have viewed a copy of the film on Sunday.

It is now obvious that it was the CIA that requested, most likely on Saturday, that C. D. Jackson take ownership and control over Zapruder's film so that he could have *LIFE* magazine permanently suppress it as its "private property." That's obviously what caused Jackson to change his mind and decide that *LIFE* should buy all rights to the film rather than simply the print-media rights to the film.

Reflect on what Jackson was doing. *LIFE* initially bought the print-media rights for $50,000 (the equivalent of $454,000 today). Two days later, he was offering an additional $100,000 (or an additional $900,000 in today's money) for a film that he intended to lock away in a vault and never let anyone see, thereby forgoing a large amount of money in licensing fees in order to supposedly protect Americans from being exposed to the violence depicted in the film.

It's a virtual certainty that by Saturday, the day after the fraudulent autopsy was performed, the CIA had decided to alter the Zapruder film at its top-secret "Hawkeyeworks" lab that was secretly located inside the "Hawkeye Plant" corporate research and development facility at Kodak's headquarters in Rochester, New York. Did they have the capability to do that? During a visit that Brugioni had made to "Hawkeyeworks," Ed Green, the Kodak manager who ran the "Hawkeye Plant," told Brugioni that the facility could "do anything" with film.

That meant that the CIA needed to take ownership and possession of the original film as well as the first-day copy that Zapruder still retained. That's the role that CIA acolyte and *LIFE* magazine publisher

C. D. Jackson would have played. He could purchase the film and then have *LIFE* suppress it under the rubric of private-property rights, and no one would be the wiser. To avoid the risk of Zapruder selling the film rights to someone else, Jackson made the new offer so high that Zapruder couldn't turn it down, especially given his favorable bias toward *LIFE*.

You will recall from chapter 8 that on March 6, 1975, Geraldo Rivera showed a bootleg copy of the Zapruder film on his nationwide television show. As I previously noted, people were so angry after viewing the film that Congress was pressured into opening a new investigation into the assassination. That investigation was carried out from 1976 to 1978 by the House Select Committee on Assassinations. The HSCA's report was published in 1979.

Why were people so outraged? If you have seen Oliver Stone's movie *JFK*, you will recall the jury argument by Kevin Costner, who was portraying District Attorney Jim Garrison. In his argument to the jury, Costner kept repeating the phrase "back and to the left" — "back and to the left" — "back and to the left."

What Costner was referring to was the violent movement of Kennedy's body back and to the left at the moment he was struck by a fatal shot to the head. That movement of back and to the left obviously implied that a fatal head shot came from the right front, which was contrary to the official lone-nut theory, which held that three shots had come only from the president's rear.

That back-and-to-the-left movement is actually the most striking and memorable part of the Zapruder film. It was that movement that generated the outrage among the American people that led to the reinvestigation of the assassination by the House Select Committee.

But consider this: No one, including Zapruder himself, ever emphasized that back-and-to-left movement on the weekend of the assassination. There is a likely reason for that: The back-and-to-the-left movement was likely in the original film, only not at the speed and with the violence shown in the extant Zapruder film. By optically deleting frames from the film, the resulting time-compression of the remaining frames, when played back in a projector at standard speed, may well have dramatically speeded up the back-and-to-the-left motion and made it appear much faster and more violent than it was in the original film. Of course, that could explain why there was a still a need to keep the altered film sequestered under the laughable guise of protecting sensitive Americans from viewing violence.

After the outrage arising from Rivera's showing of the film on national television in March of 1975, *LIFE* magazine had had enough. It decided that it wanted to rid itself of the Zapruder film. And after all, Jackson's mission to keep the film suppressed, ostensibly to protect the American people from seeing the violence in it, had now been squelched by Rivera.

That was when *LIFE* magazine rejected Henry Zapruder's very generous offer of $60,000 for the film, which, again, translates to $309,000 in today's dollars. Instead, *LIFE* agreed to accept only one dollar from the Zapruder family in return for giving the film back to them on April 9, 1975.

Why would *LIFE* magazine make the highly unusual decision to walk away from the equivalent today of $309,000? As you will recall from chapter 8, Alexandra Zapruder claimed that the likely reason is that Time Inc., the owner of *LIFE* magazine, wanted to garner positive publicity by appearing to not be profiting off the film. Another possibility — and this is entirely speculation — is that it might well have been the CIA that provided the money to Jackson for the extra $100,000 paid to Zapruder for his film.

After all, by Monday morning, November 25, the CIA needed the film much more than *LIFE* magazine did, especially when we see what the CIA was doing with the film on Saturday night and Sunday, when Zapruder still owned the film. If the CIA fronted the additional money for the second purchase of the film on Monday, November 25, it would have made sense that *LIFE* might feel reticent about accepting Henry Zapruder's extremely generous offer when they were selling the film back to him. In this regard, it's worth recalling a portion of the Drew Pearson quote from Spartacus Educational that was mentioned in chapter 8: "I always was suspicious that a lot of dough was coming from unexplained quarters and didn't learn until sometime later that *the CIA was footing the bill.*" (Emphasis added.)

Of course, even though *LIFE* executives might have known that the CIA had fronted the additional $100,000 for the film ($900,000 in today's money), it is unlikely that Jackson would have shared with anyone at *LIFE* that he was suppressing the film on behalf of the CIA or the reasons for the suppression. (The one possible exception might have been Henry Luce, the magazine magnate who launched *Time* and *LIFE* magazine who himself was a fierce Cold War anti-communist who had a close relationship with the CIA.) In fact, it's a virtual certainty that the CIA did not tell Jackson about the film alteration, given the dangerous possibility that Jackson could leak the information. All that the CIA would have needed to do was request Jackson to suppress the film on grounds of "national security." Being the loyal CIA acolyte that he was, Jackson would have willingly agreed to do so, no questions asked, without advising anyone else at *LIFE* (except possibly Luce) that he was doing the bidding of the CIA.

Please permit me another relevant digression. In 1977, *Rolling Stone* published an article entitled "The CIA and the Media" by Carl Bernstein. The article revealed "more than 400 American journalists who in the past twenty-five years have secretly carried out assignments for the Central Intelligence Agency." Included among the journalists was Henry Luce of Time Inc., the owner of *LIFE* magazine. Bernstein wrote: "Some of these journalists' relationships with the Agency were tacit; some were explicit. There was cooperation, accommodation and overlap. Journalists provided a full range of clandestine services — from simple intelligence gathering to serving as go-betweens with spies in Communist countries. Reporters shared their notebooks with the CIA. Editors shared their staffs. Some of the journalists were Pulitzer Prize winners, distinguished reporters who considered themselves ambassadors-without-portfolio for their country. Most were less exalted: foreign correspondents who found that their association with the Agency helped their work; stringers and freelancers who were as interested in the derring-do of the spy business as in filing articles, and, the smallest category, full-time CIA employees masquerading as journalists abroad. In many instances, CIA documents show, journalists were engaged to perform tasks for the CIA with the consent of the managements of America's leading news organizations. The history of the CIA's involvement with the American press continues to be shrouded by an official policy of obfuscation and deception. . . . By far the most valuable of these associations, according to CIA officials, have been with *The New York Times*, CBS, and Time Inc."

Returning to the overall context of the Zapruder film mystery, once those two men who identified themselves as Secret Service agents delivered the film to Dino Brugioni's team at NPIC on Saturday night, Brugioni and his team, at the direction of the two agents, carefully examined the film and made enlargements of selected frames. Those enlargements were placed on briefing boards, where each photograph was labeled by Brugioni by its frame number. (The reconstructed 16mm-wide Zapruder film delivered to Homer McMahon on Sunday night by "Bill Smith" consisted of 486 frames; the extant film today in the Archives has 480 frames because six damaged frames were removed by *LIFE* technicians when they accidentally broke the film in two places. The two Secret Service copies today each have 486 frames, which is how we know that 6 frames were removed when LIFE damaged the film. On that Saturday night at NPIC, the total number of frames was not recorded anywhere, but Bill Banfield, the head of NPIC's photo lab and graphics department, counted the frame numbers himself for each print they made of a still frame, and Brugioni placed those frame numbers on his briefing boards below the enlargements of the frames that were displayed.)

After Brugioni's Saturday-night team created the internegatives of the individual movie frames desired for blow-up by the Secret Service agents and made a couple of test prints to prove NPIC could make good enlargements, the two Secret Service agents departed with the original Zapruder film about 3 a.m. (i.e., early Sunday morning), before Brugioni's briefing boards were completed.

Once the ARRB learned from Homer McMahon in 1997 that Secret Service agent "Bill Smith" brought the 16mm film to NPIC from "Hawkeyeworks," on Sunday night, it became easy to deduce that the Zapruder film had been transported to "Hawkeyeworks" some time after leaving Dallas. Once Janney and Horne uncovered the Saturday-night event through their interviews with Brugioni in 2009, it became clear that the film had gone from Dallas to Chicago, from Chicago to NPIC in Washington, from Washington to "Hawkeyeworks" in Rochester, and, in altered form, from Hawkeyeworks back to NPIC.

Furthermore, recall that according to Brugioni, who had personally visited "Hawkeyeworks," the Hawkeye Plant could "do anything" with photography, per Ed Green, the plant manager of Kodak's state-of-the-art R&D facility in Rochester. Brugioni told Doug Horne during his video interview in July of 2011 that while he personally did not visit the unclassified portions of the "Hawkeye Plant," he was confident they had sophisticated motion-picture equipment, such as optical printers, because that was the site where Kodak did its research and development on new types of motion-picture film for the Hollywood movie industry. Brugioni told Peter Janney in May of 2009 at his home in Virginia that he was absolutely sure the "Hawkeye Plant" had the ability to duplicate motion-picture films, based on what Green had told him. Brugioni reiterated several times to Janney Green's comment that the plant could "do anything."

Upon the film's arrival at "Hawkeyeworks," photographic experts would have immediately gone into action, with the following basic goals: one, optically delete the frames showing the car's wide, sloppy turn onto Elm Street; two, optically delete the car stop or near stop; three, optically delete the frames showing bloody exit debris leaving JFK's head toward the left rear; four, limit the massive head explosion to one frame only by repainting it as a much lower (and redder) eruption (thus removing almost all of the large cloud of white mist and biological debris well above his head); five, black out the large exit wound on the back of Kennedy's head in frames 314–337; and six, paint a large apparent wound on frames depicting the side and top of Kennedy's head (called "the blob" by most researchers), which would have been generally consistent with the damage shown in many of the fraudulent Kennedy autopsy photos.

It is, of course, impossible to know which photographic experts would have been used for the alteration project. One possibility is photographic experts who were employed by the CIA. They could have then used equipment, including an optical printer, within the Hawkeye Plant. No evidence has ever surfaced that any Kodak employees were involved in the operation or that Kodak was even aware of the operation, but it certainly would not have been beyond the realm of reasonable possibility that the CIA enlisted the unwitting assistance of Kodak photography experts by citing "national security," just as it did with Dino Brugioni, Homer McMahon, and Ben Hunter. It is also within the realm of reasonable possibility that Kodak personnel willingly cooperated in the alteration project under the rubric of Cold War cooperation and without suspecting anything nefarious, especially given the close and secret relationship between the CIA and Kodak to wage the Cold War together.

After all, Kodak had given the CIA the authority to locate and operate a top-secret facility inside its "Hawkeye Plant" in support of the CIA's U-2 and Corona surveillance photography. Homer McMahon, the person in charge of the Sunday-night team at NPIC, told the ARRB in 1997 that the CIA was "in bed with the Yellow God," referring to Kodak. Explaining what he meant by that, he stated, "We had their top scientists and photochemists and optical people working in the 'world beyond;' we had their best people — I shouldn't even talk about it, I'm sorry. And there was a definite link, on the national level, where we had 'the best there was' working with us."

While writing this chapter, I asked Doug Horne how photography experts, whoever they were, would have altered the film. The following was his response:

[Beginning of Horne response] "They would first have copied Zapruder's film in an optical printer by blowing it up into a 16mm or 35mm format — almost certainly 35mm — and would have then used that 35mm enlargement to make the necessary changes to the film. The machine used would most likely have been an Oxberry optical printer, modified with an animation stand. This was known as an *aerial optical printer*. In such a set-up, the "aerial image" of each frame, one at a time, was always displayed in a flat plane about waist-high, on an animation stand (10.5 x 7.5 inches in size), upon which artwork could then be applied, located directly above a set of condenser lenses (9 x 13 inches in size) in the middle of the optical printer.

"The artwork would be overlaid onto the displayed film frame image by painting the desired visual effect on a clear acetate cel positioned on top of the animation stand. (The animation stand was positioned directly on top of the condenser lenses that relayed the 'aerial image' of each frame from the playback camera at the bottom of the machine.) The artwork painted on the transparent acetate cel — whether it was a black patch, or a pink 'blob,' or a new head explosion — was always superimposed on top of the image of the existing film frame displayed on the animation stand via the condenser lenses. If the artwork was opaque, it would automatically 'matte out' or block that portion of the film frame in the 'aerial image.' Therefore, film professionals describe aerial imaging as 'self-matting.'

"After the alteration of each frame through the application of artwork — paint — on the animation cel, each composite frame would be rephotographed, one at a time, by a 16mm, 'double 8' format 'process camera' positioned directly above the animation stand. In this way, a new film would be created one frame at a time. The opaque paint applied to the animation cel overlaid on top of the aerial image of each frame in an aerial optical printer was always self-matting, and the composite image could be rephotographed by only one pass of the film in the process camera. Any frames that needed to be deleted would be optically excised from the new film by simply not rephotographing them in the process camera. The end result would have been a new, 16mm-wide, 'double 8' film that mimicked a camera-original, unslit 'double 8' film. The new film would have had the turn from Houston to Elm optically removed and the brief car stop optically removed. It would have displayed wounds very different in character than those on the true camera-original film: namely, with the back of JFK's head blacked out (and the large exit wound obscured), and a huge red blob on the side of his head and top of his head and, in some frames, even in front of his face, that was not seen by anyone at Parkland Hospital.

"Because a picture is often worth a thousand words, I encourage the reader to go to the PODCAST page for archival episode #107 at Midnight Writer News, at this link:

https://midnightwriternews.com/mwn-episode-107-douglas-horne-on-the-zapruder-film-alteration-debate

"On that PODCAST page you will find a schematic diagram of an optical printer modified with an animation stand, and an actual photograph of an Oxberry optical printer modified with an animation stand

— that is, an *aerial optical printer* — taken in the 1950s. These images were taken from the first textbook ever published on the 'black arts' of Hollywood, in 1965, titled, *The Technique of Special Effects Cinematography* by Professor Raymond Fielding of the University of Houston's School of Communications. In the book, Fielding describes in intricate detail that there were two basic techniques used by the movie industry up until that time (1965) to alter images in motion-picture films: traveling mattes and aerial imaging. The technique called *aerial imaging* is undoubtedly the technique employed to alter the Zapruder film. It was a quick process and simple to perform, compared to the multiple passes in a process camera required by traveling mattes. Oxberry optical printers were standard equipment in the movie industry in that era and one such printer was almost certainly present at the 'Hawkeye Plant' in Rochester, Kodak's principal research and development facility, where Kodak developed new motion-picture film products and worked with the motion-picture movie industry." [End of Horne response.]

At this point, it's worth asking an important question: What would be the purpose of sending the film to "Hawkeyeworks" if it wasn't to alter it? Remember: They could watch the film at NPIC on the 8mm movie projector that Brugioni's team procured on Saturday night. Therefore, the only conceivable reason for sending it to"Hawkeyeworks" in Rochester would have been to alter it.

There is something else to consider. Recall that *LIFE* magazine published muddy black-and-white photographs of frames from the film in its November 29 issue. Why would *LIFE* do that? The Zapruder film was in color, not black and white. Color was everything, especially for a magazine like *LIFE,* whose aim, as a profit-seeking business, was to sell as many copies of the magazine as possible. Alexandra asserts that *LIFE* simply did not have sufficient time to process and print color images in order to make the November 29 deadline. I submit that's nonsense. As I previously noted, that issue began hitting the newsstands in Chicago on Tuesday, November 26. There was no inherent reason why that had to be the case. They could have had it hit the newsstands on Friday, November 29, the date of the issue, which would have given them three more days to process and print the color photographs. Moreover, even if they were to miss the November 29 deadline and have the issue hit the newsstands on, say, the following Sunday, it's not as though anyone would have sued them for missing the publication date by a couple of days.

I submit that there is a better explanation for *LIFE*'s decision to go with those muddy, black-and-white photographs in its November 29 issue. Since Jackson could not be certain as to when the CIA would send *LIFE* the color film, *LIFE* had to settle for publishing what the CIA had given it — that is, three black-and-white copies, probably made on a contact printer, which would explain the soft, "muddy" nature of the images in the November 29 issue. Those three black-and-white film copies were actually discovered in December of 1999 when the Zapruder family turned over all of its film elements to the Sixth Floor Museum in Dallas, which included reproductions of the 16mm-wide unslit version of the altered Zapruder film masquerading as the "camera-original." Later on, after the CIA sent *LIFE* the new (altered) "original" film, *LIFE* used striking color blow-ups of individual frames from that film in a special JFK memorial issue of the magazine published in December 1963 and in subsequent issues in 1964 and 1966.

After creating and then copying the altered film at the "Hawkeye Plant" in Rochester on Sunday, November 24, the altered Zapruder film, now masquerading as a "camera-original" 16mm-wide, unslit "double 8" film was then brought back to the NPIC facility in Washington on Sunday night, where it was represented to be a "camera original" film to the McMahon/Hunter team. It's worth reemphasizing that Brugioni's team was not summoned back on Sunday night to make photo enlargements and briefing boards from the new film. The reason is obvious: Brugioni would have known that the film had been altered. Instead, a different team headed by McMahon and Hunter was summoned to perform those tasks. The 16mm-wide, unslit "double 8" film that had been created using a top-of-line Oxberry aerial optical printer at the "Hawkeye Plant," where they could "do anything," was so good that McMahon and Hunter were convinced that it was, in fact, an original film.

There were two major slip-ups, however, in this deception. As I noted in chapter 13, the new "original" was bought to NPIC on Sunday night in a 16mm-wide unslit "double 8" format, rather than slitting it at the "Hawkeye Plant" and converting it to an 8mm format, so that it would then match up with the format of Zapruder's true original film, which had been slit in Dallas and converted into an 8mm film, and, most important, had arrived at NPIC in that condition the day before. The proof that something was seriously amiss was the fact that the film that arrived Sunday night — and that was represented to be the original — was *not* in the same format as the original film that had arrived Saturday night. It had somehow, miraculously, transformed itself from a slit 8mm original film into an *unslit,* 16mm-wide "double 8" film purported to *also* be the "camera original."

Of course, it's possible that it wasn't a slip-up at all. Recall that NPIC did not have an 8mm projector, which is why Brugioni had someone go out and purchase one on Saturday night. Thus, it's entirely possible that Bill Smith, not knowing that Brugioni's team had purchased an 8mm projector the night before, intentionally brought the altered film in its 16mm format to NPIC so that it could be viewed in NPIC's 16mm projector.

The other slip up was the visual appearance of the three copies of the film made at the "Hawkeye Plant" in Rochester. As the three color-copy films are viewed today, they each have a different density: one looks "just right," one looks too dark, and one looks too light. In other words, their exposures were "bracketed." When copying a film, bracketed exposures are made when the person doing the copying job is unsure what the best exposure should be. Bracketing usually ensures that at least one of the copies will be perfect.

However, sometimes copies are not bracketed, in which case the person copying the film makes the best guess as to how much light to use when exposing each copy and then ensures that all three copies have that same exposure. That's how the copies were made at the Jamieson Film Company in Dallas — using the same light-and-filter-pack for the exposure of each of the three "same day copies" — something that the film experts at "Hawkeyeworks" were obviously not aware of. Remember: the CIA managers in Rochester had only the camera original 8mm Zapruder film; they did not have any of the three "first-day copies." Thus, the three "first-generation copies" that exist today (called Secret Service 1, Secret Service 2, and LMH2) should all have the same density, or exposure, if they are what they purport to be — but they most certainly do not. (In chapter 15, we will discuss Roland Zavada, a retired Kodak official who did a limited authenticity study of the Zapruder film for the ARRB. For now, it should be noted that the "bracketing" of the extant so-called "first-generation copies" was definitively revealed in a December 1999 addendum to Zavada's September 1998 report for the ARRB.)

In summary, copies of the camera-original Zapruder film made on November 22, 1963, at the Jamieson Film Company lab should have exactly the same density and look exactly the same visually; however, the three extant "first-generation copies" today look markedly different from one another. This is a give-away that they were made later, from the altered Zapruder film masquerading as the original film, by technicians at "Hawkeyeworks" who didn't know better and thus created three "bracketed" exposures. Those copies were obviously swapped out with the true "first-day copies" the week after the assassination, probably by Tuesday, November 26, 1963.

Nonetheless, given the top-secret nature of the entire operation, the people involved in the alteration could not have been too concerned about these two slip-ups adversely affecting their overall operation. After all, let's not forget that the CIA was able to keep the Saturday-night operation run by Dino Brugioni secret for more than 45 years and the details of the Sunday-night operation run by Homer McMahon secret for more than 33 years.

15

Alteration

(Part 3)

In her book, Alexandra Zapruder writes. "Late on Saturday (or possibly Sunday) night, Ben Hunter and Homer McMahon, two employees of the CIA's National Photographic Interpretation Center (NPIC), were called in to the lab." She goes on to state, "Nearly nothing was known about the NPIC handling of the Zapruder film until the midseventies, when first-generation assassination researcher Paul Hoch came across CIA Document 450 among other materials he had received in response to a Freedom of Information Act request. This record confirms that the NPIC analysis took place and establishes that two sets of four large briefing boards with enlargements of the film were created, though the document does not state when or by whom. Much later, NPIC photo analyst Dino Brugioni would state that he made two of these briefing boards, although it appears that his memory of the timing and other details was not accurate."

Alexandra is thoroughly confused. The problem isn't that Brugioni's memory of the timing and other details was inaccurate. The problem is that she obviously does not understand that there were two separate events that took place at NPIC on the weekend of the assassination, one beginning on Saturday night and one beginning on Sunday night, with different personnel participating in each event. Given her confusion on that critically important point, her understanding of the pertinent events becomes muddled and inaccurate.

Contrary to Alexandra's assertion, Brugioni never stated that he made any of the Sunday-night briefing boards. When Peter Janney and Douglas Horne showed Brugioni high-quality photos of the four-panel set of briefing boards that is part of the official record today — which is one of the three (not two, as Alexandra asserts) briefing-board sets that were made with the enlarged photos of individual Zapruder film frames made by the Sunday-night McMahon-Hunter team — Brugioni stated the opposite of what Alexandra ascribes to him. He did not make "two of these briefing boards," as she asserted in her book. Rather, Brugioni specifically denied that he made *any* of the panels in the briefing-board set that is now part of the official record (and that was made on Sunday night by the McMahon/Hunter team).

How could Brugioni be so sure? Because the way that he prepared the Saturday-night briefing boards was different from how the Sunday-night briefing boards were prepared. For example, the briefing boards he prepared consisted of two-panel sets, 20 x 22 inches in size, with a hinge in the middle that would enable the set to close in on itself. The Sunday-night briefing boards (one set of which is in the National Archives today) consisted of four separate panels that were each much wider than Brugioni's two panels. The four Sunday-night briefing-board panels were *not* connected to each other in any way. That's not all. Brugioni also stated that the labeling of the enlarged photographs on the Sunday briefing boards was entirely different from the labeling that he used for his Saturday-night briefing boards.

In her book, Alexandra criticized Horne for relying on "impressions and memories of several former CIA agents who were interviewed nearly thirty years after the fact." What she fails to criticize is why it took so long for this story to come out. She doesn't seem bothered one whit by the fact that the CIA kept its complete relationship to the Zapruder film secret from the American people for more than 45 years (until Dino Brugioni revealed the rest of the story in 2009) — and officially continues to do so to this day. At the risk of belaboring the obvious, if the CIA had not kept its complete role with the Zapruder film secret for some 45 years, then we would have heard the accounts of Brugioni, McMahon, and Hunter a long time ago. Not surprisingly, there is no call by Alexandra for the CIA to release all of its remaining records relating to the Zapruder film, both at NPIC in Washington and at "Hawkeyeworks" in Rochester. If it was all legitimate, surely the CIA kept reports and records relating to the activities at "Hawkeyeworks" and could easily release them to the public.

It seems that for Alexandra, there is nothing unusual about the CIA's secret role in the Zapruder film. In fact, it is obvious that in her mind the CIA was simply working together with the Secret Service to investigate the Kennedy assassination.

Not surprisingly, Alexandra also doesn't seem bothered by the fact that the CIA lacked any legal authority to investigate criminal acts within the United States. Remember that the Kennedy assassination was a murder case under Texas state law. Since when does the CIA have jurisdiction to investigate a state murder case? Since when does the CIA have the authority to engage in any domestic operations?

Moreover, if the CIA took possession of the Zapruder film on the weekend of the assassination simply to help investigate Kennedy's murder, where are the results of that investigation? They certainly weren't turned over to the Warren Commission, which was the official body whose ostensible purpose was to investigate the assassination. Why not? And they also weren't turned over to the U.S. House Select Committee on Assassinations in the mid-1970s, which was reinvestigating the Kennedy assassination. Why not? And they certainly were not turned over to the ARRB in the mid-1990s, when the law required the CIA to disclose its assassination-related records. Why not? In fact, they still haven't been disclosed to the American people to this day. Why not? That's the strangest "investigation" I have ever heard of. Just think: investigating a crime and then keeping the results of that investigation secret from everyone, including the people who have the legal authority to investigate the crime.

As I observed in chapter 4, Alexandra Zapruder obviously could not bring herself to condemn the CIA in her book for the dark, nefarious, and evil things it has done in the past in the name of "national security," including secretly hiring former members of the Nazi regime, conducting illegal drug experiments on unsuspecting people, engaging in state-sponsored kidnappings and assassinations of innocent people, initiating coups that destroyed democratic regimes in foreign countries, installing and supporting brutal foreign dictatorships, conducting secret surveillance on American citizens, torturing people, and intentionally destroying evidence of its own criminal conduct, like it did with MK-ULTRA and, more recently, its videotaped torture sessions.

Alexandra obviously cannot bring herself to acknowledge the possibility — much less the likelihood — that the CIA engaged in the same type of evil on the weekend of Kennedy's assassination, just as she cannot bring herself to acknowledge that the U.S. military establishment engaged in the same type of evil at the Bethesda morgue on the evening of the assassination. She cannot bring herself to acknowledge the possibility that the national-security establishment was the centrum of evil that enveloped her grandfather, destroyed his life, and ended up producing a family taboo against discussing his film.

Another omission by Alexandra, which we discussed in chapter 8, obviously gains added significance once we realize that the CIA played an important role with the film on the weekend of the assassination. You will recall that when she mentioned *LIFE* magazine publisher C. D. Jackson, Alexandra failed to disclose that he was a longtime fiercely loyal acolyte of the CIA. Why would Alexandra fail to mention that fact, especially given the discovery of the CIA's role with the film on Sunday night more than 33 years after the assassination and the discovery of its role on Saturday night more than 45 years after the assassination? Given the obvious compartmentalized operation conducted at NPIC the weekend immediately following the assassination, why would she consider Jackson's long-standing affiliation with the CIA so unimportant a fact as to not share it with her readers?

Alexandra goes to great lengths to criticize Jim Garrison's prosecution of Clay Shaw in New Orleans and goes on to criticize Oliver Stone for his movie *JFK,* which was based on Garrison's prosecution of Shaw. Yet, if it hadn't been for Garrison's prosecution, Oliver Stone would never have made his movie, which means that the JFK Records Act and the ARRB would never have come into existence. Without the ARRB, we would never have learned about the creation of the Sunday-night briefing boards, which revealed that the Zapruder film was brought from "Hawkeyeworks" in Rochester to NPIC in Washington. We also would never have learned about the two big lies that Secret Service agent "Bill Smith" told Homer McMahon about the film — that the film had been donated by a citizen from Dallas and that the camera-original film had been developed at "Hawkeyeworks."

It's now time to address the matter of Secret Service agent "Bill Smith," who brought the 16mm-wide, unslit film to NPIC on Sunday night, and, for that matter, the two Secret Service agents who brought the original 8mm Zapruder film to NPIC on Saturday night. In her book, Alexandra expresses skepticism about "Bill Smith," noting, correctly, that "there is no record" of him.

Not surprisingly, she draws the wrong inference from this. She apparently concludes that the "Bill Smith" story is reason for doubting Homer McMahon's veracity. She misses an obvious point: that the briefing-board set that is in the National Archives today contains the photographs that McMahon and Hunter took and enlarged, which means that *someone* brought them the film on Sunday night.

Who was that someone? What Alexandra refuses to see is the obvious — that "Bill Smith" wasn't a Secret Service agent at all, and neither were the two couriers who identified themselves as Secret Service agents on Saturday night to Dino Brugioni. It is a virtual certainty that all three couriers were CIA agents posing as Secret Service agents. After all, it is common knowledge that it was — and still is — regular procedure in the world of covert operations for CIA personnel to operate "under cover" and use false names and false identification.

How can we be so sure that all three couriers were CIA agents posing as Secret Service agents? The CIA's "Hawkeyeworks" operation at Kodak's headquarters in Rochester was a top-secret operation. Such being the case, there is no reasonable possibility that the CIA would disclose that operation to the Secret Service. That's why it's a virtual certainty that it was CIA agents posing as Secret Service agents who retrieved the Zapruder film in Chicago on Saturday afternoon, transported it to NPIC on Saturday night, took it early on Sunday morning to "Hawkeyeworks" in Rochester, and then brought the new 16mm-wide, unslit film masquerading as an "original" from "Hawkeyeworks" back to NPIC on Sunday night.

After all, let's not forget that the arrangements to acquire the Zapruder film would have been made with CIA acolyte C. D. Jackson. Therefore, it would only have made sense that it would be the CIA handling this part of the operation.

Why was Alexandra unable to draw this logical inference about Secret Service agent "Bill Smith?" For the same reason that she was psychologically unable to disclose Jackson's close relationship with the CIA to the readers of her book. I submit that at this point — the point at which she was so close to the centrum of evil that took the life of a U.S. president — her subconscious was practically screaming at her with a dire warning: "Danger! Danger! Do not go down this road. It leads to the dark secret behind the destruction of your grandfather and behind the taboo that has held your family in its grip for five decades."

In fact, my hunch is that this is when she experienced the greatest amount of internal stress, albeit at a subconscious level, given that she was getting exceedingly close to the family's dark secret and, more important, to the evil force that not only snuffed out the life of a U.S. president but also, in the process, ended up destroying the happy and joyous life that her grandfather Abe had been living prior to his encounter with evil. In fact, Alexandra implicitly alluded to this deep subconscious internal discomfort when she wrote in her book that "tangling" with the "alterationists" during her research had caused her to experience "despair," "resignation," and "the desire to take a nap."

There is something else interesting to note — how Alexandra labels Dino Brugioni in her book. She labels him simply as "photo analyst Dino Brugioni." That's it. Just a "photo analyst." This becomes important because Brugioni told Janney and Horne that he was certain that he was handling the original film, not a copy of the film, during that Saturday-night operation. Alexandra, on the other hand, questions his judgment and claims that he must have been mistaken and was instead dealing with the copy of the film that the Secret Service shipped to Washington late Friday night and that arrived in Washington before dawn on Saturday.

You will recall that in chapter 13, I pointed out that Brugioni had served as NPIC's Chief Information Officer for 25 years and that Wikipedia describes him as "the world's foremost imagery intelligence analyst." It's time to fill in more biographical details about Dino Brugioni — details that, for whatever reason, Alexandra chose not to share with readers of her book when she referred to him as simply "photo analyst Dino Brugioni." Here is what Wikipedia states about Dino Brugioni:

"Dino Antonio Brugioni (December 16, 1921— September 25, 2015) was a former senior official at the CIA's National Photographic Interpretation Center (NPIC). He was an imagery analyst and also served as NPIC's Chief of Information. During his 35-year career, Brugioni helped establish imagery intelligence (IMINT) as a national asset to solve intelligence problems. Even after retirement, Brugioni was considered to be the world's foremost imagery intelligence analyst. After retirement, he has been active in encouraging the use of declassified photographic intelligence for historical research. His book, *Eyeball to Eyeball,* is an extensive unclassified history of US imagery intelligence.... Brugioni's book, although a general history, deals extensively with the role of imagery intelligence in the Cuban Missile Crisis.

"Brugioni was one of the first historians to present photographic evidence of Auschwitz.

"Brugioni is an authority on contrived or altered photography, described in his book *Photo Fakery*.... Brugioni has written more than 90 articles, mainly on the application of overhead imagery to intelligence and other fields. He has helped with and appeared in over 75 news and historical television programs.

"Brugioni has received numerous citations and commendations, including the CIA Intelligence Medal of Merit, the CIA Intelligence Medal and the prestigious U.S. Government Pioneer in Space Medal for his role in the development of satellite reconnaissance. He twice received the Sherman Kent Award, the CIA top award for outstanding contributions to intelligence. However, he remains most proud of the commendation he received from President John Kennedy for contributions during the Cuban Missile Crisis. On April 13, 2005, he was inducted into the National Geospatial-Intelligence Agency Hall of Fame."

Based on his decades-long professional experience as an imagery intelligence analyst, Brugioni was certain that the film he was handling on that Saturday night was a camera-original film owing to the extremely sharp details in the film. He told Horne and Janney that he gave the film the "white glove" treatment during the Saturday-night operation. He also noted that the two Secret Service agents who brought him the film were extremely nervous during the time that Brugioni and his team were handling the film, something that would not likely be the case if Brugioni was dealing with a copy rather than an original.

In fact, let's return briefly to Dallas. Recall that the local Kodak facility had developed Zapruder's film and that he then took it to Jamieson Film Company to have copies made. Upon his return to Kodak, Zapruder and the Kodak personnel watched both the original and the copies of the film. Consider what Kodak's plant manager Phil Chamberlain later said about the difference between the original and the copies: "Those of us in the lab realized that the duplicate was soft, or fuzzy, compared to the original, but really of good quality, considering the circumstances."

The question naturally arises: If local Kodak representatives in Dallas could notice that first-generation copies were "soft or fuzzy" compared to the original, wouldn't it be safe to assume that the world's foremost imagery intelligence analyst could tell whether he was dealing with the original Zapruder film rather than a copy?

There is another factor to consider in Alexandra's speculation. If Brugioni was handling the copy of the film that was sent to the Secret Service in Washington on Friday night by Dallas Secret Service agent Max Phillips that arrived before dawn on Saturday morning, it would be safe to presume that the Secret Service would have delivered it to him that morning or, at the latest, early afternoon, *not* at 10 p.m. The 10 p.m. delivery time, of course, is consistent with the film leaving Dallas at 3 p.m., arriving in Chicago, and then being diverted to Washington. It's also probably worth mentioning that the two Secret Service agents who brought the film to Brugioni at NPIC had not watched it. It's also probably worth asking why the CIA would want to use a copy of the film for its briefing boards when they could easily acquire the original through the use of their devoted acolyte, C. D. Jackson.

As I previously indicated, Alexandra implied that Brugioni's recollections about that Saturday-night operation cannot be trusted because of the long passage of time. You will recall my saying in chapter 3 that in a courtroom setting, the law prefers to have witnesses testifying in court so that the jury can better assess their credibility. That's what I would like you to do with respect to Brugioni. I would invite you to go to the video entitled "The Zapruder Film Mystery" to watch a presentation on the Zapruder film by Douglas Horne that includes excerpts from the interviews that Peter Janney and Doug Horne conducted with Dino Brugioni: https://www.youtube.com/watch?v=J_QIuu6hsAc. This film is an 85-minute-long short subject that is an extra feature on filmmaker Shane O'Sullivan's main documentary program titled *Killing Oswald.*

I want you to watch Brugioni give his account of that Saturday-night operation. I have absolutely no doubt that after watching him, you will give his credibility the highest possible rating. In fact, when it comes to professionalism, competence, and commitment to truth, I would put Dino Brugioni in the same category as Dr. Robert McClelland and First Class Petty Officer Saundra Spencer.

At this point, I also invite you to read the article that I previously mentioned — Douglas Horne's article, "The Two NPIC Zapruder Film Events: Signposts Pointing to the Film's Alteration," which is posted online at https://www.lewrockwell.com/2012/05/douglas-p-horne/the-two-npic-zapruder-film-events-signposts-pointing-to-the-filmsalteration. It provides a detailed and complete account of what took place that weekend. I also invite you to read chapter 14 of volume IV of Horne's book *Inside the Assassination Records Review Board,* which gives the most complete and detailed account of the CIA's secret role in altering and studying the Zapruder film on the weekend of the assassination.

By now, you might be wondering what happened to the briefing boards that Dino Brugioni prepared on Saturday night — the ones that contained the photo enlargements from the original, unaltered Zapruder film. In chapter 4, we talked about how the CIA turned over the six photocopied pages of NPIC notes discovered with the four Sunday briefing-board panels to the Rockefeller Commission. We will now fill out more of that part of the story.

President Gerald Ford appointed the Rockefeller Commission in 1975 to investigate illegal domestic activities by the CIA, such as drug experimentation on unsuspecting Americans, illegal mail opening, and surveillance of domestic political groups. During that investigation, the CIA discovered the four Sunday-night briefing-board panels and showed them to the senior counsel for the Rockefeller Commission, Robert Olsen — but kept the panels rather than relinquish them to the commission. Later, in 1993, the CIA turned over the four briefing-board panels and the *original* NPIC notes to the National Archives, as required by the JFK Records Act. Those briefing boards are still part of the official JFK Records Collection in the National Archives today.

During the Rockefeller Commission hearings, Brugioni advised the then-director of NPIC, John J. Hicks, that he still possessed a set of the two-panel briefing boards that he and his team had prepared on Saturday night (and extending into the wee hours of Sunday morning). Even more significantly, Brugioni *showed* Hicks the Saturday-night briefing boards. Brugioni later stated in his interviews with Janney and Horne that Hicks's response was stunning and profane: "*Goddammit, what the hell are you doing with that? Get the goddamn thing out of here!*" According to Horne's article on LewRockwell.com, "A shaken Dino Brugioni, who is still mystified today about the anger expressed by Hicks, wrapped up the two-panel briefing board, sent it over to the office of CIA Director William Colby, and never saw it again."

In fact, no member of the public would ever see Brugioni's briefing boards. There is only one possible reason for that. It's the same reason that Hicks had such an overheated reaction to seeing Brugioni's briefing boards. The reason is that Brugioni's Saturday-night briefing boards contained enlarged photographs from individual frames of the original, unaltered Zapruder film. Is it any wonder that Brugioni's briefing boards were "disappeared" and never seen again?

After all, at the risk of belaboring the obvious, if Brugioni's Saturday-night briefing boards contained enlarged photographs from the same film that the Sunday-night briefing boards contained, there would have been no reason for Hicks to react so heatedly upon seeing Brugioni's briefing boards. Moreover, the CIA would have shown *both* the surviving Brugioni Saturday-night briefing-board set *and* the surviving McMahon-Hunter Sunday-night briefing-board set to the Rockefeller Commission. But the CIA did not do that!

The fact that the CIA did not show the Brugioni Saturday-night briefing board set to the Rockefeller Commission requires us to return to the story of NPIC Director John J. Hicks, the man who, as described above, had the extremely angry and profane outburst when Brugioni delivered to him during the Rockefeller Commission hearings one of the two-panel briefing-board sets that Brugioni had prepared on the Saturday night (and the wee hours of Sunday morning) after the assassination.

Let's examine the reason for Hicks's overheated outburst and the role that he played in this series of events, including what he knew, what he withheld from Brugioni, and what he withheld from the Rockefeller Commission. As we will see, Hicks clearly had full knowledge of the compartmentalized operation at NPIC that weekend as well as full knowledge of the CIA's alteration of the Zapruder film.

As Brugioni made clear to both Horne and Janney during their interviews of him, when the CIA was forced to report its domestic activities to the Rockefeller Commission in 1975, all CIA employees were encouraged to report such activities to their superiors. Accordingly, as recounted above, in May of 1975 Brugioni reported to Hicks, the new director at the NPIC, the circumstances surrounding his creation of two briefing-board sets that Saturday night. Brugioni told Hicks that Arthur Lundahl, the then-director of NPIC, had ordered him to NPIC that night (Saturday, November 23), where two Secret Service agents delivered the 8mm-wide original Zapruder film to him. He told Hicks that he and his team had made enlarged photos of selected frames from the film and had created two duplicate sets of briefing boards (with two panels each, displaying 12–15 photos per briefing-board set). He also recounted to Hicks that the two Secret Service agents were interested in the timing between shots, but that Brugioni's team advised them this was not possible to do accurately because the camera was spring wound and the timing between shots would be continuously changing as the spring mechanism unwound while operating the camera.

Most important, Brugioni reported to Hicks that one of the two-panel briefing-board sets that he created still existed and, in fact, he proceeded to show it to him. That was when Hicks went ballistic, exclaiming *"Get the goddamn thing out of here!"*

Stepping back a moment, it is beyond any reasonable doubt that Arthur Lundahl, the NPIC director on the weekend of the assassination, was fully aware of the compartmentalized operations on Saturday night and Sunday night. That's because it was Lundahl who had directed both teams to NPIC on Saturday night and Sunday night and emphasized the highly classified nature of the operations to each team. In other words, it was Lundahl who ensured that the Saturday-night team would never know about the Sunday-night team and that the Sunday-night team would never know about the Saturday-night team.

But what about Hicks? What did he know at the time of the Rockefeller Commission hearings in 1975? Hicks was an intelligence officer with the CIA but he was not with NPIC in 1963. However, he later went to work at NPIC and served as Lundahl's executive director for four years before Lundahl retired in 1973.

Based on Hicks's highly charged outburst and obvious displeasure when Brugioni dutifully came forward with one of his Saturday-night briefing-board sets (*"Get the goddamn thing out of here!"*), it is a virtual certainty that Hicks knew that there was a difference between the Sunday-night briefing-board set (which he already possessed) and the Saturday-night briefing-board set that Brugioni was showing him. Undoubtedly, Lundahl, prior to his retirement, had filled Hicks in on the Zapruder film shenanigans that had taken place on the November 23–25 weekend. Otherwise, why would Hicks have had such an overheated reaction to Brugioni's set of briefing boards?

Later that month, on May 13, Hicks reported to his CIA superior via a handwritten memo the discovery of four briefing-board panels (which formed one briefing-board set) as well as six pages of associated notes. (The associated notes covered two separate subjects: three of the six pages were about the creation of prints for the four panels and the other three pages were a complex shot-and-timing analysis of the motion-picture film itself, specifically three different interpretations of what happened in the limousine, based on only three shots having been fired.) The four briefing-board panels discovered and reported by Hicks, of course, were created during the Homer McMahon / Ben Hunter event at NPIC that began Sunday night.

In other words, Hicks (who was now the new NPIC director) knew about both sets of briefing boards found at NPIC — Brugioni's Saturday-night briefing boards and the McMahon / Hunter Sunday-night briefing boards — because he himself had seen both sets! And this was the same month Hicks was required to report to the Rockefeller Commission.

Equally important, we also know that Hicks was approached by Brugioni before he reported to his superior (the CIA's deputy director for science and technology) — the discovery of the Sunday-night briefing-board panels and the associated notes on May 13. We know that because an unsigned but typewritten report based largely upon what Brugioni had told Hicks was sent to Senior Counsel Robert Olsen of the Rockefeller Commission on May 7. That document describes the creation of two sets of briefing boards (not the three sets created from Homer McMahon's three sets of prints), accurately states that the customer represented himself to be the Secret Service, and describes accurately the inability of NPIC personnel to provide accurate timing between shots because Zapruder's camera was spring-wound. Those were facts that had been provided to Hicks by Brugioni, not by McMahon and Hunter, which confirms that Hicks knew about the Brugioni Saturday-night event prior to May 7.

This unsigned typewritten summary of briefing-board activity was a tricky document, and intentionally so. Consider this: It did not report the date of the briefing-board activity (except to say it was "late in 1963") or the names of the personnel who made them. Neither Brugioni nor McMahon was mentioned in this document. It falsely reported that a copy of the film was delivered to CIA Director McCone.

And worst of all, the document falsely stated that the two sets of briefing boards created were four panels each! Hicks knew better, because Brugioni had shown him his two-panel briefing board set made from the original film, in which the two panels were connected by a hinge in the middle. The only logical explanation here is that Hicks (the obvious author of the report) was intentionally conflating the two briefing-board events to make them seem like only one event. His objective was obviously to confuse and to avoid having to tell the whole story of what had happened on the weekend of the assassination. This document, which the CIA provided to Douglas Horne in 2011 in response to a Freedom of Information Act (FOIA) request, is a classic example of the way that the CIA lies in an official capacity to hide the truth from others. A facsimile of this document (the typewritten, unsigned statement about briefing-board activity forwarded to the Rockefeller Commission from the CIA on May 7, 1975) is provided for your review in appendix B.

What did NPIC Director John J. Hicks do and say during his May 14, 1975, oral briefing to Senior Counsel Olsen of the Rockefeller Commission? Hicks gave Olsen the six photocopied pages of NPIC notes via a typewritten letter of transmittal. That letter also forwarded Hicks' handwritten memo of May 13, describing his discovery of the four briefing-board panels along with the NPIC notes. Therefore, we can be sure that Hicks showed the four panels of the Sunday-night set to Olsen (but did not give them to him). He must have showed them to him because they are mentioned in both the NPIC notes as well as in Hicks' internal, handwritten memo of May 13. We know that Hicks did not give Olsen the four Sunday-night panels because they were retained by the CIA and then were turned over to the National Archives in 1993 in accordance with the JFK Records Act.

And consider this: NPIC Director Hicks did not invite Brugioni to the meeting with Olsen nor did he show Olsen the 2-panel briefing-board set that Brugioni had shown to him. (No doubt Brugioni had gotten rid of it by this time, as ordered by Hicks, by sending it to CIA Director William Colby's office.) And even more damning, Hicks never told Brugioni about the discovery of the four briefing-board panels made beginning Sunday night, November 24, using prints created by Homer McMahon and Ben Hunter. The CIA, therefore — specifically NPIC Director John J. Hicks — was withholding crucial information from both Dino Brugioni (one of its own), and from the Rockefeller Commission. Of course, we know that lying is a way of life for the CIA. John Hicks was clearly hiding the fact that there was a compartmentalized operation at NPIC the weekend of the assassination from both Dino Brugioni and Rockefeller Commission Senior Counsel Robert Olsen — and he got away with it.

Let's now return to the Paul Mandel article that we discussed in chapter 1. You will recall that was the article in which *LIFE* staff writer Mandel lied when he stated that the Zapruder film, which by that time was owned and possessed by *LIFE* magazine, showed President

Kennedy turning around and facing the Texas School Book Depository when he was shot in the throat.

Mandel's article also contains some of the exact language present in the shot-and-timing analysis of the Kennedy assassination in the NPIC notes, specifically the following phraseology: "74 frames later," and "48 frames after that," and "4.1 seconds," and "2.7 seconds." These quotes are taken verbatim from the column in the NPIC shot-and-timing analysis labeled "*LIFE* magazine." That would suggest, of course, the likelihood that the CIA was communicating information to C. D. Jackson, the publisher, who, in turn, was communicating the information to Mandel or, alternatively, that a CIA official was communicating with Mandel directly, with Jackson's approval and consent.

Why is Alexandra Zapruder so intent on blocking out of her mind the Brugioni Saturday-night event or conflating the Saturday-night event and the Sunday-night event into one event? I have no doubt that it is her subconscious once again kicking into full gear, practically screaming at her: "Danger! Danger! Do not proceed down this road. Avoid it at all costs because it will lead you to the dark evil force that enveloped and destroyed your grandfather."

After all, why would deep-state officials have two separate teams doing photo enlargements of the same film? If someone simply wanted more photos from the film enlarged, why not bring Brugioni's team back on Sunday night to make those additional enlargements? If it's the same film on both Saturday night and Sunday night, why keep Brugioni and his team in the dark about the Sunday-night event, and why keep the Sunday-night McMahon / Hunter team in the dark about the Brugioni event on Saturday night?

In her book, Alexandra makes the following assertion: "The original film seems to have remained unslit, while the three duplicates were slit into 8mm strips that were spliced together."

That would appear to be a rather nonchalant sentence, but it actually has profound implications.

What Alexandra is referring to is what occurred at the Kodak facility in Dallas, where Abraham Zapruder took his film for developing. Recall from chapter 13 that the normal procedure after developing what starts out as a 25-foot long, 16mm-wide, "double 8" film, like the one that Zapruder had, was to slit it down the middle and then splice together the two strips, side A and side B, so that the customer ends up with one 50-foot-long film that is only 8mm wide.

You will recall, however, that Zapruder wanted to make copies of his film, which Kodak lacked the equipment to do. That's why they sent him to the Jamieson Film Company in Dallas. Jamieson's equipment could make copies of 16mm film but not 8mm film. Therefore, Kodak left Zapruder's film in its original 16mm format rather than slitting it down the middle after it was developed. Moreover, while Jamieson could make copies of the 16mm film, they would be *undeveloped* copies. To get the copies developed, Zapruder would have to take them back to Kodak.

Thus, Jamieson made three undeveloped copies of the film on his contact printer, pursuant to Zapruder's instructions. Zapruder then returned to Kodak, where they developed his three copy films. Kodak then proceeded to slit all four 16mm films — the original and the three copies — down the middle, converting all four films into 8mm films rather than 16mm films.

Except that Alexandra asserts, "The original film *seems* to have remained unslit."

Why does she make that assertion? Again, subconsciously, she has to recognize the extreme importance of the major slip-up that occurred on Sunday night. Recall that the person who identified himself as Secret Service agent "Bill Smith" brought what he represented was a 16mm-wide, unslit original of the Zapruder film. If the Kodak people in Dallas actually did slit the original film down the middle before Zapruder departed that evening, then that would confirm that the 16mm film on Sunday night had to be a copy masquerading as a camera-original film — because, again, a 16mm film that has been slit down the middle, thereby converting it into an 8mm film, cannot be reconstituted into a 16mm film (except by state-of-the-art optical processes, in sophisticated equipment at a high-tech photo lab).

Therefore, by asserting that "the original film *seems* to have remained unslit," Alexandra, no doubt operating on a subconscious level, is suggesting that there was nothing unusual about that 16mm "double 8" film that was brought into NPIC on Sunday night. The implication is that it was the same original 16mm film that her grandfather took of the assassination. In other words, no film alteration at all.

But there is one big problem with Alexandra's unfounded assertion: The people at the Kodak facility in Dallas affirmed that they slit both the original and all three copies of the film.

Phil Chamberlain was the Kodak production supervisor in Dallas. He was in charge of the Zapruder film operation on Friday afternoon of the assassination. In a statement he gave to Roland Zavada, the retired Kodak film chemist who the ARRB commissioned to do an authenticity study on the Zapruder film from 1996 to 1998, Chamberlain stated that they had in fact slit both the original and the copies of the film. A report by Zavada dated July 28, 1997, details minutes of a meeting between Zavada and Dallas Kodak representatives Dick Blair and Phil Chamberlain, in which Zavada stated: "After the dupes [from the Jamieson Film Company] were found satisfactory, the original film was slit to 8mm. Mr. Zapruder, possibly his lawyer, Phil and several laboratory personnel viewed the 8mm film on an 8mm projector at least twice." This conclusion was repeated in Zavada's final report to the ARRB in September of 1998.

Moreover, in June 1997, Chamberlain sent Zavada a copy of a manuscript he had written back in the late 1970s, which stated in part: "Less than an hour later, he [Zapruder] was back [from Jamieson Film Company] with the two [sic] rolls of film.... This time, we slit and spliced the films and put them on regular 8mm projector spools, and once again trooped to the conference room — this time to see the film at normal size and speed, and several times, if we wished!"

As we will see in chapter 16, Alexandra Zapruder attacked Douglas Horne for supposedly impugning the integrity of her grandfather. Thus, notice the irony when she implicitly impugns the integrity of the Kodak personnel who developed her grandfathers's film by insinuating that they didn't really slit the original film, despite the fact that that is precisely what they did.

Let's reflect on this point a bit longer. Recall Alexandra's speculation that Secret Service agent Forrest Sorrels might have been lying when he quoted Abraham as saying that he intended to get as much money as he could for his film, despite the fact that the evidence overwhelmingly establishes that that is exactly what Abraham Zapruder did. I know we have already gone over this point, but please permit me to recap the salient facts before I ask a very important question.

From the moment he filmed the assassination, Zapruder knew he had a valuable asset and was determined to get as much money as he could for it. His grief over having witnessed the president's death certainly did not interfere with his immediately heading out to get his film developed and copied. It also didn't interfere with his taking the time to contact his lawyer, who advised him to get affidavits so that he could prove to any prospective buyers that there were no unauthorized copies of the film floating around and that the film had not been cut or edited at the processing plant. He met with *LIFE* magazine's Dick Stolley the morning after the assassination and negotiated a deal for $50,000, which in today's value is $454,000. On the Monday following the assassination, he was in his lawyer's office showing the film to various media representatives in the hope of getting top dollar for the motion-picture rights to the film.

Thus, here is the very important question: Given that Zapruder was intent on getting as much money as he could for his film, is it logical that he would want to show prospective buyers a copy of his film rather than the original, especially given that Dick Chamberlain, the Kodak plant supervisor in Dallas, had noted that the copy of the film was "soft" or "fuzzy" compared to the original? Keep in mind that Zapruder could not show people a 16mm film in his 8mm home movie projector. To show prospective buyers the original film, it would necessarily have had to be slit down the middle, thereby converting it to the 8mm format. I submit that as determined as he was to get top dollar for his film, there is no reasonable possibility that Zapruder would have wanted to show prospective buyers a "soft" and "fuzzy" copy rather than a clear and sharp original. That means that the 16mm-wide "double 8" film that Secret Service agent "Bill Smith" brought from "Hawkeyeworks" to NPIC on Sunday night had to be a copy, an alteration of the true original film that was then optically edited to remove certain scenes and add special visual effects to other scenes *masquerading as the unslit, 16mm-wide camera-original film.*

16

Alteration

(Part 4)

In her book, Alexandra Zapruder placed a lot of emphasis on an authenticity report prepared by Kodak's Roland Zavada in which he concluded that the Zapruder film is "consistent" with authenticity. What she doesn't mention, however, is that the report isn't worth the paper it's written on, given what had to be one of the gravest ethical violations that could ever be committed by Zavada's company, Eastman Kodak.

In 1996, owing to the controversy surrounding the Zapruder film, the ARRB decided to commission a limited authenticity study of the film. The study was "limited" because it would examine and analyze physical aspects of the film but not the content of it. Given Kodak's reputation in the film industry, the ARRB approached the company about doing such a study.

Kodak agreed to do the study and, no doubt to the ARRB's pleasant surprise, offered to do it for free. Kodak called Zavada, a retired film chemist who formerly worked for the company, out of retirement to conduct the study. However, in offering to do the study, Kodak failed to inform the ARRB of an important fact: The CIA had a highly classified, top-secret codeword film facility named "Hawkeyeworks" within Kodak's research and development laboratory, known as the "Hawkeye Plant," at its headquarters in Rochester, New York.

In the field of ethics, that's what is called a "conflict of interest." In this case, it's about the gravest conflict of interest that could ever occur. After all, Kodak was undoubtedly aware of the fact that Oliver Stone's 1991 movie *JFK* posited that the U.S. national-security establishment, including the CIA, had orchestrated and carried out Kennedy's assassination and that the movie had led directly to the JFK Records Act and the ARRB, the agency to which Kodak was now offering its free services.

Suppose, for example, that the CIA did, in fact, use its top-secret "Hawkeyeworks" facility to alter the Zapruder film. That would clearly mean CIA complicity in the Kennedy assassination, given that there is obviously no innocent explanation for a fraudulent film any more than there is an innocent explanation for a fraudulent autopsy. Of course, we don't know whether Kodak was part of the alteration operation at "Hawkeyeworks," and there certainly is no evidence of such. Nonetheless, imagine the difficulty that Kodak would have, from an ethical standpoint, in finding that the Zapruder film had been altered at the "Hawkeyeworks" facility. Kodak would indirectly be finding that the CIA participated in the assassination of President Kennedy and that it covered up the assassination by using a facility that was secretly located within Kodak's headquarters.

That's why there are rules against conflicts of interest in ethics. By the time the ARRB learned about that secret relationship between Kodak and the CIA, in 1997, Zavada was already deep into his authenticity study. At that point, the ARRB should have simply terminated the project and ceased doing business with Kodak. But given that Zavada had already done so much work on the project and that Kodak was doing it for free, the ARRB's senior management effectively waived the conflict of interest and let the project proceed, which it should not have done. Under ethical principles, there are some conflicts of interest that are so grave that they simply cannot be waived, and this clearly was one of them.

Just think about what was being asked of Zavada. What if he concluded that the CIA had altered the Zapruder film at its "Hawkeye-works" facility? Could that not have adversely affected his former company, even if only indirectly? How could anyone reasonably be expected to be totally objective in that type of situation? Again, that's why there are prohibitions against this sort of thing in the field of ethics.

What does Alexandra say about this grave ethical violation? Nothing. She doesn't mention it, much less condemn or even mildly criticize it.

Equally significant, she doesn't express any concern whatsoever about what seems to have been a very close relationship between a major private-sector company — Kodak — and a government entity that has secretly hired Nazis, performed drug experiments on unsuspecting Americans, spied on political groups within the United States, assassinated people and conspired to assassinate people, initiated regime-change operations against foreign officials, and engaged in other evil and nefarious actions. Recall from chapter 14 what CIA and NPIC official Homer McMahon said about the close working relationship between the CIA and Kodak — that the CIA was "in bed with the Yellow God," referring to Kodak. Explaining what he meant by that, McMahon stated, "We had their top scientists and photochemists and optical people working in the 'world beyond;' we had their best people — I shouldn't even talk about it, I'm sorry. And there was a definite link, on the national level, where we had 'the best there was' working with us."

Recall Operation Mockingbird, the secret CIA operation to acquire assets within the mainstream press whose mission was to expound the CIA's propaganda to the American people and the people of the world. The mindsets of the journalists who agreed to become CIA assets were the same as that of Kodak and *LIFE* magazine publisher C. D. Jackson. They were of the belief that they were doing their patriotic part to win the Cold War against "godless communism" and the supposed international communist conspiracy to take over the world.

A secret close working relationship between a journalist and the CIA is no different, in principle, from a close working relationship between a private-sector company and the CIA. They are equally morally reprehensible.

I can't help but wonder what the reaction was among Kodak executives when President Kennedy delivered his Peace Speech at American University in June 1963 in which he effectively declared an end to the Cold War racket and announced that America would henceforth live in peace and harmony with the Soviet Union and the communist world. I can't help but wonder whether those Kodak representatives considered Kennedy to be as much a threat to "national security" as their CIA ally did.

Alexandra points to McMahon's candid admission during his ARRB interview in 1997 that he had suffered from drug abuse and alcoholism to suggest that he couldn't be trusted. But the fact is that both McMahon and Ben Hunter were very clear about what they remembered and did not remember about that Sunday-night event. None of McMahon's comments about the film activity at NPIC on November 24 and 25, 1963, exhibited any evidence of senility, dementia, or an untrustworthy memory.

In fact, I would like you to read the entire transcript of the ARRB's interview of Homer McMahon. (The interview was not videotaped.) The transcript is found at the end of this book in appendix C. I have no doubts that you will find Homer McMahon to be an honest and trustworthy individual whose statements are worthy of belief. I have no doubts that you will find him as credible a witness as Dino Brugioni, especially as he details what he remembers and doesn't remember about the Sunday-night event at NPIC. I also believe that you will find McMahon to be a sincere and genuine individual, which is best reflected by his open acknowledgment of having experienced a drug-abuse and alcohol-related problem.

At this point, it's worth reminding ourselves that under the JFK Records Act, the CIA was required to disclose all of its assassination-related records to the ARRB. There is no question that the records at "Hawkeyeworks" relating to the Zapruder film would be considered assassination-related. At the risk of belaboring the obvious, the CIA never delivered such records to the ARRB.

In 2009, long after he had left the ARRB, Doug Horne served a Freedom of Information Act (FOIA) request on the CIA seeking information about what it did with the Zapruder film at its "Hawkeye-works" facility. Keep in mind, after all, that there was absolutely no reason for the CIA to send the Zapruder film to Rochester. If all they wanted to do was watch the film and make photo enlargements and briefing boards from it, they could do that — and did do that — in Washington, at NPIC. The only reason for sending the film to Rochester would have been to alter it. As Dino Brugioni related, at the "Hawkeye Plant," they could "do anything."

What was the CIA's response to Horne's request? It responded, "The CIA Information Act ... exempts CIA operational files from the search, review, publication, and disclosure requirements of the FOIA." According to the CIA's website, "The CIA Information Act, 50 U.S.C. 431, exempts from the search, review, and disclosure provisions of the FOIA all operational records of the CIA maintained by its National Clandestine Service, its Directorate of Science and Technology, and its Office of Security. By the term operational records, we mean those records and files detailing the actual conduct of our intelligence activities."

That sure sounds to me like an implicit admission that the CIA was running some sort of top-secret domestic intelligence operation involving the Zapruder film at "Hawkeyeworks" and that it claims the authority to keep details of that operation secret from the American people. But why would the CIA be running a top-secret intelligence operation on the Zapruder film at "Hawkeyeworks" if the operation didn't involve altering the film? If the CIA was instead assisting with the investigation into Kennedy's murder, as Alexandra Zapruder seems to believe, why hide what the CIA was doing with the Zapruder film at "Hawkeyeworks?" Moreover, why keep the results of that investigation secret from the Warren Commission in 1964, the House Select Committee on Assassinations in the 1970s, and the Assassination Records Review Board in the 1990s? Indeed, why keep the results of that investigation secret from the American people today, some 58 years after the assassination?

What does Alexandra Zapruder say about the CIA's failure to comply with the JFK Records Act with respect to its "Hawkeyeworks" operation on the Zapruder film and about Horne's Freedom of Information Act request and the CIA's response to it? By now, you should know the answer: She doesn't mention them.

What the CIA did do when it belatedly responded to Horne's FOIA was to provide him with documents that had *already been released* — the NPIC briefing-board notes and related documents that the CIA had already forwarded to the Rockefeller Commission in May of 1975, which had already been released in the form of "CIA document 450" in response to a FOIA request by researcher Paul Hoch, circa 1978. Thus, the CIA was trying to *appear* responsive to Horne's request, when in reality, the agency was not responsive at all. The CIA did not address Horne's central questions about "Hawkeyeworks" activity with the Zapruder film.

Let's now examine the nasty and quite overblown attack that Alexandra Zapruder leveled against Doug Horne. It involved Abraham Zapruder's efforts to get his film developed immediately after the assassination. It was an extremely strange attack given both its hyperbolic tone and the fact that it related to a rather innocuous point. As a matter of fact, Alexandra's entire critique of Doug Horne's work on the Zapruder film comes across as particularly vituperative. Interestingly, this acerbic side of Alexandra Zapruder never seems to manifest itself in her in-person presentations about her grandfather's film — at least not in the ones that I saw online. In those presentations, she comes across as nothing less than nice, genial, genuine, good-natured, and sincere. Interestingly, she implicitly acknowledged this dichotomy in a presentation she made at the 2017 San Antonio Book Festival, where she laughingly said to the audience, "And then there is a larger alteration theory which I won't get into now because of the time but I went into at great length in the book, possibly not very nicely."

Given Alexandra's particularly caustic attack against Horne, I would like to say a few things about Doug Horne before we examine the attack she leveled against him. After I read Horne's five-volume book about the medical evidence and the ARRB (*Inside the Assassination Records Review Board*), we met each other and became friends. We have worked closely together during the past several years. One of our bestselling books at The Future of Freedom Foundation, where I serve as president, is *JFK's War with the National Security Establishment: Why Kennedy Was Assassinated,* which Horne authored.

Horne has also spoken at two conferences that FFF has sponsored, one entitled "The National Security State and JFK" and the other entitled "The National Security State and the Kennedy Assassination," which can be viewed in the multimedia section of FFF's website (fff.org). His Powerpoint presentation on the medical evidence at that conference, entitled "The JFK Medical Coverup," which is almost three hours long, is the best presentation on this subject I have ever seen. You can watch it here: https://www.fff.org/freedom-in-motion/video/the-jfk-medical-coverup.

In 2014, Horne did an absolutely excellent five-part video presentation on the assassination for FFF, which is also posted in the multimedia section of FFF's website. It is entitled "Altered History: Exposing Deceit and Deception in the JFK Assassination Medical Evidence."

In my entire life, I have never met a writer with a fiercer commitment to truth and accuracy than Douglas Horne. In fact, his commitment to truth and accuracy actually borders on the obsessive. For example, when we were working on his video presentation "Altered History," we initially figured that it would simply entail several hours of video, for which we were prepared to pay a professional videographer to record for us. Not so. After the presentation was completed, Horne insisted on carefully editing and revising it, which was significantly increasing our videographer costs, which we had not anticipated. But we came to understand that that was Doug Horne. He simply would not let us publish a presentation that in his mind was not perfect. When the expensive ordeal was finally over, however, we had an absolutely fantastic product to share with people. "Altered History" is FFF's most-watched video presentation ever.

Another example of Horne's perfectionism is this: In our recent online conference "The Kennedy Assassination and the National Security State," Horne had completed recording one of his presentations, which was almost three hours long, when he telephoned me to advise me that he was going to have to rerecord the entire presentation. When I asked him why, he explained to me that he had made a factual mistake within the presentation, which to me was rather minor, but not to him. That's Doug Horne. I finally convinced him to keep the presentation and issue a correction at the end of it.

At that same online conference, Horne and I were doing a Q&A session together, and he deemed it necessary to correct a factual error that I made during that session. That's Doug Horne.

As I was reading Alexandra's caustic and overwrought attack on Horne, therefore, I kept thinking that at least on a subconscious level, she has a deep-seated fear of Doug Horne. It's as if her subconscious was once again practically screaming at her with "Danger! Danger! If you go down the road this man has uncovered, you will be getting so close to the evil that destroyed your grandfather."

In my opinion, her subconscious would be absolutely right in raising those danger signals, because in my estimation, Doug Horne is the assassination researcher — more than any other — who has put the Kennedy assassination into a coherent and logical context. Or to put it another way, he has placed all of the available pieces to the Kennedy assassination puzzle in a way that they all fit, and in a way that reveals that what occurred on November 22, 1963, was a national-security state regime-change operation. His book *Inside the Assassination Records Review Board* was a watershed development with respect to the Kennedy assassination. For years, I have read and studied books and watched videos relating to the assassination. While many of them made excellent points and expanded my understanding of the assassination, most of them were nonetheless unsatisfying because they didn't incorporate all of the existing facts, especially the fraudulent autopsy that was conducted on Kennedy's body, into an overall, consistent, logical, and coherent thesis of the assassination. That's what Horne's book was able to do. He put it all together. As I stated in chapter 2, there is a good reason why I dedicated my book *The Kennedy Autopsy,* which essentially is an easy-to-read synopsis of Horne's five-volume book, to Doug Horne and why I have dedicated this book to him as well.

Let's now examine the nasty and overblown attack that Alexandra Zapruder leveled against Doug Horne on what was actually a very innocuous point. It involves Abraham Zapruder's efforts to get his film developed immediately after the assassination.

You will recall that after Zapruder returned to his office shortly after filming the assassination, he was visited by two Dallas policemen and then, shortly after that, by Secret Service agent Forrest Sorrels. Zapruder, Sorrels, and the two cops then drove to a local television station to see if it could develop Zapruder's film. The television station was unable to develop the film and directed Zapruder to the local Eastman Kodak facility. It was there that Zapruder had his film developed and, according to Alexandra, "apparently spoke with an attorney who advised him about having affidavits made to certify the safe handling and processing of the film and the duplicates." After getting his film developed, Zapruder headed to the Jamieson Film Company to have three (undeveloped) copies made of the film. He then returned to Kodak with the original and the three copies, where, after the three copies were developed and all four films (the original and all three copies) were slit, Zapruder, Erwin Schwartz, and the Kodak people viewed the films.

Zapruder secured affidavits from Kodak and Jamieson attesting to the procedure by which the original film was developed and copied and verifying that only three copies were made of the film. The notarial acknowledgments on the affidavits were dated November 22, the date of the assassination.

In his book *Inside the Assassination Records Review Board* and later in an interview, Horne speculated as to whether those affidavits were really executed on Friday rather than on the following Monday morning. He simply found it hard to believe that Zapruder had those affidavits in hand within a few hours of having filmed the assassination.

Horne was clearly not accusing anyone of dark, nefarious conduct. He was simply engaging in speculation on what was a rather innocuous point. After all, it would not have been unusual for a lawyer to have prepared and dated the affidavits on Friday and then directed the client to have them executed on Monday. It would also not have been unusual if the notary public failed to change the date on the affidavit when he or she notarized the documents.

But for Alexandra, Horne's speculation was obviously a horrific, grave offense. In her book, she went ballistic, even suggesting that

Horne was accusing her grandfather of being a liar. She wrote, "But, for reasons that are not entirely clear, he [Horne] says that Abe lied about having the affidavits signed by the lab technicians on that day.... In other words, I don't believe my grandfather was a liar."

It was a strange attack for three reasons.

First, it was an extremely overblown reaction to Horne's speculation. When I read her attack, my immediate reaction was: Wow! Why in the world would she go off on this tangent in such an angry manner, especially since she had to know that its prejudicial effect would be to discourage readers of her book from reading and seriously considering Horne's substantive arguments on the important issues regarding the Zapruder film itself?

Second, she never actually cited any statement in which Horne actually accused her grandfather of lying.

Third, and, equally important, she never cited any statement by her grandfather as to when he had the affidavits signed. His signature certainly does not appear on the affidavits. You would think that if Abraham had ever made such a statement, she most certainly would have quoted him. Thus, how can Alexandra say that Horne accused her grandfather of lying about when he got the affidavits signed if her grandfather never stated when he got the affidavits signed?

After reading Alexandra's attack on Horne, I decided to look up those affidavits that had caused her to go ballistic. On examining them, I concluded that she did in fact have the better of the argument and that Horne's surmising about the affidavits being signed on Monday was probably incorrect. I base that on the fact that the Kodak affidavit actually appears to be an existing, standard form that Kodak may have used when legally certifying the development of people's films. The Jamieson affidavit seems to track the language of the Kodak affidavit, and so it's possible that Jamieson had the same type of standardized form that Kodak had. It's also possible that Zapruder just had Jamieson copy the language of the Kodak form and incorporate it into the affidavit signed by Jamieson. In any event, the entire matter certainly did not warrant Alexandra's overheated response to Horne's innocuous speculation as to when the affidavits were actually executed.

As I pondered that attack on Horne, as well as her wondering whether Secret Service agent Forrest Sorrels might have been lying when he stated that Abraham had told him he was out to get as much money as he could for his film, I wondered whether these obvious overreactions were the result of a mindset ingrained in Alexandra and the other Zapruder grandchildren by their parents and their grandmother Lillian.

In her book, Alexandra wrote, "In addition to what I absorbed from our family culture and watching my parents, I remember a few very clear messages that were conveyed to me — to all of us, I think — about the Zapruder film. First and foremost, whatever the rest of the world thought, Papa Abe was remembered in our family for his true self, not for anything having to do with the film. I must have heard my mother say a hundred times, 'Your grandfather should have been famous for who he was, for being a good person and a funny, wonderful man, and not for the film.' Surely this feeling came naturally to my parents, but it was handed down as an imperative to us.... She was fiercely proud of him — as she was of everyone in her family — and she made sure to attend to his memory and legacy for the benefit of posterity.... How he was represented to the public remained a sensitive topic even after he died."

Alexandra also recounts an interview conducted with Lillian Zapruder in 1973 by Richard Stolley, the *LIFE* magazine representative with whom her husband had negotiated for the purchase and sale of the film: "Toward the end of the conversation, when she was thoroughly finished contradicting him on every last point, Stolley gently pointed out, 'You might be slightly prejudiced, Mrs. Zapruder.' And she finally agreed. 'Well, yes, I think I must be because ... he absolutely, honest to God, my husband was a man of integrity. I've never met anybody like him yet."

My hunch is that once Abraham passed away, Lillian, trying to suppress the dark secret that Abraham had lived a lie for the last seven years of his life, bent over backwards to make certain that everyone, especially her grandchildren, knew that her husband had been nothing less than a paragon of honesty, virtue, and integrity. Lillian Zapruder was not only determined to protect the dark secret that had consumed her husband but also to make absolutely certain that her grandchildren knew that their grandfather was a man of impeccable honesty, morality, ethics, integrity, and honor. If that mindset was ingrained in Alexandra from childhood, it would certainly explain her overblown reaction to anyone who even hinted at the notion that her grandfather was less than perfectly honest or perfectly good.

There is actually an ironic and also revealing twist to Alexandra's attack on Horne regarding those affidavits. The fact that Abraham was taking the time to secure the affidavits and the fact that he had apparently sought legal advice about them would indicate that he really was, in fact, trying to get top dollar for his film, which would indicate that Forrest Sorrels had told the truth after all when he stated that Abraham Zapruder had told him that that he hoped to get as much money as possible for his film.

17

Alteration

(Part 5)

Author's note: Douglas Horne, who served as chief analyst for military records for the Assassination Records Review Board in the 1990s, granted me permission to include the following two items in my book: (1) "Partial Transcript of the July 2011 HD Video Interview of Dino Brugioni" and (2) "Partial Transcript of Thom Whitehead HD Video Interview of Paul Rutan, Jr., and Garrett Smith in 2013." The text below is written by Horne, and the emphases added throughout both transcripts have been provided by him. In January 2022, he received the consent of both Thom Whitehead and Sydney Wilkinson for the partial transcript of Thom's 2013 interview of Paul Rutan, Jr., and Garrett Smith to be published in this book.

Partial transcript of the July 2011 HD video interview of Dino Brugioni conducted by Peter Janney and Douglas Horne

In this portion of the interview, Dino Brugioni was examining individual Zapruder film frames on a large, 17.5-inch high-definition screen on a high-quality laptop computer. This extensive film interview was recorded by professional videographers in HD video. Significant portions of this interview of Dino Brugioni have previously appeared in public already in Shane O'Sullivan's film *The Zapruder*

Film Mystery. However, the portions of the interview represented by this transcript *have never before been released to the public*.

The frames examined by Brugioni during this interview were some of the state-of-the-art "high definition" (6k) digital scans made of individual Zapruder film frames by independent researchers Sydney Wilkinson and Thom Whitehead in Hollywood. After purchasing their Zapruder film from the National Archives in November 2008, they decided to use a then-state-of-the-art Northlight 6k digital scanner to digitize the Zapruder film, creating digital scans of *each frame* in their 35mm film that were 6144 x 4668 pixels each, with an effective size of 114.7 Mb of digital data per frame, which is *more than ten times greater* than the amount of information displayed in a traditional 2k, or "1080p," HD television image. (In contrast, television HD images that are 2k are only 1920 x 1080 pixels per frame, with only about 9.7 Mb of digital information per frame.)

Wilkinson and Whitehead created their digital scans of the Zapruder film in "logarithmic color," which reveals more information about the film frame than does the "linear color" you watch on TV in documentaries and television dramas, in movie theaters, and on your computer screens. *Logarithmic color* (which is the totality of all color information in the film frame) reveals *all* of the available information in each film frame and brings out much more detail in blacks and mid-blacks (by "stretching" the blacks into grays) than you would see in a "linear color" image of the same frame.

In the "linear color" images you are all familiar with in movies and TV shows, and on your computer screens, the contrast and color balance in each frame have always been adjusted to make the images more pleasing to the eye — and the very bright and very dark areas of the images have been "clipped" in order to make the majority of each image appear "correct" to your eyes.

To the untrained eye of a non-film-professional, logarithmic color film images appear to be "muddy" and "flat;" but they are actually the best way to retain and study all of the color information in a film. Without color correction, logarithmic color images appear "washed out," but the amount of information about the blacks is substantially increased. (By the way, using logarithmic color does not make a shadow look like a patch.)

The Zapruder film element that was digitally scanned by Wilkinson and Whitehead was the third-generation, 35mm dupe negative they purchased from the National Archives in 2008 — hence, its images faithfully represent what is on the extant film in the Archives today.

Examination of Zapruder Frame 313 (The Head Explosion)

Horne: Can I show you the one frame of the head explosion that's in the existing film? There's only one frame in the film that shows with any graphic violence the head explosion where there's any red mist or blood.

Brugioni: Well, I remember it — that shocked all of us when we saw it. I thought it was —

Horne: This is frame 313 of the extant film [referring to the laptop screen Brugioni was examining with the aid of a metal pointer of the type used at lectures].

Brugioni: — *I thought I remembered a chunk of head here* [gesturing to the air well above and slightly to the right of JFK's head in frame 313 with the tip of his pointer] *and this was misty, bigger* [pointing well above JFK's head again with his pointer, and comparing the head explosion he remembered seeing in the Zapruder film on Saturday, November 23, 1963 with the head explosion in the extant Zapruder film today].

Horne: How far would you say the mist or the explosion was above his head, in real terms? *How many inches or how many feet above his head?*

Brugioni: *I'd say about a foot and a half, and it was high, it was above, this way* [gesturing again with his pointer to the air well above and slightly to the right of JFK's head in frame 313].

Horne: It was high.

Brugioni: *Yeah.*

Horne: I can enlarge this even more [displaying a magnified image of frame 313, and then increasing its magnification further].

Brugioni: *No, I saw much more than that.*

Horne: Much more than that.

Brugioni: *Um hmmm. Like up here* [gesturing with his pointer well above and slightly forward of JFK's head].

Horne: Did it hang in the air for a moment?

Brugioni: [With amazement on his face] *Well, there should be — you say there's not another frame? There should —*

Horne: *I'll show you now the adjacent frames on either side* [and Horne proceeded to do so on the laptop screen]. *This* [displaying frame 313 again] *is the only frame that shows any red color or blood —*

Brugioni: *No, what I remember — was something, it was white, and then there was a white mist around it* [gesturing again with his pointer above the head of JFK in frame 313].

Horne: That's frame 313, and there's 314, and 315 [quickly displaying the three frames in sequence].

Brugioni: *I remembered more.*

Horne: You remember more?

Brugioni: *Um hmmm.*

Horne: *How certain are you about that?*

Brugioni: *I'm certain, because that's what shocked me.*

Horne: The dramatic nature of it?

Brugioni: *Yeah.*

Horne: The horrific —

Brugioni: *Yeah, we weren't expecting it, you know.*

Horne: If you had to estimate how many seconds the cloud of mist or the explosion lasted, can you estimate how many seconds it lasted, when you watched it [as a motion picture on November 23, 1963]?

Brugioni: *It lasted longer than what's showing on there, on what you have* [referring to frame 313, followed by 314 and 315, which show no head explosion].

Horne: And was it much more dramatic then?

Brugioni: *Yeah.*

Horne: Higher in the air?

Brugioni: *Yes. And this one shows it* [referring and pointing to the red head explosion in frame 313] *fairly close by; what I remember was I thought there was a chunk in the air* [gesturing again to the open air above JFK's head with his pointer].

Examination of Zapruder Frame 317

Horne: Now, this is four frames after the head explosion [referring to the digital scan of frame 317]. This is frame 317. I'm going to magnify this now, I'm going to blow it up, because there is a really unusual looking anomaly in this image which is of serious interest to a lot of people.

Brugioni: *My god, that's a different change of color there, that's for damn sure* [using his pointer, referring to the very dark, sharply delineated "black patch" on the back of JFK's head in frame 317].

Brugioni: [After studying the "black patch" for quite a long time in silence, using his pointer, Brugioni finally spoke, while pointing at the "black patch."] *That doesn't look right.*

Horne: I don't think it does either, but I'm not a photoanalyst and you were, for decades. So, your opinion is of great interest to us. [Brugioni continued to study frame 317 for a long time, in silence, using his pointer.]

Horne: *Have you ever seen a shadow on somebody's head that had straight edges like that?*

Brugioni: *No, not with hair.* See, here's an example, right there, you know [pointing at the softly delineated shadows in Jacqueline Kennedy's hair in the same frame, in which no sharp or straight edges were visible]. *That's an anomaly* [referring again to frame 317].

Dino Brugioni Examines and Comments on the Zapruder Film as a Motion Picture, Repeatedly Viewing the LMH Company's Commercial DVD Product Titled "Image of An Assassination," First Sold in 1998.

Horne: Do you think that this film you're watching now ... do you think this is the film you watched on Saturday, November 23rd [1963]?

Brugioni: I watched a good quality film, that's for sure. *I don't know, I thought the blast to the head lasted longer.... I thought I saw a white glob in the air, higher, and there was a mist.*

[Break in dialogue; new dialogue begins below after Brugioni views the Zapruder film on the DVD in slow motion]

Brugioni: *I don't know, sometimes I just have a feeling that something has been cut out of this, you know, the killing.*

Horne: Regarding the head explosion?

Brugioni: *Yeah.*

Horne: Does it appear too brief to you, is that what you're saying?

Brugioni: *Yeah.*

[Break in dialogue; new dialogue below commences after Brugioni examined what are called "Close Up Frames" on the DVD, specifically still close-ups of frames 313, 314, 315, 316, and 317]

Horne: *Now* [after pausing the image on the laptop screen on the magnified blowup of frame 317 from the DVD], *this anomaly* *that we saw in the logarithmic color scan* [i.e., the "black patch"] *is still present, it's just harder to see because of all the contrast in the picture, but it's still present, its in exactly the same spot, and it's still got straight lines* [i.e., edges]. *This is a frame that's getting a lot of attention right now, since it happens to have unnaturally straight edges —*

Brugioni: [using his pointer, and directing it in frame 317 toward what is commonly referred to as the large red "blob" on the right side of JFK's head] — *I would agree because this [pointing at the "blob"] is an anomaly right here, too.*

[Break in dialogue; new dialogue below begins after repeated viewing by Brugioni of the Zapruder film as a motion picture in slow motion, including the head shot]

Brugioni: *I don't know, I saw more matter in the air than that.*

Horne: And you're certain about that?

Brugioni: *Yeah, I'm certain about that. I'm sorry the other guys are not here* [Brugioni was referring to his two former partners at NPIC on November 23, 1963 — Bill Banfield and Ralph Pearce — who were both deceased at the time of the interview] ... *but I mean it was just, we were all awed when we saw it* [the head explosion].

Horne: And the two Secret Service agents had not seen it yet, right?

Brugioni: Yeah, they hadn't seen it [the head explosion] and they were awed.

[Break in dialogue; dialogue below resumes after Brugioni watches the film again, in slow motion, with the focus on the head shot]

Horne: Is this what you recall seeing Saturday [November 23, 1963]?

Brugioni: *I saw more, No, I saw more than that.* [Brugioni was shaking his head from left to right in negation.]

Horne: *How certain are you about that on a scale of one to ten?*

Brugioni: *TEN. I'm sure I saw more.*

Horne: Are you, ah, do you believe that with that exception this is the same film you worked on, the same general film, or do you think this might be a different film?

Brugioni: *No, I think it's the same film but I just thought there's missing frames — I thought there's something missing out of this.*

Horne: Now I'm going to ask you to estimate something, it's just an estimate. Based on the actual camera speed, average camera speed of 18 frames a second, how many frames do you think might be missing from the head explosion?

Brugioni: *It would be a few. I just thought when I saw it I just — I remember the white* [biological material] *above the head and the white mist around the — around it.*

Horne: *Was the mist white or red?*

Brugioni: *White.*

Horne: Um hmmm. *Do you remember seeing red mist at all?*

Brugioni: *No, I remember just the white.*

Horne: *You don't remember seeing a bloody color? A blood color — like you see here?*

Brugioni: *No.*

Horne: *You don't. [Are] you sure about that?*

Brugioni: *Yeah.*

[Break in dialogue; dialogue below resumes after Brugioni again views the film, and the head shot, as a motion picture]

Brugioni: *I saw more than just that.* [Brugioni was shaking his head from left to right, in negation.]

Horne: It's apparent to me that you're very certain about that.

Brugioni: *Yeah, yeah.*

[End of partial transcript of Dino Brugioni interview]

Partial transcript of Thom Whitehead HD video interview of Paul Rutan, Jr., and Garrett Smith in 2013

Thom Whitehead is a seasoned Hollywood television and feature-film mastering editor specializing in the post-production processing and restoration of motion pictures. In the summer of 2013, he interviewed Paul Rutan, Jr., (a film restoration and film lab expert) and Garrett Smith (VP Production Technology and Digital Mastering Operations, Paramount Pictures) for the purpose of future inclusion in a documentary tentatively titled "Alteration" (currently in production by Thom Whitehead and Sydney Wilkinson).

This is the first time that any part of this interview has been published. Rutan and Smith are among the dozens of film professionals (editors, colorists, and restoration experts) who have seen the 6k scans of the Zapruder film made by Wilkinson and Whitehead. Although nearly all of those movie-industry film professionals who evaluated the scans expressed a strong opinion that the Zapruder film had indeed been altered, only a few have had the courage to appear for a formal interview and express that conclusion on camera.

Paul Rutan and Garrett Smith were among the first to do so.

Professional Background

Smith: ....Now, as to my credibility, thirty-seven years in the movie business, I'm not sure how much lower you can go than that; and [I] just got done with nearly twenty-five years at Paramount, where I basically ran their mastering for most of those years and spent the last few years investigating new digital production technology.

Rutan: [I've] been doing this since 1968, I was delivering film in New York City; and then full time from '74 I got hired to work for my Dad, and I worked for him for 12 years — started out as janitor, and then shipping, and then film cleaning, and then film repair, and then optical lineup, and then optical printing. So, ever since then I've worked for a couple of companies, set up a department at COMPAC video, and I had my own company for 14 years doing restorations.

[Break in conversation; interview resumes with Rutan examining and commenting on frame 313]

Whitehead: Do you see any signs of alteration?

Rutan: *Yes.*

Whitehead: Where do you see them?

Rutan: *Well* [speaking while pointing at frame 313 on a large HD monitor], *in the — this explosion right here doesn't look, it's, see* [pointing] *— it's got defects on it — but it just doesn't look real, it doesn't look like blood, it just doesn't look real.*

[Break in conversation; interview resumes with Rutan looking at a large display of frame 317 — the "black patch" on the back of JFK's head]

Rutan: *I think you're looking at a patch, at a photographic patch that they put on the back of his* [JFK's] *head. It's crude, but if you run the film* [Thom Whitehead did so, displaying the frames immediately after the so-called "head shot" in rapid sequence as a motion picture], *you'll see that it moves — differently than his head does, as well. So, it's an optical, some sort of an optical [effect] that they put on there, to not show the back of his head.*

Whitehead: In your opinion, what do you think would have been the most likely way this would have been accomplished?

Rutan: *With an optical printer, with an aerial optical printer ---*

Whitehead: What they call an aerial imaging machine?

Rutan: *Yes, yes — aerial optical printer, where they could create that patch as an overlay, and then lay it on there. Just like old-time, optical special effects stuff.*

Whitehead: And how long do you think that a process like this might have taken?

Rutan: *Overnight.*

[Break in conversation]

Rutan: *Well, they did have optical printers for 8mm because they would take 8mm and blow it up to 16mm, so they did have that capability at that time. I have 8mm gates myself.*

[Break in conversation; interview resumes with Rutan examining frames 317, 321, and 323 on an HD monitor]

Rutan: *...My opinion is that it's an overlay they did, that's black, so it doesn't have the effect of the sun on his hair....*

Whitehead: OK, Paul, we're looking here [again] at frame 317 — this is the one that first caught my interest as having something wrong.

Rutan: *Well, the only thing I can see really is how predominant the black patch is in this particular frame* [pointing]. *I mean, it's clear to me that that is not the back of his head, that that is some kind of a [sic] optical effect, that has been laid on the back of his head by an optical house. And this* [pointing at the large pink "blob" on the right side of JFK's head] *is also an optical effect. But the back of his head is what always — what I'm always drawn to, because you — it's almost like he's wearing a toupee, because there's the top of his head* [pointing at JFK's auburn hair on the very top of his head] *and that's basically the color it should be, and then it's black, it's just solid black.*

[Break in conversation; interview resumes with Garrett Smith commenting on frame 317, showing the "black patch" on the back of JFK's head]

Smith: *You know, the density doesn't match — the shoulders don't match that* [meaning that the shadow on the back of JFK's shoulders does not match the black patch on the back of his head] *and* [the black patch] *doesn't match the top of his head* [pointing to JFK's auburn colored hair on top]. *So, it looks to me like somewhere in here* [pointing] *somebody did a hold-back and let-through matte or essentially blocked in a part of the area in an in-between thing — in-between generation, and then made a film* *copy so you've got some grain structure over the superimposed element, that is consistent with the rest of the frame; but you've got an irregular-shaped — I don't know if you'd call that a trapezoid — but you've got an irregular shape, superimposed over the head where the density values that — from the hair that we saw in the previous frame are completely different — very noticeable ... but that clearly shows it to me that something has been added to that frame; that's what it looks like to me.*

[Break in conversation]

Smith: *It just seems really obvious that the frames where they've matted out the back of the head, and added in the pink splash, the pink water-balloon — whatever it is that's supposed to be the blood — it's just not even believable ... maybe fifty years ago that might have passed muster, but for anybody — I mean — my impression is if I showed it to a 12-year old kid, they would say it was a cartoon...*

Rutan: *So, I think, you know, I think fifty years ago, it was perfectly believable — [where] as today, you know, with this major blow-up we've made, and the 6k scan, the faults are very apparent ... every time I look at it, it's hard for me to look at it, because it's not real.*

Smith: *....this is good enough for broadcast TV fifty years ago ... somebody had an agenda to — whatever that agenda was, they obviously doctored this film ... that film looks like it was doctored; I don't know why, I don't know who — but it seems really obvious.*

[End of Rutan / Smith interview excerpt]

Readers who wish to view images of the digital scans of frames 313, 317, and 323 should go to the Midnight Writer News archive online and view the PODCAST page for archived interview #107 at this link: https://midnightwriternews.com/mwn-episode-107-douglas-horne-on-the-zapruder-film-alteration-debate.

18

The Plot

(Part 1)

The plot to kill President John F. Kennedy was a highly sophisticated operation, one that in my view was jointly conceived, orchestrated, and implemented by the U.S. military establishment and the Central Intelligence Agency.

Dealey Plaza in downtown Dallas, where the assassination took place, was a perfect spot for an ambush. They thought of everything. Since it was at the end of Kennedy's parade route, there would be fewer people taking pictures and films. The established custom entailed having a flatbed truck with cameramen on it traveling directly in front of the presidential limousine so that the press could easily take pictures and films of the president. This time, it was announced at Love Field just prior to the departure of the motorcade that the flatbed press truck had been cancelled. Instead, cameramen were placed in three open convertible automobiles several cars back in the motorcade. This ensured that fewer professional photographers would be taking photographs and films of the presidential limousine and its occupants during the assassination and that there would be no close-up shots of what happened in the car during the shooting.

The turn from Houston Street onto Elm Street reportedly violated Secret Service protocols against making turns of more than 90 degrees. This excessively wide turn, however, ensured that the presidential limousine would be traveling at an extremely low rate of speed when the assassins began shooting from both the front and the back. Windows in high-rise buildings in the area would not be sealed.To ensure that the shooters would have a clear line of sight at the president, Secret Service agents would be directed not to stand on the back bumper of the presidential limousine, and motorcycle cops would be directed to stay even with, or behind, the rear wheels of the limousine so that there were no motorcycle escorts immediately abreast of the limousine or immediately in front of it. (In a planning meeting prior to JFK's arrival, the Secret Service also directed the Dallas police department to cut the number of motorcycle escorts around the limousine from eight to four.)

The Secret Service agent driving the limousine would not step on the accelerator once gunshots began ringing out. Instead, to make certain that the gunshots actually killed, and not just wounded, the president, the driver would stop or nearly stop the limousine until the president was hit by a fatal shot. The Secret Service agent who was in the front passenger seat would do nothing to save the president's life after the gunshots began. The few bystanders with cameras would have their photos and films confiscated, destroyed, altered, or never returned. Men falsely identifying themselves as Secret Service agents would be positioned in Dealey Plaza to divert people so that the assassins could escape.

It is a virtual certainty that the grand design or "architecture" of the assassination plot, including the cover-up, was designed by the CIA. At that time, the CIA was headed by brilliant people, many of whom were Ivy League graduates. Moreover, practically from the beginning of the CIA in 1947, CIA officials had been studying and specializing in not only the dark art of assassination but also in hiding the CIA's role in state-sponsored assassinations.

In fact, one can go online and Google "A Study of Assassination" and read what was an early version of a CIA assassination manual, one that was being used as early as 1952. It makes for eerie reading. Not only does it explain different methods of assassination, it also emphasizes the importance of carrying out assassinations in ways that prevent people from proving or even knowing that the CIA was deeply involved in the assassination.

There were two important aspects to the plot to kill Kennedy. One was brilliant and the other one was absolutely ingenious. One wouldn't expect anything less from the Ivy Leaguers who were running the CIA.

The brilliant part involved framing a purported communist for the killing of President Kennedy.

Why a communist?

In 1963, we were at the height of the Cold War, which had been raging for more than a decade. Since even before World War II, Americans had been indoctrinated with the notion that communism and communists posed a grave danger to America. Many people were convinced that the United States was in danger of falling to the Reds.

Recall the McCarthy hearings in the 1950s. Innocent Americans were being hauled up to Congress to answer whether they were or ever had been members of the Communist Party. People were convinced that there were communists everywhere who needed to be ferreted out and exposed. There were supposedly communists in Congress, in the executive-branch bureaucracies, and in the army. In Hollywood, screenwriters and others were being ostracized and boycotted. Some suspected communists, such as noted screenwriter Dalton Trumbo, were prosecuted, convicted, and jailed for contempt. People who had had any connection to communism in their past were fired and had difficulty finding new employment. Nothing worse could befall a person during the Cold War than to be labeled a communist.

By framing a purported communist for assassinating President Kennedy, the national-security establishment could rest assured that few people, if any, would come to his defense. If anyone did come to his defense, he could immediately be labeled a communist or a communist sympathizer and thereby have his own life damaged or destroyed.

That's what happened to New York City attorney Mark Lane, the man with whom Abraham Zapruder had the unpleasant encounter that I described in chapter 11. As one of the first people who questioned the official lone-nut theory of the assassination, Lane was immediately labeled a communist sympathizer by U.S. officials. Federal officials even began secretly monitoring his activities in the belief that he was acting on behalf of the purported international communist conspiracy to take over the world that was supposedly based in Moscow.

As we also discussed in chapter 11, the deep fear of being labeled a communist would necessarily have been a critically important factor in Zapruder's decision to not make waves about the alteration of his film. If Zapruder had chosen the same road that Mark Lane chose, the result would have been much worse for Zapruder, given that he had emigrated from Russia, was a Jew, and lived in Dallas, arguably the most right-wing city in the country. If Zapruder had accused *LIFE* magazine of lying about his film or altering his film, the national-security establishment and its army of assets in the private sector would have done everything to destroy him by smearing him as a communist or communist sympathizer or even a Russian mole whose mission was to infiltrate America and help pave the wave toward a communist victory in the Cold War.

By framing a purported communist, the plotters knew that no conservative would ever come to his defense. Conservatives hated and feared communists, and they were the biggest supporters of the Cold War and the anti-communist crusade.

But the strategy also worked to paralyze people on the left. There was so much animosity and fear after Kennedy's assassination that many leftwing groups did not dare to challenge the official story for fear of being labeled communist sympathizers and, consequently, losing donations to their organizations and causes. One of the best examples of this phenomenon was the Fair Play for Cuba Committee, the national organization for which Oswald was proselytizing in New Orleans a few months before the assassination. After Oswald was accused of killing the president, the FPCC permanently shut down its operations, which, of course, was what the FBI and the CIA had been striving for.

There was one big problem with this blame-a-communist strategy, however. How would the plotters arrange things so that they could frame a real communist? In other words, what are the odds that a communist would be at the right place at the right time during an assassination so that he could be framed for the crime? Moreover, right-wing Dallas was probably the last place one would find a communist to frame.

Imagine a CIA agent approaching a communist in New York City and saying, "Hi! There is a great job opening in Dallas, Texas. It's in a place called the Texas School Book Depository. Would you be interested? You'll have to move down to Dallas by November." The probability is that that New York City communist would respond, "Not on your life. Get out of my face."

How did the plotters resolve this problem? They did so by doing the second-best thing: They framed a secret government operative who had been secretly trained to act like a communist.

We know that both the CIA and the FBI were infiltrating leftist organizations during the Cold War. Sometimes this involved converting people within the organization into federal spies. Other times, however, it involved training agents to act as communists. It was obviously necessary that these agents be well-versed and highly educated in the principles of communism and socialism. Otherwise, it would be easy to uncover them as secret government agents posing as communists.

As the evidence surrounding the Kennedy assassination surfaced in the years and decades following the assassination, it became increasingly clear that Lee Harvey Oswald, the accused assassin, was, in fact, a government agent, one who was trained to be a communist infiltrator.

In fact, soon after the Warren Commission was organized to investigate the assassination of President Kennedy, its chairman, Earl Warren, summoned the members of the commission to a top-secret meeting at which Warren announced that he had received very discomforting information. The information was that Oswald had been serving as an informant for the FBI or U.S. intelligence.

How was this discomforting information resolved? The commission decided to simply ask the FBI and the CIA whether the information was true. When they both responded in the negative, that was considered the end of the matter. It was considered inconceivable that the FBI and the CIA would lie about such a thing. Warren ordered the members of the commission to keep the information secret. He ordered the court reporter who was transcribing the meeting to destroy her transcript and to keep the information secret as well. The last thing the Warren Commission wanted was for the American people to become aware of this possibility.

Oswald had served in the U.S. Marines. How many communists have you ever heard of in the U.S. Marines? I'll bet none. Communists hate Marines, and Marines hate communists. In fact, Marines had only recently killed hundreds of thousands of communists in the Korean War. That war was never formally ended, only suspended. Thus, there was always the possibility that U.S. Marine Oswald would be required to fight and kill his supposed communist allies. Why would any self-respecting communist put himself in that position?

Proponents of the official story — that a communist killed Kennedy — point to the fact that Oswald was studying Marxism when he was in high school. What they don't point out, however, is that his favorite television show as a child was *I Led Three Lives,* which revolved around a secret government agent whose job was to infiltrate communist cells within the United States and bust them.

While he was a Marine, Oswald was studying Marxism, so much so that his fellow Marines started calling him "Oswaldovich." What are the chances that the Marines would permit a possible communist spy to remain in the Marine Corps, especially at the height of the Cold War, when everyone was ferreting out, ostracizing, firing, and boycotting communists?

Oswald also became fluent in the Russian language while serving in the Marines. How does a high-school dropout do that without professional assistance? Learning a foreign language is extremely difficult, and learning to speak it requires conversing with other people. Thus, it is a virtual certainty that Oswald had to have had the assistance of the military's language-school experts in becoming fluent in Russian.

The military stationed Oswald at U.S. Naval Air Station Atsugi in Japan, where the CIA's top-secret U-2 spy plane was based. Would the military really station a genuine communist at such a base, especially given that that was where top-secret U-2 spy flights were originating?

After persuading the Marine Corps to grant him a "hardship discharge" in September 1959 (ostensibly to better support his sick mother), Oswald traveled to the Soviet Union. How he got the money to travel there is still a mystery. In Moscow, he loudly announced to officials in the U.S. Embassy that he was defecting to America's avowed Cold War enemy, the Soviet Union. He also announced his intention to disclose to the Soviets any top-secret, classified information that he had acquired as a Marine.

A couple of years later, Oswald announced his intention to return to the United States — with a Russian wife whose uncle had connections to Soviet intelligence. He encountered no objections or reservations from U.S. officials. In fact, the U.S. State Department actually loaned him money to return to the United States with his wife and daughter. The State Department also kindly informed a social-welfare group that assisted immigrants, Traveler's Aid Society of New York, that a 22-year-old American citizen was returning to the United States with his Russian wife and child.

On his return to the United States, was Oswald indicted or even hauled before a federal grand jury? Nope. They didn't touch him. No arrest and no torture of a man who presumably had, by popular definition, committed treason, not to mention the fact that he had greatly embarrassed the Marine Corps. There wasn't even an informal interview to ask Oswald about the secrets he had presumably given to the Soviets.

In other words, while everyone was searching madly for communists all across America and prosecuting, boycotting, ostracizing, and firing people who had any connections to communism in their pasts, one of America's most prominent communists was sauntering across the stage of history with nary a concern about being a communist — a man who had supposedly betrayed his country by defecting to America's avowed communist enemy and also vowing to disclose to the Soviets any classified information that he had acquired as a Marine. (Oswald also told the U.S. Embassy officials in Moscow, at the time of his defection, that he wanted to renounce his U.S. citizenship, but they stalled him, and he never followed through by filling out the paperwork.)

Upon his return to the United States, Oswald moved to Dallas, where he secured employment at a photography firm that — get this — was developing classified maps for the U.S. Army. He was also befriended and mentored by a man named George de Mohrenschildt, a conservative White Russian émigré who had the fingerprints of U.S. intelligence all over him.

A few months before the assassination, Oswald moved to New Orleans, where he secured employment with a company called the Reily Coffee Company, which was owned by one of the most virulent right-wingers in the country. What are the chances that an extreme anti-communist conservative would hire a self-avowed communist, especially one who had supposedly betrayed America by defecting to the Soviet Union and given up classified secrets to the Soviets?

While in New Orleans, Oswald was distributing pamphlets for the Fair Play for Cuba Committee, which the FBI and the CIA loathed and were trying to destroy. During that time, he was seen in the office of a man named Guy Bannister, a retired FBI agent and another ultra-right-winger with connections to U.S. intelligence. In what can only be seen as a monumental screw-up, Oswald stamped a return address on some of his FPPC pamphlets that led to Bannister's office.

Oswald made contact with a group of Cuban exiles called the DRE (Directorio Revolucionario Estudiantil). After the assassination, the DRE was the first group to issue a press release that advertised Oswald's communist bona fides. More than 30 years later, assassination researchers discovered that the DRE was actually a secret CIA front organization, one that was being generously funded with CIA money. At the time that the DRE released its post-assassination press release advertising Oswald's communist background, a CIA agent named George Joannides was closely monitoring and controlling the group, something that the CIA kept secret from the Warren Commission in 1964, the House Select Committee on Assassinations in the 1970s, and the Assassination Records Review Board in the 1990s.

A former *Washington Post* reporter named Jefferson Morley sued the CIA under the Freedom of Information Act for the CIA's secret files relating to Joannides's relationship to the DRE. The CIA fought the suit tooth and nail. That fight, which Morley ended up losing after some 11 years of litigation, is detailed in a book published by The

Future of Freedom Foundation entitled *Morley v. CIA: My Unfinished JFK Investigation.*

This wasn't the only time that Joannides made an appearance in matters relating to the Kennedy assassination. During the House Select Committee's reinvestigation of the Kennedy assassination during the 1970s, two law students on the staff of the committee, Dan Hardway and Ed Lopez, were charged with securing CIA records relating to Oswald's trip to Mexico City a couple of months before the assassination.

At first, believing that it was dealing with a couple of neophyte law students, the CIA played along. When the CIA realized that Hardway and Lopez knew exactly what they were doing, the CIA called Joannides out of retirement, ostensibly to facilitate the securing of CIA records. In actuality, Joannides served as the "gatekeeper" who tightly controlled the CIA records flowing to Hardway and Lopez about Oswald's trip to Mexico City some six weeks before the assassination.

Perhaps it's worth mentioning that the CIA awarded Joannides a medal for meritorious service.

As we will see in chapter 19, there was good reason for the CIA to be concerned about disclosing its records relating to Oswald's trip to Mexico City. That trip played a critically important role not only in framing him for the Kennedy assassination but also in securing an immediate shutdown of the investigation.

There is something else we need to consider: motive. No one has ever come up with a motive for Oswald to kill Kennedy. The most popular argument among proponents of the lone-nut theory of the assassination has been that Oswald was a little man who suddenly decided that he could become a big man by killing a big man.

But there is one big problem with that argument. Oswald claimed he was innocent. If he was a little man who was trying to become a big man by killing a big man, he would have been bragging that he had, in fact, done the dirty deed. He not only denied doing it, he went one step further and declared that he was being framed for the crime. That's what he was alluding to when he described himself as a "patsy."

Moreover, keep in mind the "breakthrough" that Kennedy achieved after the Cuban Missile Crisis. Kennedy had clearly come to the realization that the Cold War was nothing more than a dangerous racket, one that not only risked nuclear war but also one that was enriching the national-security establishment and its ever-growing army of "defense" contractors. Recall that in his Peace Speech at American University in June 1963, Kennedy effectively declared an end to the Cold War and a commitment to establishing peaceful and friendly relations with the Soviet Union and the rest of the communist world.

Why would a genuine communist want to kill a president who was leading America in that direction, especially given that his vice-president, Lyndon Johnson, was on the same page as the national-security establishment? It would not be difficult to see that right-wingers, which included the Pentagon and the CIA, would want to get rid of Kennedy for his "treasonous betrayal," but it makes no sense that a communist would want to do that.

Not surprisingly, Alexandra Zapruder does not address any of these anomalies, contradictions, and mysteries surrounding Oswald in her book. Subscribing to the lone-nut theory of the assassination, she simply settles for repeatedly mocking and ridiculing "conspiracy theorists" and "alterationists."

19

The Plot

(Part 2)

Whenever someone kills a cop, the police immediately pull out all the stops to bring the killer to justice. That's to be expected. To protect themselves, they have to send out a powerful message that the police will come after the killer with everything they have.

This is also true on a federal level. Many years ago, a Mexican drug cartel kidnapped, brutally tortured, and executed a DEA agent named Kiki Camarena. DEA agents pulled out all the stops to uncover the identities of the people who had participated in the crime, then orchestrated their kidnapping and forced rendition to the United States for trial.

In the 1970s, a federal judge in San Antonio named John H. Wood, Jr., believed that it was important for federal judges to do their part to "win" the "war on drugs." He was known as "Maximum John" for the maximum jail sentences that he would mete out to people who were convicted of drug offenses in his court. In 1979, Wood was assassinated. The feds pulled out all the stops to discover everyone who was involved in the assassination plot, including secretly monitoring communications between lawyers and their clients.

Deep-State officials knew full well that this phenomenon would be even more pronounced with the assassination of a U.S. president. The plotters in the Kennedy assassination knew that the full investigative might of the entire federal government, as well as that of state and local governments, would come to bear in an effort to bring every single person involved in the assassination to justice.

Therefore, the plotters had to figure out a way not only to assassinate the president but also a way to ensure that no investigation would ever lead to the national-security establishment. That is where the ingenious part of the plot comes into play.

Keep in mind, once again, that the people at the top of the CIA, many of whom were Ivy League graduates, were extremely brilliant people who had decided to devote their minds and their talents to the dark arts of assassination and cover-up. Recall that top-secret assassination manual from 1952 that I mentioned in chapter 18, which not only detailed ways to assassinate people but also ways to ensure that the crime could never be traced to the CIA.

On Monday, November 25, 1963 — only three days after the Kennedy assassination — U.S. Deputy Attorney General Nicholas Katzenbach issued one of the most remarkable memoranda in the history of U.S. criminal justice. The memorandum, addressed to presidential aide Bill Moyers, stated in part: "The public must be satisfied that Oswald was the assassin; that he did not have confederates that are still at large and that the evidence was such that he would have been convicted at trial."

Just the day before, on Sunday — the very same day that Oswald was assassinated by Jack Ruby — FBI Director J. Edgar Hoover issued a secret memo in which he stated, "There is nothing further on the Oswald case except that he is dead.... The thing I am concerned about, and so is Mr. Katzenbach, is having something issued so we can convince the public that Oswald is the real assassin." That memo indicates that Katzenbach, like Hoover, had actually reached this conclusion on November 24.

The FBI kept that Hoover memo secret from the Warren Commission, the House Select Committee, and the Assassination Records Review Board. You will recall that the congressional mandate in the JFK Records Act of 1992, which the ARRB was charged with enforcing, was that federal agencies disclose all of their assassination-related records to the public. However, there was a loophole in the law. If any records revealed "sources or methods" or whose disclosure posed a threat to "national security," federal agencies were authorized to keep them secret for another 25 years.

That 25-year deadline came due in 2017, during the Trump administration. While Trump granted the CIA's request for another four years of secrecy, a few of the assassination-related records were released. Among them was Hoover's memo.

The question naturally arises: How in the world would that Hoover memo have revealed "sources" or "methods" or threatened "national security," whatever definition is placed on that nebulous and meaningless term, if it had been released back in the 1990s?

It wouldn't have. The FBI simply lied to the ARRB when it claimed that that the disclosure of that memo would constitute a threat to national security.

How in the world could these two high-level federal law-enforcement officers — Hoover and Katzenbach — have been so certain so quickly that Lee Harvey Oswald did not have confederates who had assisted him with the assassination? Indeed, how could they be so certain that Oswald had, in fact, committed the assassination and that he wasn't the victim of a sophisticated frame-up? Don't forget, after all, that Oswald was saying that he was innocent and that he was being framed.

There is no way that Hoover and Katzenbach could have been so certain. There is no way for anyone to have known who was involved in the assassination within a day or even weeks of the assassination, especially without a full-blown investigation.

What was going on here? The president of the United States had just been assassinated. Everything we know about law enforcement says that they will pull out all the stops when a government official is murdered. Law-enforcement officials will stop at nothing to bring every single suspect to justice.

Yet, here were two of the top federal law-enforcement officials in the country immediately shutting down any further investigation into the assassination by immediately declaring that Oswald was the lone assassin of the president.

The answer to this mystery lies in the ingenious strategy devised by those brilliant assassination specialists within the CIA. They figured out a way to not only successfully assassinate Kennedy but to also ensure that a fierce investigation that could have led to them was immediately shut down.

You will recall that immediately after the assassination, two of the treating physicians at Parkland Hospital, Dr. Kemp Clark and Dr. Malcolm Perry, held a press conference, where they announced that Kennedy had suffered two wounds: a small bullet-sized wound in the throat and a massive hole in the back of his head.

During that press conference, Perry stated three times that the wound in Kennedy's throat had the appearance of an entry wound and that the bullet that punctured his throat was coming at him from in front of him. That would mean, of course, that Kennedy had been shot from the front, which also meant that Oswald, in the School Book Depository behind the limousine during the shooting, could not have fired that shot.

How did Perry arrive at his conclusion that the throat wound was an entrance wound? After all, that determination is ordinarily the job of a pathologist, a specialized physician who conducts an autopsy on the victim to determine entrance and exit wounds and bullet trajectories. Perry wasn't a pathologist and he certainly had not performed an autopsy. He was one of the president's treating physicians.

When a bullet enters a person's body, the entrance wound is ordinarily the size of the bullet. As it proceeds through the body, it is pushing mass and creating a shock wave in front of it. The bullet then exits with a "blowout" wound, one that is much larger than the entrance wound. A "blowout" wound is often called an "avulsed" wound, a term that some physicians used to describe President Kennedy's large defect in the right rear of his head.

That's how Perry reached the conclusion that Kennedy's throat wound appeared to be an entrance wound. Having treated countless gunshot wounds at Parkland, the 34-year-old Perry knew what entrance wounds and exit wounds ordinarily looked like. Kennedy's throat wound appeared to be an entrance wound because it was the size of a bullet's diameter and had smooth edges leading inward, not ragged edges leading in an outward direction.

Keep in mind also that Parkland Hospital was one of the best trauma hospitals in the country. It specialized in things like gunshot wounds and was also a teaching hospital. Thus, its surgeons had lots of experience in recognizing and treating gunshot wounds, in a part of the country where gun ownership was high and many people suffered from gunshot wounds.

Moreover, the massive hole in the back of Kennedy's head clearly looked like an exit wound, which implied that that this shot had also come from Kennedy's front.

Immediately after the shots rang out, many bystanders and several police officers, certain that shots had come from Kennedy's front, rushed toward the "grassy knoll" and stockade fence that were situated to Kennedy's right front.

That obviously raises the $64,000 question: If you're going to frame a person who is purportedly firing from the rear, why in the world would you have shots fired from the front? That's pretty dumb, isn't it? How could those brilliant Ivy League graduates not see that?

Actually, that is the absolutely ingenious part of the entire plot to assassinate Kennedy. Being able to prove with certainty that shots had been fired from the front as well as from behind meant that there was crossfire and therefore a conspiracy — an absolutely essential part of the plot. Because of that crossfire, those brilliant Ivy League graduates at the CIA were able to get the investigation of the assassination, an investigation that could have led to them, shut down immediately after the assassination.

Now, bear with me at this point because this is where things get very sophisticated and very complicated. *This is the most important part of the coverup of the Kennedy assassination.* So, I'm going to be very methodical and deliberate to make certain that this part of the cover up is crystal clear.

The thing that the American people feared most in 1963 was the possibility of nuclear war. Everyone knew what had happened to Hiroshima and Nagasaki when U.S. forces dropped atomic bombs on those two cities near the end of World War II. Both cities were immediately destroyed and most everyone within or near the city was either incinerated or gravely burned or got very sick from radiation poisoning. Those images had been seared into the minds of every American.

During the early 1960s, many Americans were building fall-out shelters under, or adjacent to, their homes. There were nuclear drills in the public schools, where American schoolchildren were taught to "duck and cover" in the event of nuclear war.

Moreover, don't forget that only one year before the Kennedy assassination, the United States and the Soviet Union had come within an inch of all-out nuclear war during the Cuban Missile Crisis.

Indeed, as we learned in the buildup to President George W. Bush's invasion of Iraq in 2003, this deep-seated fear of nuclear war has not significantly dissipated. Once Bush and his national-security team suggested that Iraqi dictator Saddam Hussein was preparing to unleash "mushroom clouds" over American cities, the American people overwhelmingly supported his plan to invade Iraq.

The CIA plotters understood this phenomenon perfectly and used it to bring about the immediate shutdown of the investigation into the Kennedy assassination that could have — and most likely would have — led to them.

Here is how the plot operated. They have a purported shooter firing from the rear. That's Oswald. He's a communist. But he isn't just a "stand-alone communist." He's got confederates helping him to assassinate the president, and they are firing from the front. That was the purpose of intentionally having shots hit the president from the front. The plotters wanted to establish that Oswald, the presumed assassin firing from the rear, definitely had confederates firing from the front.

Thus, when Dr. Perry announced three times at the press conference immediately following Kennedy's death that the wound in Kennedy's throat appeared to be an entrance wound, he was unwittingly doing precisely what the plotters wanted him to do: confirming a conspiracy.

The question naturally arises: Who are those people who fired from the front? Were they friends or relatives of Oswald? Fellow employees at the Texas School Book Depository?

This is where Oswald's trip to Mexico City a couple of months before the assassination now comes into play. Oswald (or someone portraying Oswald) went to both the Soviet embassy and the Cuban embassy in Mexico City. While at the Soviet embassy, Oswald is supposed to have met with a Soviet officer named Valery Kostikov, who was the head of what was called "wet affairs" — that is, assassinations — for the USSR in the Western Hemisphere.

Therefore, Oswald's confederates who had fired from the front had to be Soviet and Cuban agents. The conspiracy had been solidified in Mexico City. There is no other reasonable conclusion that could be drawn. That meant that President Kennedy had been assassinated as part of the international communist conspiracy to take over the world that undergirded the Cold War.

What did that mean? That obviously meant all-out nuclear war. The idea was that once the American people discovered that the communists had killed their admired and beloved president, they would demand immediate retaliation.

In what form would that retaliation come? Well, it's not as though Soviet leader Nikita Khrushchev and Cuban leader Fidel Castro would present themselves to be easily assassinated. So, the only way to retaliate would be by bombing Moscow and Havana or anywhere else the two communist leaders might be.

At the risk of belaboring the obvious, a massive attack against Moscow and Havana or any other parts of the Soviet Union or Cuba would quickly have escalated to all-out nuclear war.

To recap the plot: There would be no doubt in people's minds, based on planted evidence, that Oswald had shot at the president from the rear — from the Texas School Book Depository. Oswald would be immediately presented as a communist. That's where the DRE, the CIA's front organization in New Orleans, would come into play. It would immediately issue a press release detailing Oswald's communist background and his pro-Cuba activities in New Orleans shortly before the assassination.

But — and here is where Mexico City comes into play — Oswald would not be just some stand-alone communist. He would be a communist who had lived in the Soviet Union after defecting there and who had just recently made contact with Soviet and Cuban officials in Mexico City, including an important Russian assassination official.

There is no doubt that Kennedy was hit by shots fired from the front. That is established by the small throat wound and the massive exit-sized blowout in the back of his head. Who were the shooters in the front? There could also be no doubt that the shooters from the front had to have been agents of the Soviet Union and Cuba. Operating through Oswald firing from the rear and other communist agents firing from the front, the international communist conspiracy would appear to have snuffed out the life of a U.S. president.

That ostensibly leaves President Johnson and the U.S. national-security establishment with a horrific choice: Should they retaliate or not? If they retaliate, that would mean all-out nuclear war, which would leave tens of millions of Americans dead and much of the United States destroyed.

In order to avoid nuclear war, therefore, they decide not to retaliate and settle instead for pinning the crime on Oswald, who was now dead. That's how they induced the entire federal bureaucracy, including the FBI, to immediately shut down the investigation into the assassination. Avoiding nuclear war became a foremost matter of "national security."

Let's go back and review that memorandum that Deputy Attorney General Katzenbach sent to presidential aide Bill Moyers on Monday, November 25 — only three days after the assassination: "The public must be satisfied that Oswald was the assassin; that he did not have confederates that are still at large and that the evidence was such that he would have been convicted at trial." FBI Director J. Edgar Hoover's memo the day before had said, "There is nothing further on the Oswald case except that he is dead.... The thing I am concerned about, and so is Mr. Katzenbach, is having something issued so we can convince the public that Oswald is the real assassin."

According to *The Presidential Recordings: Lyndon B. Johnson: The Kennedy Assassination and the Transfer of Power: November 1963–January 1964,* President Johnson met with CIA Director John McCone on the Saturday morning after the assassination — November 23. That volume states, "Nonetheless, there was one piece of disturbing information that had been confirmed by the CIA in the hours since the assassination. Just weeks before November 22, Lee Harvey Oswald had traveled to Mexico City and visited the Soviet Embassy. This contact raised the ante on direct Soviet involvement, and it was agreed that McCone would personally brief Johnson for at least the next few days on this development. Three hours later, McCone stopped by the EOB to tell Johnson more troubling news. Oswald, while in Mexico City, had apparently visited the Cuban Embassy as well."

On December 15, 2021, the National Archives released a CIA report entitled "SUMMARY of Relevant Information on Lee Harvey OSWALD at 0700 24 November 1963." The report detailed Oswald's supposed visits to the Soviet and Cuban embassies in Mexico City. In the first sentences of the report, the CIA refers to Kostikov, the Soviet assassination specialist: "Our first Information on OSWALD came from a technical operation in Mexico City and was cabled in on 9 October 1963. It revealed that on 1 October 1963 Lee OSWALD had been in touch there with Soviet Consul Valery KOSTIKOV about a telegram which the Soviet Embassy was supposed to send on him to the Soviet Embassy in Washington. The data showed that OSWALD had also been at the Soviet Embassy in Washington."

That report was prepared at 7 a.m. on the Sunday morning after the assassination. It is a virtual certainty that it was sent to President Johnson, which would have enabled him to easily convince federal officials of the imminent danger of nuclear war with the Soviet Union. That memo, combined with evidence of shots fired from the front, would explain why Hoover and Katzenbach concluded that very same day — Sunday, November 24 — that the investigation needed to be shut down immediately after Oswald was assassinated.

There is also the Mafia to consider. Remember: The CIA had secretly entered into a partnership with that criminal organization to assassinate Fidel Castro. It would have been easy to shift the focus of that assassination partnership to Kennedy when the need arose. At that point, it would not have been difficult to induce FBI director

Hoover to immediately shut down any investigation by the FBI. All that the Mafia or the CIA would have had to do was show Hoover photos of himself in compromising sexual activity with his FBI deputy director, Clyde Tolson. Hoover, who himself was an expert in that type of blackmail game, would have immediately done whatever was asked of him, especially given his deep antipathy toward the Kennedy brothers.

Moreover, the Mafia could be counted on to silence Oswald so that a trial would never be held. That's where Jack Ruby came into play.

Thus, the plot was operating on two levels: One level was internal, within the federal government, and shrouded in "national-security" secrecy — that is, the belief that a conspiracy involving communist gunmen in Dealey Plaza, acting on behalf of the USSR or Castro (or both), killed JFK in a crossfire (with shots fired from both the front and the rear). That "fact," known to insiders in the federal government, had to be covered up to prevent World War III. The other level on which the plot was operating was this: the way to prevent World War III was to convince the American people that Oswald was the lone assassin of the president, simply a nut who acted alone. If the public could be convinced that he acted alone, then the public would not believe there was a communist conspiracy to kill the president. There would then be no risk of World War III because the public would not demand immediate retaliation against the Soviets.

In reality, the World War III scenario would undoubtedly not have played out because it is difficult to imagine that Americans would overwhelmingly be demanding military retaliation that they knew would lead to nuclear war, especially given that Nikita Khrushchev and Fidel Castro would have been vehemently denying that they had had any role in the assassination. The Peace Speech made by JFK in June 1963 would have made it difficult to persuade the American people that Khrushchev had killed Kennedy. (Kennedy was proceeding secretly, and cautiously, in the fall of 1963 to also normalize relations with Castro, but the American people did not know about that. Only the NSA and CIA did!) Castro would have pointed out that he was having lunch with a Kennedy emissary, French journalist Jean Daniel, at the very moment of the assassination. Why would Khrushchev and Castro want to assassinate a president who was about to end the Cold War and establish peaceful and friendly relations with the communist world, especially when his vice-president vehemently disagreed with Kennedy's vision for the future direction of America and instead aligned himself with the vision of the U.S. national-security establishment?

But that false notion that the American people would demand immediate retaliation was a perfect way of selling the desperate need to shut down the investigation within the federal bureaucracy by pinning the crime solely on Oswald. It was ostensibly the way to protect the American people from all-out nuclear war.

That's how the entire assassination got shrouded within the cloak of "national security," notwithstanding the fact that it had been supposedly committed by a "lone nut" who just happened to be at the right place at the right time. All that Johnson and the national-security establishment had to do was to convince key people within the federal bureaucracy of the need to settle for pinning the crime on Oswald and immediately shut down any further investigation. The federal bureaucracy would pick up the cue and follow suit, as reflected by those memos from Katzenbach and Hoover and, as we will see, by the three military pathologists who would be tasked with conducting a fraudulent autopsy on Kennedy's body to hide from the American people the fact that shots had been fired from the front.

In fact, we know that President Johnson employed this World War III cover story more than once. When he asked Earl Warren to become a member of the commission to investigate the assassination, Warren initially refused to do so. He said that it would be a conflict of interest given his position as Chief Justice of the United States. Johnson told him that his country needed him because America was facing the possibility of all-out nuclear war that would inevitably kill forty million Americans. That's what caused Warren to change his mind and agree to serve on the commission.

Warren had clearly been read in on the facts of the frontal shots. Otherwise, he would have asked the natural question: How could an assassination committed by a lone nut possibly lead to nuclear war? Johnson would have shown Warren that November 24 memo detailing Oswald's visits to the Soviet and Cuban embassies as well as the evidence establishing that there were shots that hit Kennedy from the front to convince him of the vital importance of proving that Oswald alone killed the president.

When Johnson asked Sen. Richard Russell, Jr., to serve on the commission, he, too, initially refused because of personal enmity that he bore against Earl Warren. Johnson used the World War III cover story on him as well, telling him that his service was needed to avoid nuclear war. Undoubtedly, he was also shown that CIA report along with evidence of shots having been fired from the front.

Given that Johnson employed the World War III cover story on two members of the Warren Commission, it is likely that he did so with others as well. That would have ensured that the commission's investigation would focus on establishing that Oswald alone had shot the president, especially since Allen Dulles, the former CIA director who Kennedy fired after the Bay of Pigs disaster, would be serving on the commission and be able to control its operation and direction.

But what if Warren, Hoover, or any other federal bureaucrat had asked the obvious question: Given that the communists have killed our president, why shouldn't we retaliate against them, even if it does mean nuclear war?

Johnson would have had the perfect response: "I've learned that those Kennedy boys were doing everything they could to oust Castro from power, including through assassination and terrorism. It's obvious that the Reds got to him first. I'll be damned if I'm going to head this country into nuclear war to retaliate for an assassination war that the Kennedys started and ended up losing to the Reds. The damned Murder Inc. that their CIA was operating in the Caribbean got the Kennedys burned and that's just the way things will have to remain."

Who could argue with that reasoning?

As an aside, it should be noted that Johnson would have been speaking falsely about Kennedy's policy on assassinations. As Prof. John Newman, a former Army intelligence officer, has documented in his books *Countdown to Darkness* and *Into the Storm,* one of the biggest lies told by the CIA since the mid-1970s has been that the Kennedy brothers sanctioned Castro's assassination. In actuality, the assassination plots against Castro were always CIA-directed, had begun under Eisenhower, and then continued under Kennedy without his knowledge or approval.

Johnson was raising the World War III cover story at Parkland Hospital even before Kennedy expired. While waiting for Kennedy to be declared dead, he alluded to the possibility that the assassination was the first step in a Soviet nuclear attack on the United States. Yet, he continued waiting at the hospital rather than immediately going to Dallas's Love Field and getting up in the air to direct America's response to such an attack.

Then, while Johnson was heading to Love Field after Kennedy had been declared dead, Johnson scrunched down in the car, saying that there was a danger of a communist ambush if the assassination was actually the first step in a Soviet nuclear attack.

Yet, when Johnson arrived at Love Field, his actions belied any concern whatsoever for the possibility that the assassination was, in fact, the first step of a nuclear attack by the Soviets. Knowing that the team of Secret Service agents headed by Roy Kellerman would soon be arriving with Kennedy's body, he had aides begin removing seats from the back of Air Force One to make room for the heavy, bronze ceremonial Dallas casket. Although Air Force One and Air Force Two were near-duplicates of each other, he decided to use Air Force One. He then ordered aides to transfer the luggage from Air Force Two to Air Force One, notwithstanding the fact that both planes were going to the same destination. He also took the time to summon a Dallas federal judge to come to Love Field to swear him in as president even though Attorney General Robert Kennedy had advised him that no such swearing in was necessary.

President Kennedy was declared dead at 1 p.m. Yet, Johnson didn't depart Love Field until 2:47 p.m. — about one and three quarter hours later.

Thus, Johnson's actions belied any concern whatsoever for the possibility that the assassination was the first stage in a Soviet nuclear attack on the United States. In fact, his actions expressed a certainty that no such possibility existed. After all, if Johnson truly believed that there was even a 1 percent chance that the assassination was the first stage in an attack, he would have gotten into the air immediately in order to direct America's defenses to repel such an attack. The obvious reason he didn't do that, even while lying about his supposed concern about a possible Soviet nuclear attack, was that he knew for certain that the Soviets had not assassinated Kennedy. And the only reason he could be so certain is that he knew who really killed the president.

20

The Autopsy

(Part 1)

In the mid-1990s, two key members on the staff of the Assassination Records Review Board — Jeremy Gunn, the general counsel of the ARRB, and Douglas Horne, the ARRB's chief analyst for military records, made a startling discovery. They discovered that there were actually two different brain examinations following the autopsy that the U.S. military conducted on President Kennedy's body on the evening of the assassination. The two brain examinations took place during the week-and-a-half following the Kennedy autopsy.

Why is that significant?

One reason is that for 33 years — until the ARRB began to take the depositions of people involved in the autopsy — the pathologists who conducted the autopsy had been falsely claiming that there had been only one brain examination. Indeed, a supplemental brain examination after an autopsy — after the brain has had time to "fix" in formalin solution (formaldehyde) — is customary in an autopsy involving a gunshot to the head.

Another reason is that the second examination was of someone else's brain but nonetheless falsely represented, in photos taken at that exam, to be Kennedy's brain.

How was this fraud uncovered?

Horne served as Gunn's primary assistant for medical-evidence issues and, as such, would assist Gunn to prepare for the ARRB's depositions of persons associated with Kennedy's autopsy. As they were preparing in 1996 for the deposition of the third of the three pathologists at the autopsy, former Army forensic pathologist Lt. Col. Pierre Finck, Gunn asked Horne to draw up a timeline of when "the brain exam" had taken place, to determine the identities of the people who attended the exam, and to study the circumstances surrounding the event. To develop this timeline, Horne's task was to study all the relevant testimony before the Warren Commission and the House Select Committee on Assassinations as well as the pertinent documents relating to the brain exam. In the process of developing that timeline, Horne determined that there actually had been two brain examinations rather than only one. Once he presented his findings to Gunn, Gunn expressed his agreement with what Horne had discovered.

The first of the two exams was conducted on the morning of November 25, 1963. It was attended by Navy autopsy pathologists CDR James J. Humes and CDR "J" Thornton Boswell, two of the three pathologists who had conducted the Kennedy autopsy the previous Friday night, and by Navy civilian John Stringer, who was the official photographer for the autopsy.

The second brain exam, Horne concluded, was conducted sometime between November 29 and December 2, 1963. It was attended by Humes, Boswell, Finck, and an unknown Navy photographer.

Thus, significantly, Humes and Boswell, the two Navy pathologists, were present at both events and, therefore, were fully aware of the fraud in which they were engaging at the second brain exam.

Stringer told the ARRB that at the first brain exam, the brain was "serially sectioned" or cut like a loaf of bread, which is standard procedure in gunshots to the head. At the second brain exam, the brain was not "serially sectioned." There is something important to note about this: Once a brain is sectioned, it cannot be put back together. It remains sliced up. Assuming that the brain at the first brain exam was that of President Kennedy, which is almost certainly the case, that means that the brain at the second brain exam necessarily had to be someone else's brain, not Kennedy's.

None of the photographs that Stringer took at the first brain exam, on November 25 (when the brain was "sectioned"), ever made it into the official collection of autopsy photographs. As Stringer told the ARRB staff, the reason for making "coronal sections" (i.e., sections that separate the brain into anterior and posterior slices) was to reveal the damage caused as the bullet(s) traveled through the brain tissue — by showing, section-by-section, the bullet track in the brain tissue. He photographed each coronal section of Kennedy's brain on top of a "light box," which was illuminated from both below, by the light box itself, and above, by his strobe light.

The official brain photographs in the autopsy records depict the brain used at the second exam. They depict a damaged but essentially intact brain — one that has not been sectioned or sliced up like a loaf of bread. Not surprisingly, the general pattern of damage in the brain at that second brain exam is consistent with the official scenario of the assassination — that Kennedy was shot from the rear.

It's also worth mentioning that when the ARRB showed Stringer the official autopsy photographs of the brain, he stated that the photographs were not — and could not be — the brain photographs that he took. He cited three reasons: first, the film images of the brain in the National Archives are not recorded on the type of film he shot; second, there are no photos of coronal sections (and most of the images he shot were of those coronal sections); and third, he did not shoot the underside of the brain (so-called *basilar* views) — he shot only *superior* views of the top of the brain, yet one half of the brain photos in the Archives are basilar views.

It would be extremely difficult to find a better example of fraud than those two brain examinations.

Soon after Horne made his discovery that there had been two brain exams, he meticulously documented his finding in a lengthy, footnoted research "memo for the record." Soon afterward, two articles on the matter appeared in the mainstream press, both of which can be found online: (1) "Archive Photos Not of JFK's Brain, Concludes Aide to Review Board" by *Washington Post* staff writer George Lardner, Jr. (https://www.washingtonpost.com/wp-srv/national/longterm/jfk/jfk1110.htm) and (2) "Newly Released JFK Documents Raise Questions About Medical Evidence" by Associated Press writer Deb Reichmann (https://www.washingtonpost.com/wp-srv/national/longterm/jfk/ap110998.htm).

While many newspapers published one or both of those articles, to my knowledge, not one mainstream newspaper ever published any editorial or op-ed about this occurrence. By the same token, no investigative reporter (or anyone else) ever conducted a follow-up investigation to get to the bottom of what had taken place. By this time (November of 1998) — some 35 years after the assassination — the mainstream press had either become indifferent to the Kennedy assassination or simply too fearful of doing anything that would smack of questioning the official lone-nut theory of the assassination.

Moreover, don't forget something important about the ARRB and the JFK Records Act: While the law enabled Horne and Gunn to "clarify the record" by uncovering the fraud surrounding the two brain exams, it also prohibited them from investigating the matter. Recall also that the ARRB board members strictly enforced that prohibition on the staff. Staff members well understood that advocating a reinvestigation by the ARRB was a sure way to get fired. Therefore, even though Horne forwarded his detailed memo to Gunn (the ARRB's general counsel) and ARRB Executive Director David Marwell, there was never any follow-up questioning or investigation by the ARRB staff. Moreover, the ARRB board members failed to request Congress to grant the ARRB the power to investigate clear evidence of criminal activity.

The question naturally arises: Why was the U.S. military, on the evening of November 22, 1963, conducting a fraudulent autopsy on the body of a president who had just been assassinated a few hours before and a fraudulent brain examination in the days following the autopsy?

As we saw in chapter 19, to ensure that the investigation into the assassination would be shut down immediately, it was essential to the assassination plot to have the federal bureaucracy, especially the FBI and the Warren Commission, secretly (but not publicly) know that shots had been fired from the front. Those frontal shots, combined with Oswald's purported shots from the rear, established that a communist conspiracy had killed America's president, which inevitably meant nuclear war. That prospect of nuclear war provided the perfect pretext for moving the federal bureaucracy toward immediately shutting down the investigation and settling for pinning the crime solely on Oswald, who was now dead. With the investigation shut down, no one would ever discover that the assassination was actually a regime-change operation orchestrated and carried out by the national-security establishment.

But there still remained a big problem: how to convince the American people that there weren't actually people firing from Kennedy's front. Don't forget that Parkland Hospital treating physician Dr. Malcolm Perry had already publicly announced at that press conference following the president's death that the shot that hit Kennedy in the throat had the appearance of an entrance wound, and his colleague Dr. Kemp Clark, who was present at the press conference, had not expressed disagreement with him. Don't forget as well that the treating physicians at Parkland stated that Kennedy had a massive exit wound in the back of his head, which implied another frontal shot.

And as I wrote earlier, many bystanders and police officers had rushed toward the grassy knoll and the stockade fence in the president's right front because they heard shots fired from that direction.

That's where the fraudulent autopsy came into play. Its purpose was to convince the American people, through the persuasive power of forensic evidence, that Kennedy had been assassinated by a lone nut, one who did not have confederates assisting him. The official autopsy report, which is sometimes referred to as the "best evidence" in a murder case, would serve to negate the assertions of the Dallas physicians and other witnesses whose statements indicated that the president had been shot from the front.

After all, what better evidence as to the actual condition of the back of President Kennedy's head than official autopsy photographs? Photographs don't lie, do they? And who in the world is ever going to suggest that the U.S. military, one of the most trusted institutions in the country, would falsify official autopsy photographs? Such an accusation would clearly be over the top, at least in 1963 America, when Americans had an overarching trust in the national-security establishment, which, don't forget, was keeping them safe from the communists. The official autopsy photographs would establish that those Dallas doctors and all the other witnesses who saw that massive exit wound in the back of Kennedy's head must have just imagined that wound, given the stresses and strains of the situation. In fact, this strategy worked well with the House Select Committee on Assassinations in the mid-1970s. The HSCA's forensic pathology panel determined that the autopsy photos were the ground truth in the assassination and reluctantly decided that all of the Parkland treating physicians had to be wrong.

It now becomes clear how ingenious it was to alter the Zapruder film rather than simply destroy or lose it. Who in the world would ever believe that the film had been altered, especially given that no one would ever discover that the CIA took possession of the film on the weekend of the assassination? Certainly no one could say that *LIFE* magazine, which purportedly had possession of the film that weekend, could have altered the film, given that it lacked the capability (e.g., a top-of-the-line optical printer and highly skilled personnel to operate it) of performing a highly sophisticated alteration of the film.

A fraudulent Zapruder film would reinforce the fraudulent autopsy photographs that showed the back of Kennedy's head to be intact. Anyone suggesting that the photography was fraudulent would implicitly be suggesting that the Zapruder film was fraudulent as well, in which case he could be mocked, ridiculed, and smeared both as an "alterationist" and a "conspiracy theorist," as Alexandra Zapruder does repeatedly in her book.

It would not have been difficult to secure the cooperation of military pathologists to the fraudulent autopsy scheme. The first step would be to select pathologists who were not board-certified *forensic pathologists,* such as Humes and Boswell. They would be more susceptible to following orders and deferring to authority given that they were embedded in a military culture, one in which people are accustomed to following orders and keeping secrets.

The pathologists would have been included in the World War III cover story. They would have been told that their job was to hide the fact that the president had been shot from the front and to ensure that the autopsy report would conclude that the president had been shot only from the rear. They would have been told that they were protecting the nation from a nuclear war and that "national security" required a false autopsy. They would have been required to vow to never disclose what they had done and to take the secret with them to the grave.

There isn't a military officer alive who would not have followed that directive and taken that oath in the hours immediately following the assassination of the president, especially when told that "national security" depended on it.

It now becomes clear why it was imperative that the military have the job of conducting the autopsy — because of the culture of secrecy and the propensity to obey orders that pervade the military structure.

To conduct a fraudulent autopsy obviously required the cooperation of many people, most of whom were not part of the assassination itself. Secrecy was essential. If people were free to talk about what they had seen or done, it would obviously have increased the chances that the fraud would be uncovered.

Thus, it shouldn't surprise anyone that people who participated in the autopsy were led to believe that this was a highly "classified" operation. Everyone in the military knows what "classified" means. It means you never talk about it, not even after you leave the military. Recall, for example, how Navy First Class Petty Officer Saundra Spencer had kept her story secret for more than three decades, until the ARRB released her in the mid-1990s from her vow of secrecy.

That's not all. Autopsy personnel in the Navy were also required to sign written secrecy oaths in which they promised to never reveal what they had seen or done. These secrecy oaths threatened them with court martial if they even talked about what they had witnessed at the autopsy. The Navy personnel who signed these oaths included Humes and Boswell (the two Navy pathologists); Dr. John Ebersole (the radiologist); Jerrol Custer and Ed Reed (the two Navy x-ray technicians), and Paul O'Connor and James Jenkins (the two Navy corpsmen assisting the pathologists).

It now becomes clear why it was imperative that the Secret Service team at Parkland Hospital in Dallas do whatever was necessary, including threatening the use of deadly force, to get Kennedy's body out of Parkland without letting the Dallas County medical examiner, Dr. Earl Rose, conduct the autopsy on Kennedy's body. There is no way that U.S. officials could have ensured that Rose and the people assisting him would have followed orders to conduct a fraudulent autopsy and keep quiet about it.

But the military's autopsy was always the "Achilles heel" of the assassination. The plotters could always count on silence on the part of the people who were involved in the assassination itself. Murder is not something that murderers freely talk about, especially when the victim is the president of the United States. Thus, it's not surprising that we still do not know, for example, who it was that killed Mafia figures Jimmy Hoffa or Johnny Rosselli, the Mafia member who served as liaison between the Mafia and the CIA during their partnership to assassinate Fidel Castro.

The autopsy is something completely different. Since participants to the fraudulent autopsy didn't have the same incentive to keep their lips sealed, they were more willing to talk once they were released from the vows of secrecy that the military had imposed upon them.

At this point, it would be helpful to recap the events surrounding the fraudulent autopsy that was conducted on President Kennedy's body and fill in some of the gaps that we haven't yet discussed.

The scheme was launched at Parkland Hospital at the moment that President Kennedy was declared dead. That was when a team of Secret Service agents, operating under orders and brandishing guns and screaming profanities, forced their way out of Parkland, in the process prohibiting Dr. Rose from conducting an autopsy, which was required by state law.

That team of Secret Service agents transported the body in an expensive, ornate, extremely heavy casket to Dallas's Love Field, where it was loaded onto Air Force One, the plane that President Lyndon Johnson was now using. Johnson transported the casket to Andrews Air Force Base in Maryland, where he delivered it into the hands of the military.

At some point between Dallas and the Bethesda morgue, the president's body was secretly removed from the heavy bronze Dallas casket and placed in a cheap, lightweight aluminum shipping casket. That most likely happened in the following manner: President Kennedy's body was secretly removed from the Dallas casket shortly after it was taken onboard Air Force One at Love Field, most likely before the swearing-in of President Johnson and *certainly* before takeoff. After Air Force One landed at Andrews Air Force Base a little over two hours later, and after LBJ gave a short speech and then departed for the White House in a military helicopter, President Kennedy's body was then secretly transported by a helicopter in the dark of night to the grounds near Bethesda Naval Hospital.

After the helicopter landed in the darkness at the officer's club parking lot, Kennedy's body was met by federal agents, placed in a zippered body bag and put inside the aluminum shipping casket brought to the scene by the funeral-home hearse that met the helicopter. The shipping casket was then driven the very short distance from the officer's club parking lot to the loading dock of the Bethesda Naval Hospital Morgue, which was located in the back of the facility and out of public view, where it was offloaded and carried into the anteroom outside the morgue by Navy sailors at 6:35 p.m. (Recall Marine Sergeant Roger Boyajian's report mentioned in chapter 2.)

Meanwhile, the Dallas casket was transported from Andrews AFB to the front of Bethesda Naval Hospital in a motorcade, inside a light-gray Navy cardiac ambulance, which did not arrive outside the front of Bethesda until 6:55 p.m. Of course, the public could not — and did not — know that the casket was empty.

After taking an initial series of quick photos that depicted the real wounds and which never made it into the official autopsy collection, Humes conducted pre-autopsy surgery for the purpose of removing all evidence of frontal shots from JFK's body. He did this by expanding the large exit wound in the right rear of Kennedy's cranium to five times its original size (so as to get access to the brain). Bullet fragments were removed, as were bullet tracks, by removing substantial portions of brain tissue in the frontal portion of the cerebral cortex. Humes used first a scalpel, and then a bone saw, to perform a "modified craniotomy" (or skull-cap removal), in the process creating a massive head defect that encompassed the right half of the top of the head, the right side of the head, and the right rear of the head, which included the original exit wound in the back of the head seen in Dallas. As described by Army pathologist Dr. Pierre Finck in his 1965 typewritten notes provided to his superior, General Joseph Blumberg, the defect thus created was "fronto-parietal-occipital." (It should be pointed out here that Finck did not witness the clandestine pre-autopsy surgery on JFK's cranium; he arrived at the Bethesda morgue after the formal 8:15 p.m. start of the autopsy and after the brain had already been removed in front of a large audience. In his report to Blumberg, he was simply describing the defect he had observed.)

There were actually two witnesses to the pre-autopsy surgery — Tom Robinson, one of the morticians for Gawler's Funeral Home, and Navy x-ray technician Ed Reed. The surgery they witnessed had to have taken place during the 6:35 p.m. to 8:00 p.m. time period because it is undisputed that there was no craniotomy performed during the official autopsy.

Humes also surgically expanded the tracheotomy performed by Dr. Perry at Parkland Hospital to at least twice its original width, turning it into an ugly gash that did not look like any tracheotomy that anyone at the morgue had ever seen. It was now much too large and had widely gaping, irregular edges. This was done to get access to the bullet — the frontal shot — that had punctured Kennedy's throat and trachea and had lodged on top of his right lung. Conveniently, this surgery on the tracheotomy site also transformed a neat entrance wound with a small incision in it to what looked like a jagged exit wound in the throat.

As soon as the illicit post-mortem surgery on the deceased president was concluded, the skull x-rays were taken, and then a quick set-up was done for photography purposes. The president's head was placed in a metal head brace that supported the back of his head, a Bethesda towel was placed under his head on the examining table, and many photographs were taken. None of those photos showed the condition of the back of the head; they all showed massive damage to the top and right side of the head, and they all depicted the metal head brace — which significantly, was not used at the formal autopsy which began at 8:15 p.m.

Moreover, the skull x-rays do not depict the condition of JFK's cranium at Parkland. They reflect the condition of Kennedy's skull *after post-mortem surgery* to remove evidence of frontal shots. Likewise, the massive cranial defect that showed such damage to the top and right side of JFK's head was *misrepresented* ever after as "damage done by the assassin's bullet," even though this damage was in no way similar to the localized damage to the back of JFK's head seen at Parkland.

The skull x-rays were probably completed no later than about 7:15 p.m., followed by an initial round of head and upper-body photographs. Meanwhile, the light-gray Navy cardiac ambulance that contained the (empty) Dallas casket — and in which Jacqueline Kennedy and Bobby Kennedy were traveling — had arrived at the front of the facility at 6:55 p.m. Jacqueline and Bobby exited the vehicle and headed to an upstairs floor, where they wait until the autopsy and embalming were completed. After sitting out in front of the Bethesda facility for 12 minutes (after arriving there at about 6:55 p.m.), the ambulance with the empty Dallas casket inside was driven to the morgue loading dock.

At about 7:17 p.m., a four-man team consisting of Secret Service agents Roy Kellerman and William Greer and FBI agents Francis O'Neill and James Sibert moved the empty bronze Dallas casket into the morgue anteroom using a wheeled conveyance called a "church truck." Significantly, the two FBI agents, who did not know the Dallas casket was empty, were not allowed entrance into the morgue examining room and were initially shepherded down the hall to another room and told to wait while the "preparations for the autopsy" were underway. The initial round of photos using the head brace (which conveniently obscured the condition of the back of JFK's head) was probably completed by 7:30 p.m.

After the conclusion of the post-mortem surgery, the taking of the skull x-rays, and the taking of the initial round of "autopsy" photos using the head brace — most likely between 7:30 p.m. and 7:45 p.m. — the president's body was placed back into the Dallas casket, which was then carried out and put back into the light-gray Navy ambulance. The Navy ambulance was then driven back to the front of the facility, where it was reunited with the military honor guard — the "Joint Service Casket Team," which consisted of personnel representing the different branches of the military. That honor guard then carried the Dallas casket into the morgue at 8:00 p.m., as documented in their official after-action report. The autopsy officially began at 8:15 p.m.

It is worth recalling that it was also at 8:00 p.m. that Humes telephoned Finck to invite him to participate in the autopsy. During that telephone call, Humes told Finck that they already had a set of developed x-rays of the president's head. There were no skull x-rays taken in Dallas. The ARRB staff learned from its depositions of the two Navy x-ray technicians that it took about 30 minutes to develop and dry the x-ray films once they got them back up to their lab on the fourth floor of Bethesda Naval Hospital. At the risk of belaboring the obvious, the only way Humes could have already had a set of developed x-rays ready for examination is if the x-rays had already been taken well before the official entry time for the Dallas casket of 8:00 p.m. — that is, during the 6:35 p.m. to 8:00 p.m. time period after the president's body had been sneaked into the morgue.

At this point, it's also worth recalling Saundra Spencer's testimony before the ARRB. She had been asked, on a highly classified basis, to develop what she thought were the official photographs of the Kennedy autopsy on the weekend of the assassination. When the ARRB showed her one of the official autopsy photographs showing the back of Kennedy's head to be intact, she testified that that was not the post-mortem photograph of the back of the head that she developed on the weekend of the assassination. The one she developed, she stated directly and unequivocally, showed a large, two to two-and-one-half-inch "blown out chunk" missing from the back of Kennedy's head, which was consistent with the statements of the Dallas treating physicians and many other witnesses some 36 years earlier.

Even more significant, it became clear during Spencer's ARRB deposition that the photos of President Kennedy that she developed on the weekend of the assassination were not actually taken during the autopsy; based on the appearance of the body, they had to have been taken after the conclusion of Kennedy's embalming and after the reconstruction of his body by the embalmers. This is important because it means that the original damage to the back of Kennedy's head (the exit wound seen at Parkland) was obviously so severe that it could not be covered up even by the embalmers, using their restorative art.

If Spencer's testimony was truthful and accurate — and if the statements of Dr. McClelland, Dr. Crenshaw, and others were correct — then that could mean only one thing: The military's photographs showing the back of Kennedy's head to be intact are false and fraudulent.

21

The Autopsy

(Part 2)

What about the throat wound, the one that Dr. Malcolm Perry at Parkland Hospital had stated had the appearance of an entrance wound?

Here, it is important for me to once again go slowly and deliberately because the events surrounding that wound are complex. At the same time, they go a long way toward revealing the difficulty that the pathologists and the plotters were having in their attempts to explain away the throat wound.

The best synopsis of the events surrounding the neck wound is a video presentation made by Douglas Horne at an online conference entitled "The National Security State and the Kennedy Assassination," held by The Future of Freedom Foundation in the spring of 2021. The entire conference can be accessed in the multimedia section of FFF's website (fff.org). Horne's presentation is entitled "The Evolving JFK Autopsy Report" and is embedded in a presentation entitled "The JFK Medical Coverup Q&A." Just go to 1:15 of that presentation to access Horne's one-hour talk.

The autopsy conducted on President Kennedy's body ended around 11:00 p.m. on Friday night, the day he was shot. At that point, FBI agents O'Neill and Sibert left the morgue and went to the FBI laboratory to deliver two small, minuscule bullet fragments removed from JFK's cranium at the autopsy. They then summarized the autopsy results that Dr. Humes had given them in a telegram that they dictated over the phone early Saturday morning. That telegram transmitted the results of the autopsy from the Baltimore office (which they had telephoned) to FBI headquarters. That's how we know what the official conclusions of the pathologists were at the end of the autopsy. Those same conclusions were also repeated in their official FD-302 report, written on November 26, the day after Kennedy's funeral. Those conclusions, as reported by O'Neill and Sibert, were the following: Kennedy had been hit by two shots from the rear. One shot had hit him in the back of the head, and the other shot had hit him high in the back, near his right shoulder, and did not exit the body on the other side.

What about the neck wound? It wasn't mentioned! Humes later claimed that he didn't know that there was a wound in the front of the neck because, he said, the tracheotomy that the Dallas doctors had performed had obscured it. He later intimated to the Warren Commission that he didn't learn that there was a bullet wound in the throat until he spoke to Dr. Perry the following morning.

We now know that had to be a lie, however, because of testimony that Pierre Finck gave in 1969 at the Clay Shaw trial in New Orleans.

Finck had been called to testify by Shaw's team of attorneys. On cross-examination, the state's attorney asked Finck why they hadn't dissected the neck wound as part of the autopsy. Finck hemmed and hawed and did everything he could to avoid answering the question. The prosecutor, however, would not let him off the hook. Exasperated by Finck's refusal to answer the question directly, the prosecutor finally asked the judge to order Finck to answer the question.

When Finck finally answered the question, it became clear why he was so reluctant to answer it. He told the court that he had been ordered not to dissect the neck wound. Mind you, he didn't deny there was a neck wound. Instead, he said that he was ordered not to dissect it. When asked to identify the person who issued that order, Finck claimed he couldn't remember who that person was.

Finck's answer is powerful evidence that Humes was lying when he denied knowledge of the neck wound during the autopsy.

Furthermore, it's worth pointing out that Dr. Boswell, who conducted the autopsy with Humes, testified to the ARRB that both he and Humes were well aware *during the autopsy* that JFK had a bullet wound in his throat.

Moreover, Finck's answer also provides powerful evidence of the overall assassination plot itself. In an autopsy, the pathologists are ordinarily in charge. Yet, here was a superior force within the Deep State that was clearly controlling the autopsy. Combine that order to Finck with the fact that the president's body was secretly removed from the Dallas casket on Air Force One, transported to the morgue by helicopter, and then surreptitiously carried into the morgue, without the knowledge of the Joint Service Casket Team, before the Andrews AFB motorcade even arrived at Bethesda. Then further consider the fact that someone was manufacturing fraudulent autopsy photographs while the CIA was secretly taking possession of the Zapruder film and secretly shipping it to its photography centers in Washington, D.C., and Rochester, New York.

It all establishes that there was a highly sophisticated Deep-State regime-change operation taking place on November 22, 1963, one that was being managed and controlled by very powerful and very secretive people within the U.S. national-security establishment.

Given that the initial autopsy conclusions failed to mention the bullet wound in the throat, it is obvious what the pathologists planned to say. They were obviously going to say the same thing about the neck wound that they ended up saying about the exit wound in the back of the head — that it never existed and that the Dallas treating physicians had simply imagined it under the stress and strain of the situation.

The plotters, however, might well have concluded that that would be a stretch. It's one thing to say that the highly experienced physicians at Parkland had imagined one major wound. But two major wounds?

Some time between 11:00 p.m. and 11:45 p.m., the autopsy conclusions were changed. These new conclusions were later reported by Army Lt. Richard Lipsey, who attended the autopsy and was still there when the new conclusions were reached. Lipsey told the House Select Committee in the mid-1970s that he was certain he heard the pathologists concluding that Kennedy had now been hit from the rear by three shots: one to the head, one very low in the back of the head/high in the neck that exited the front of the neck, and one to the back, in the area of the right shoulder, which did not exit the body.

It should be noted at this point that on Saturday morning, November 23, Dr. Perry told a nurse that "people at Bethesda" had badgered him all night long, trying to pressure him into stating that the throat wound was an exit wound rather than an entrance wound.

On Saturday morning, Humes completed a first draft of the autopsy report. Presumably, it contained the three-shot scenario described by Lipsey — a scenario that denied that the president had been shot from the front.

However, early on Sunday morning, before dawn, Humes burned that first written draft of the autopsy report after rewriting it and producing a second report. He also burned autopsy notes prepared by him and others (like Dr. Finck) that he used to prepare both reports. He later claimed to the HSCA that the reason he burned the autopsy notes was because they were bloodstained — he didn't want them to become objects of morbid curiosity. Never mind that there was one autopsy record that contained the same types of blood stains — the body chart called the "Autopsy Descriptive Sheet" — that he didn't destroy.

Why the change in the autopsy report? It seems that shortly after the assassination, police officials in Dallas had learned that a bystander in Dealey Plaza named James Tague had been hit by a ricochet of a bullet that struck the curb near him in Dealey Plaza. Since the frame-up of Oswald necessitated the firing of no more than three bullets, Humes was forced to go back to the drawing board. (The Saturday-morning first draft of the autopsy report surely reported the three-hit scenario overheard by Lt. Lipsey, which would not have allowed for a missed shot. Even the Friday-night conclusion Humes gave to the FBI before 11 p.m. — that only two shots hit JFK — was inconsistent with the missed shot reported by James Tague because, as everyone knew, a bullet also hit and severely wounded Gov. John Connally.)

On Sunday, November 24, Humes, Boswell, and Finck signed Humes's second written autopsy report after it had been typed by a secretary at Bethesda. He had finished composing the handwritten draft of this report late Saturday evening at home — before he burned the first draft in his fireplace early Sunday morning. An official autopsy report had now been signed by all three pathologists. It concluded that Kennedy had been hit by two bullets — one in the head and the other in the back of his right shoulder.

What about the neck wound? The November 24 autopsy report stated that a fragment from the "head-shot" bullet had exited through the front of Kennedy's throat, causing the throat wound.

That November 24 autopsy report later ended (in 1965) in the possession of Robert Kennedy and was never seen again. Presumably, Kennedy destroyed it. (It was not returned to the government by RFK in 1966, as the autopsy photographs and x-rays were.) According to Horne's video presentation mentioned above, we know what was in that particular autopsy report because of "official" government leaks to the press detailing the contents of the report.

For example, the December 18, 1963, issues of the *Washington Post* and the *Philadelphia Inquirer* stated that the autopsy report had concluded that "a fragment was deflected and passed out the front of the throat." In its December 27, 1963, issue, *Time* magazine (which was owned by the same company that owned *LIFE* magazine) stated that "the throat wound had been made by a fragment of the last bullet, which literally exploded in Kennedy's head."

It's worth noting that both newspapers clearly stated that the official autopsy report had still not been released to the public even though more than a month had lapsed since the assassination. They both cited unnamed official government sources who were familiar with the autopsy.

Moreover, recall that Finck testified several years later (in 1969) in the Clay Shaw trial in New Orleans, where he testified that the autopsy report described a severance of JFK's brain from the spinal cord. Actually, the official autopsy report in the record today *reflects no such thing,* which would indicate that Finck was referring to the November 24 autopsy report that ended up in 1965 in the custody of Bobby Kennedy.

In any event, the plotters obviously figured out that the conclusion expressed in the November 24 autopsy report was quite unsound, especially given that the head shot(s) and head explosion had come well after the throat shot, something that witnesses in Dealey Plaza, as well as the Zapruder film itself, could easily establish. At the risk of belaboring the obvious, if the neck wound came first, then a fragment from the head wound could not have caused the neck wound.

It was around this time that someone obviously concluded that the neck wound could be explained by claiming that Kennedy had turned around and faced the School Book Depository when he was struck in the throat by a bullet being fired by Oswald. Recall that is what *LIFE* magazine columnist Paul Mandel had written in his article in the December 6 issue of *LIFE,* which we discussed back in chapter 1.

Let's briefly return to Mandel's article. As we discussed, there is no reasonable possibility that Mandel would have simply made up his story about what the Zapruder film showed. He knew that *LIFE* magazine had the film and, therefore, that *LIFE* executives would immediately know that he was lying about its contents, in which case his career would have been over.

Therefore, it is a virtual certainty that it was *LIFE* publisher and CIA loyalist C. D. Jackson who instructed Mandel to write the article, falsely assuring him (or letting a CIA official falsely assure him) that the film showed Kennedy turning around and facing the School Book Depository when he was struck by a bullet in his throat. Mandel would not have had any reason to doubt his boss's veracity or the veracity of a CIA official.

But there is also no reasonable possibility that Jackson himself would have concocted this false story on his own. What reason would there have been for him to have done so?

Therefore, it is a virtual certainty that the notion originated within the CIA, which then turned to Jackson to enlist his help with a false story about what the Zapruder film contained. After all, since Jackson was going to prevent the American people from ever seeing the film, there was little risk that anyone would ever discover the truth.

Here is an interesting tidbit. In volume 1 of the Presidential Recordings of Lyndon Johnson, the following recorded telephone call took place on Tuesday, November 26, between President Johnson and Henry Luce, founder of *LIFE* magazine. That was the day after Jackson purchased the Zapruder film for the equivalent (in today's dollars) of $1.3 million and vowed to prevent people from ever seeing it — and three days after the film had been secretly diverted to the CIA's photography centers in Washington, D.C., and Rochester:

"5:15 p.m.

To Henry Luce

President Johnson: ... everybody in this job, and I just wanted to say hello to you, and thank you for all the good things you've done for me and tell you I never needed you as much — *Recording of conversation ends abruptly.*" (Bold, italics, and ellipses in original.)

Why did LBJ abruptly stop recording that conversation with Luce? What did he say after he abruptly stopped recording? Why would he not want people to hear the rest of that conversation?

Returning to the false scenario that Mandel expressed in his article, it must have occurred to someone at the CIA that it was also not a good scenario on which to rely, even given C. D. Jackson's determination to prevent people from ever seeing the Zapruder film. After all, there was always the possibility that someone might subpoena the film as part of some legal proceeding, in which case it would easily be discovered that Mandel had lied. In fact, in early December 1963, the Warren Commission requested to see a copy of the film, which might have been what motivated the CIA to drop the false scenario that Mandel had expressed in his December 6 article.

Finally, we have the official autopsy report that is in the record today. It is undated. It is the third written version of the autopsy report. We know that it was shown to the Parkland treating physicians, but not until December 11, 1963. It describes a two-hit scenario in which both bullets have hit the president from the rear: one bullet supposedly hitting him in the head and the other bullet supposedly hitting him in the upper back and then transiting through his neck and exiting the front of his throat. Later, Gerald Ford, who was a member of the Warren Commission, moved the location of the back wound upward by changing its description in the Warren Report to the back of the neck, in effect performing "verbal plastic surgery," so that the "magic-bullet" theory that Warren Commission attorney Arlen Specter had developed would work.

The magic-bullet theory held that a bullet hit Kennedy in the back of his neck, exited his throat, entered Gov. John Connally from the back just below the armpit, broke one of Connally's ribs, exited from Connally's chest, entered and broke Connally's wrist bone, exited his wrist, and lodged itself in Connally's thigh. After doing all this damage, it supposedly came out in a pristine, never-been-shot condition, with no visible damage at all, and especially no "mushrooming" to the tip of the bullet — which is one reason it is called the "magic bullet."

I fully realize how complex this evolving theory of the neck wound is. But simply ask yourself the following two questions: Does this seem like an ordinary and honest autopsy to you? Do you think that all those shenanigans would have occurred if Dr. Rose, the Dallas County medical examiner, had conducted the autopsy?

A small aside relating to Kennedy's head wound: During the House Select Committee on Assassinations reinvestigation of the Kennedy assassination in the 1970s, the forensic pathology panel did everything it could to pressure the three Kennedy autopsy pathologists into moving the location of a small entry wound that all three of them had specified was low in the back of Kennedy's head. The panel wanted Humes, Boswell, and Finck to agree to move the wound about four inches higher, toward the top of Kennedy's head. The reason? The new location would be more consistent with the official version of the assassination. Keep in mind that unlike Humes, Boswell, and Finck, no member of that panel was at the autopsy and, therefore, did not witness any of the president's wounds. The episode brings to mind Sir Walter Scott's famous saying, "Oh, what a tangled web we weave when first we practice to deceive."

It is also worth mentioning the matter of the head x-rays. Two physicians, Dr. David Mantik and Dr. Michael Chesser, were granted permission to study the purportedly original x-rays of President

Kennedy's skull taken at his autopsy. After multiple, repeated visits to the National Archives, including with an instrument called an optical densitometer, both of them concluded that the x-rays were fraudulent — namely, altered copy films of JFK's skull that had been light-blasted in a darkroom to cover up the massive defect and missing brain tissue in the back of Kennedy's skull. I would invite you to view videos of their respective presentations at The Future of Freedom Foundation's conference "The National Security State and the JFK Assassination," which is found in the multimedia section of FFF's website. Also, I would refer you to Mantik's website at https://themantikview.com.

There is another interesting and revealing aspect to this highly unusual saga. At no time during the autopsy did anyone express any concern whatsoever about having to testify to these events in a later criminal prosecution in Dallas of any suspected assassin. It clearly was not a concern for any of the pathologists or the people who were controlling the autopsy, which, it should be noted, took place on Friday night, when Oswald was still alive.

There can be only one reason for this phenomenon: The people who were controlling the autopsy had to have known that there was never any possibility of such a trial. Even though Lee Harvey Oswald was still alive on Friday (and Saturday), the fact is that he was a dead man walking. His remaining days were clearly numbered. Once he was killed, it would be possible to keep all the autopsy shenanigans secret from the American people.

What does Alexandra Zapruder say about all these autopsy shenanigans in her book *Twenty-Six Seconds*? By now you know the answer. She says nothing — absolutely nothing — about them. She simply could not bring herself to acknowledge and confront the fact that the dark, evil force that took the life of President Kennedy was the same dark, evil force responsible for the fraudulent autopsy on the president's body, the force that also enveloped and destroyed her grandfather and led to the family taboo against discussing the Zapruder film.

Ever since the Kennedy assassination, there have been some defenders of the lone-nut theory of the assassination who have maintained that the military pathologists who conducted the autopsy on the president's body were simply incompetent and just made mistakes. I have no doubts that if Alexandra Zapruder had addressed the medical evidence in the Kennedy autopsy in her book, that is what she would have said, just as she wrote that the points made in Paul Mandel's *LIFE* magazine article were "mistakes" rather than lies.

Thus, it becomes important to distinguish incompetence from fraud. Incompetence implies negligence or perhaps even gross negligence. Fraud involves a knowing and deliberate intent to deceive. I submit that the two separate brain examinations in the Kennedy autopsy that were falsely conflated into one brain examination constitute fraud, not incompetence. I submit that official autopsy photographs that falsely depict the condition of the back of JFK's head constitute fraud, not incompetence. I submit that secretly sneaking Kennedy's body into the Bethesda morgue almost one-and-a-half hours before the official entry time of 8 p.m. constitutes fraud, not incompetence. I submit that the secret pre-autopsy surgery that was performed on JFK's body constitutes fraud, not incompetence. I submit that the altered films misrepresented as original x-rays of the president's skull constitute fraud, not incompetence. I submit that the great weight and preponderance of the evidence establishes behind a reasonable doubt that the U.S. national-security establishment performed a fraudulent, not an incompetent, autopsy on President Kennedy's body. As I stated earlier in this book, there is no innocent explanation for a fraudulent autopsy: It necessarily incriminates the U.S. national-security establishment in the assassination of President John F. Kennedy.

22

Epilogue

(Part 1)

When I first began reading Alexandra Zapruder's book *Twenty-Six Seconds,* I couldn't help but admire her for the courage she was displaying in embarking on an exploration of the family taboo against discussing her grandfather's film. Going down that road would likely mean discovering and confronting a dark secret behind the taboo, and that's not an easy thing to do.

As I finished reading her book, however, I couldn't help but feel sorry for her. In the final analysis, she just could not bring herself to acknowledge and confront the dark evil force that assassinated President Kennedy, enveloped and destroyed her grandfather, and ultimately led to the decades-long family taboo against discussing her grandfather's 26-second film of the assassination. Instead, she subconsciously ended up settling for simplistically false explanations for what had happened to her grandfather and her family.

Let's recap what occurred in the assassination of President John F. Kennedy as well as the destruction of Dallas businessman Abraham Zapruder.

John Kennedy came into the presidency under a mark of suspicion by the U.S. national-security establishment. Although he was pretty much a standard Cold Warrior, he sympathized with third-world independence movements, which the Pentagon and the CIA, who considered themselves the experts on foreign affairs, were convinced were communist-inspired and communist-directed.

During the CIA-sponsored paramilitary invasion at Cuba's Bay of Pigs, Kennedy refused to provide U.S. Navy air support for the invaders or to land U.S. Marines to save the beachhead, which allowed the Cuban exile invasion force to be killed or captured by Castro's communist forces.

In Kennedy's mind, he was standing firm on his public promises, made prior to the exile invasion, that no U.S. military forces would be used to invade Cuba. In the eyes of the Pentagon and the CIA, however, Kennedy's decision was an act of cowardice and treason.

The CIA had told Kennedy that no American air support would be needed because, the CIA claimed, there would be a spontaneous Cuban uprising, triggered by the exile invasion. It was a lie. The CIA figured that once the battle got going, Kennedy would have to provide the needed air support to prevent the invaders from being killed or taken captive. He would then almost certainly have to follow up with U.S. ground forces to bail out the invasion and topple Castro.

Kennedy knew he had been played and was livid. He fired the highly revered director of the CIA, Allen Dulles, and he is reputed to have vowed to "splinter the CIA into a thousand pieces and scatter it to the winds." Even though some have doubted whether he actually said that (the quote was attributed to him by the *New York Times*), there is no question but that the quote expressed Kennedy's mindset toward the CIA.

For its part, the CIA was just as livid. As far as it was concerned, in the fight against the communists, Kennedy was guilty of weakness, cowardice, and even treason. Not only had he betrayed those brave Cuban exiles by letting them get killed or captured by Castro's communist forces, he also had left Cuba in communist hands, which, the CIA was convinced, posed a grave threat to U.S. national security.

The war between JFK and his national-security establishment was on. The war would continue until November 22, 1963.

After the fiasco at the Bay of Pigs, the Pentagon exhorted Kennedy to invade Cuba. On March 13, 1962, the Joint Chiefs of Staff unanimously recommended that the Secretary of Defense approve a plan called Operation Northwoods. The Northwoods plan provided *pretexts for war* that were designed to justify an American military invasion of Cuba to the American people and the world. The plan called for fake Cuban attacks on the U.S. base at Guantanamo (using friendly Cuban exiles in communist uniforms); intentionally sinking a U.S. ship in Guantanamo Bay and blaming it on Castro; launching real terrorist attacks in Miami, Florida, and Washington, D.C., which would have involved the actual wounding and killing of people and blaming it all on Castro agents; and blowing up an empty drone passenger airliner over Cuba, claiming that Castro had shot it down.

Secretary of Defense Robert McNamara never formally responded to the Northwoods plan. When Joint Chiefs Chairman Lyman Lemnitzer tried to resurrect it at a meeting on March 16, 1962, Kennedy abruptly rejected the idea of using pretexts for war or of invading Cuba with U.S. forces. Soon thereafter, on April 10, 1962, the Joint Chiefs of Staff sent a blistering memo to the Secretary of Defense recommending that the United States invade Cuba anyway, without basing the invasion on pretexts.

The Pentagon also pressured Kennedy throughout early 1961 to send U.S. troops into Laos to prevent a communist victory in that country's civil war. Kennedy instead agreed to a coalition government that included communists.

Kennedy did succumb to Pentagon pressure to send troops into South Vietnam to oppose a communist takeover of that country. However, believing that South Vietnam had to fight its own war, Kennedy decided on November 22, 1961, to greatly increase the number of U.S. military *advisors* in South Vietnam — but *not* to send combat troops, a decision from which he never wavered.

When the U.S. national-security establishment discovered in October of 1962 that the Soviet Union was installing medium-range and intermediate-range ballistic missiles with nuclear warheads in Cuba, it is not difficult to imagine its reaction. If Kennedy had provided the air support at the Bay of Pigs in April of 1961 and then bailed out the exile invasion with U.S. Marines or the U.S. Army — or if he had invaded Cuba afterwards in the spring of 1962, as the Pentagon had pressured him to do — Fidel Castro's regime would have been overthrown and the Cuban Missile Crisis would never have occurred.

Instead of bombing and invading Cuba with overwhelming U.S. military force to resolve the Cuban Missile Crisis, Kennedy imposed a blockade to prevent Soviet ships carrying offensive weapons from reaching the island. During an October 19, 1962, meeting between the Joint Chiefs and Kennedy to discuss the crisis, one member of the Joint Chiefs of Staff — USAF Chief General Curtis LeMay — brazenly compared Kennedy's "weak" action to British Prime Minister Neville Chamberlain's actions in 1938, when he gave away part of Czechoslovakia to appease Hitler.

It was Kennedy's peaceful resolution of the Cuban Missile Crisis that set the stage for his assassination. Under the deal that he made with Soviet Premier Nikita Khrushchev, Kennedy promised that the United States would not invade Cuba if the USSR removed all of its nuclear missiles and promised not to reintroduce offensive weapons in Cuba. In return for Kennedy's promise, Khrushchev did remove his nuclear missiles from Cuba and kept his promise not to reintroduce them. Kennedy also secretly agreed to remove U.S. nuclear missiles from Turkey. The missiles were removed from Turkey several months later.

In that one agreement, Kennedy had essentially guaranteed the permanency of the communist regime in Cuba, which the U.S.

national-security establishment was 100 percent convinced posed a grave threat to U.S. national security. LeMay called Kennedy's resolution of the Cuban Missile Crisis "the biggest defeat in our nation's history."

In the aftermath of the Cuban Missile Crisis, Kennedy achieved a "breakthrough." He came to the realization that the Cold War was nothing but a deadly and destructive racket, one that was threatening mankind with nuclear annihilation.

With his famous Peace Speech at American University that he delivered on June 10, 1963, Kennedy threw down the gauntlet. From that day forward, America would peacefully coexist with the Soviet Union and the rest of the communist world, including Cuba.

In the eyes of the U.S. national-security establishment, that was an unacceptable scenario. As far as the Pentagon, the CIA, the NSA, and the hawks in the State Department were concerned, the West could never live in peace and harmony with the communist world. In their eyes, this was a war to the finish.

The very next night, June 11, 1963, Kennedy went on national television and defended the U.S. civil-rights movement, which the national-security establishment was convinced was a communist front. The mission of the civil-rights movement, according to the Pentagon, the CIA, and the FBI, was to foment racial conflict and strife in order to pave the way for a communist takeover of the United States.

Later that summer, Kennedy successfully concluded the ongoing negotiations for a limited nuclear test-ban treaty with the Soviets, which banned nuclear tests underwater, on the ground, and in the air — tests that the Pentagon believed were necessary for national security. (Both sides were still permitted to conduct underground tests.)

In October of 1963, in a top-secret document called NSAM 263, Kennedy ordered the withdrawal of 1,000 troops from South Vietnam by the end of the year, as well as the complete withdrawal of American advisory forces by the end of 1965. Dramatic headlines reporting this decision were even published in the armed forces' own newspaper, *Stars and Stripes*. JFK reaffirmed to close aides and political allies that he would indeed pull out the remaining troops after he won the 1964 presidential election. He said that he could not do it for political reasons before the election because it would open him up to attacks by his likely GOP opponent, Barry Goldwater, of being "soft on communism." In the eyes of the Pentagon and the CIA, Kennedy's decision to end the U.S. advisory effort and withdraw from Vietnam meant that the dominoes in Southeast Asia would begin falling to the communists.

Kennedy fully understood the dangers he faced in trying to move America in a totally different direction from that of the national-security establishment. For one thing, he had listened to President Eisenhower's Farewell Address in 1961, in which Ike warned Americans about the grave danger to the liberties and democratic processes posed by the military-industrial complex.

Moreover, to deliver a similar warning, Kennedy had prevailed on friends in Hollywood to produce a film based on the novel *Seven Days in May,* which posited a military takeover of the federal government.

After Kennedy's Peace Speech at American University, it was clear that there was no way to peacefully resolve his war with the national-security establishment. After all, if Kennedy's vision prevailed, there was a good chance that the American people in the 1960s would have demanded the restoration of their founding governmental system of a limited-government republic. That necessarily would have meant the dismantling of the national-security state, the governmental system that was adopted to fight the Cold War.

Scoffing at the notion that the November 22 assassination was a regime-change operation, the mainstream media has never addressed an important question: What happens if a president really does pose a threat to national security? What is the national-security establishment supposed to do? Is it supposed to just sit idly by and let the president take the country down?

In 1963, the Constitution set forth only two ways to remove a president — through impeachment or through the next election. It does not provide for the removal of the president by the national-security establishment.

But the view of the Pentagon and the CIA was that the Constitution is not a "suicide pact." In other words, if the only way to save the nation is by violating the Constitution, the national-security establishment would not hesitate to violate the Constitution.

How do we know that was (and is) the mindset of the national-security establishment? We know it through the U.S. regime-change operations that took place in 1954 in Guatemala and then later in the early 1970s in Chile. The U.S. national-security establishment advised their national-security counterparts in both countries that they had a moral duty to remove their democratically elected presidents from office on the grounds that they posed a grave threat to their country's national security, notwithstanding the fact that such action would be illegal under the countries's own laws.

For decades, the mainstream media has mocked and ridiculed the notion that the U.S. national-security establishment would orchestrate and carry out Kennedy's assassination. In the process, they have failed to note an important fact: What President Kennedy was doing in reaching out to the Russians, Cubans, and the rest of the communist world in a spirit of peace and friendship was no different from what President Arbenz was doing in Guatemala and what President Allende would do in Chile, which is why they were targeted for regime change.

If those two democratically elected presidents posed such a grave threat to the United States (as well as to their own countries), then why wouldn't a U.S. president pose an even greater threat given that he would be undermining national security from within the federal government?

Moreover, if a poll were undertaken today asking the mainstream media whether they would want the national-security establishment to take out a president that really was posing a threat to national-security, my hunch is that the overwhelming majority would say yes, especially if the state-sponsored role in the assassination was kept secret.

When the federal government was converted into a national-security state after World War II to oppose the supposed international communist conspiracy, a deal was implicitly entered into between the American people and the national-security establishment. Under this implicit agreement, the national-security establishment would exercise dark-side powers, including assassination, against anyone who posed a threat to national security. At the same time, however, the deal implicitly entailed keeping what it was doing secret from the American people, so that their consciences would not be troubled. It was a bargain with the devil.

It would be difficult to find a better example of an evil form of governmental structure than a national-security state. To put things into context, North Korea is a national-security state. So are China, Russia, Cuba, Pakistan, Egypt, and Myanmar.

A national-security state wields and exercise omnipotent powers, including assassination, torture, kidnapping, indefinite detention, denial of due process, denial of trial by jury, and suppression of free speech. It also engages in coups, invasions, bombings, wars of aggression, and other regime-change operations.

That's not all. The U.S. national-security establishment has also undertaken secret drug experiments on unsuspecting Americans. That's what MKULTRA was all about. When that operation came to light, the CIA knowingly and intentionally destroyed its MKULTRA records to ensure that the American people would never learn the full extent of the operation.

There was also the CIA's secret hiring of former Nazi officials, knowing full well what the Nazi regime had done during the Holocaust.

It was all justified by the U.S. anti-communist crusade. And it was all evil. But the problem was that it wasn't recognized as evil by all too many Americans because the crusade had stultified the consciences of the American people.

Where was the moral outrage among the American people when the assassination of Congo leader Patrice Lumumba and the assassination attempts against Cuban leader Fidel Castro came to light? The moral outrage was essentially non-existent.

The CIA had persuaded President Eisenhower that as a third-world leader, Lumumba was aligning himself with communism. Consequently, according to Prof. John Newman in his book *Countdown to Darkness,* Eisenhower authorized Lumumba's assassination. Even if it was true, however, that Lumumba was leaning toward communism, so what? Why didn't Lumumba or anyone else have the right to orient toward any philosophy and any nation they wanted, including communism, the Soviet Union, Cuba, and Red China?

Declassified high-level NSC meeting minutes have revealed that President Eisenhower, who bought into the CIA's reasoning about the communist threat, also authorized Castro's assassination. For decades, the U.S. mainstream press has nonchalantly and even jokingly treated the CIA's assassination attempts against Cuban President Fidel Castro as no big deal or even as a necessary action to protect America's national security. In actuality, those assassination attempts were nothing more than attempts to commit murder.

The CIA claimed that it had the moral authority to assassinate Castro because he was a communist. For decades, all too many Americans have gone along with that justification. But since when does anyone have the right to kill another person because of his particular political or economic ideology? If the CIA wields the moral authority to kill people with communist beliefs, then does that mean that American citizens have the authority to do the same thing to people who hold communist or socialist beliefs?

In 1953, the CIA destroyed Iran's experiment with democracy by initiating a coup that ousted the country's democratically elected prime minister, Mohammad Mossadegh, from power and replaced him with one of the cruelest and most brutal dictators in the world, the Shah of Iran. Adding insult to injury, the CIA then helped to organize, train, and maintain the Shah's SAVAK, one of the most tyrannical agencies in the world.

In 1954, the national-security establishment orchestrated the ouster of the democratically elected president of Guatemala, Jacobo Arbenz. As part of that operation, the CIA even drew up a list of people to be assassinated. The CIA will still not let us see that kill list on grounds of national security, but there can be no doubt that Arbenz was at the top. That regime-change operation led to a 30-year civil war in Guatemala that ended up killing more than a million people.

In late 1960 through 1963, the CIA entered into an assassination partnership with the Mafia, the world's most evil criminal organization. The purpose of that assassination partnership was to eliminate Cuban President Fidel Castro. Moreover, U.S. officials implemented a brutal economic embargo targeting the Cuban populace with death and impoverishment, with the aim of inducing the Cuban people to oust their communist regime from power and replace it with a pro-U.S. regime. That embargo is still in existence today and harshly enforced.

In 1950s and 1960s, the CIA launched regime-change operations in Indonesia, which led to the brutal murder, torture, or imprisonment of hundreds of thousands or possibly even millions of innocent people.

From 1970 to 1973, the CIA initiated a regime-change operation in Chile whose aim was to oust the country's democratically elected president, Salvador Allende, from office. Allende's "crime?" He was a socialist who was befriending the Soviet Union and Cuba. Once Allende was violently removed from power, his replacement, Gen. Augusto Pinochet, proceeded to round up some 60,000 innocent people. Pinochet's goons then tortured or raped most of them and killed or disappeared some 3,000 of them, including, with the approval of the U.S. national-security establishment, two young American men named Charles Horman and Frank Teruggi. The Horman saga was memorialized in a move called *Missing,* which starred Jack Lemmon and Sissy Spacek. Pinochet's tyrannical reign of anti-communist terror, which lasted 17 years, was fully supported by the Pentagon and the CIA, both of whom thought it great that Pinochet and his goons were bringing death and destruction to "communists."

In the process of the Chilean regime-change operation, the CIA orchestrated the violent kidnapping and murder of Gen. Rene Schneider, the overall commanding general of Chile's armed forces. His crime was that he opposed the U.S. plans for a coup in his country. He held that the Chilean constitution, which he swore to uphold, did not provide for a coup as a way to remove a president from office. His widow and four children were left mourning the loss of this innocent man.

There was also the CIA's participation during the 1970s in the top-secret international kidnapping, torture, and assassination program known as Operation Condor that was run by brutal right-wing dictators in South America.

The worst mistake the American people ever made was to permit U.S. officials to convert the federal government from a limited-government republic to a national-security state. Not only is this form of governmental structure the epitome of evil, it also has had a highly deleterious effect on the consciences of the American people.

That's not to say, of course, that everyone who works for the national-security establishment is evil. We know that is clearly not the case when we consider people like Saundra Spencer, Dino Brugioni, Homer McMahon, Ben Hunter, and most members of America's armed forces. But it is appropriate to say that all of them are working for or serving an evil institution — the national-security establishment — an institution that engages in highly evil acts and, in the process, convinces good people to participate unwittingly in its evil.

As we have seen in this book, evil sometimes manipulates good people into making choices that come with horrific consequences, sometimes destroying such people or significantly altering their lives for the worse. It would be difficult to find a better example of this phenomenon than Abraham Zapruder.

There is something else that should be noted about the evil of the national-security state. The people who knowingly participated in all of its evil actions, including the Kennedy assassination, never considered themselves to be evil or felt that they were committing evil acts. On the contrary, all of them considered themselves patriots who were doing what they believed was necessary to protect national security and the American people from the Reds. What could be more evil than an institution that causes people who are engaged in evil to believe that they are actually doing something good and patriotic?

In a 1983 interview on New Jersey PBS, psychiatrist M. Scott Peck stated, "Actually, when you go into a jail, you can give psychiatric diagnoses to just about everybody in the jail. And rather seldom are these people people who I would call evil. What people in jail say is that the real bad guys are not in here, they're out there. And while there is a certain sort of self-justificatory quality to this, there is also a certain correctness. The people I'm calling people of the lie are into looking good. And they place a high premium on that. And they're into disguising their own evil from themselves as well as from others. And so they place a high premium on respectability. And their crimes are often much more subtle than those that get people in jail."

23

Epilogue

(Part 2)

Let us continue with our recap of the assassination of President Kennedy and the destruction of Abraham Zapruder.

The regime-change operation against Kennedy involved a classic military ambush in Dealey Plaza in Dallas, Texas. The big problem that the national-security establishment faced was that an assassination of a U.S. president was certain to bring an all-out, fierce investigation that would likely disclose that the assassination had been orchestrated and carried by the CIA and the Pentagon.

Their solution was both brilliant and ingenious.

The brilliant aspect of the plot was to frame a communist. This was the height of the Cold War. Everyone hated and feared communists. Framing a communist for assassinating Kennedy would ensure that hardly anyone would come to his defense. If people did come to his defense, they could be immediately smeared and destroyed as communist sympathizers.

Since it was virtually impossible to frame a real communist, the plotters did the next-best thing. They framed one of their own government agents, Lee Harvey Oswald, who had been trained to act like a communist.

After all, how many communist U.S. Marines have you have ever known? Communists hate Marines, and Marines hate communists. Would the Marines really have permitted a self-avowed communist to remain in their midst at the height of the Cold War, especially given that he could have been reporting radar secrets and troop movements to the Soviet Union? Would the Marine Corps really have stationed a self-proclaimed communist Marine at Naval Air Station Atsugi, from which the CIA's top-secret U-2 spy plane was taking off to conduct illegal surveillance flights over Red China? Moreover, how could Oswald have learned to be fluent in the Russian language without receiving specialized assistance from the military's language experts?

When he arrived in the Soviet Union, Oswald defected to America's avowed Cold War enemy, asking for and receiving permission to live and work there. He also vowed to disclose to the Soviets any radar secrets he had learned while serving as a Marine radar operator.

Yet, on his return from the Soviet Union, U.S. officials didn't do anything to him. They didn't take him into custody and torture him. They didn't indict him. They didn't subpoena him to testify before Congress. Officially, based on what the military said shortly after the assassination of JFK, they didn't even interrogate him.

That's not the way that U.S. officials treat "traitors."

As soon as Oswald was arrested after Kennedy was assassinated, the DRE, a self-proclaimed pro-Cuba group in New Orleans, put out a press release announcing Oswald's communist *bona fides*. What no one knew at the time and would not know for another 30 years was that the DRE was in effect a CIA front organization, one that was being generously funded by the CIA and closely controlled and monitored by a CIA agent named George Joannides.

But here is the ingenious part of the plot, the one that succeeded in getting the investigations into the assassination immediately shut down: Oswald was not presented as simply a stand-alone communist, one who just happened to be at the right place at the right time.

Instead, he was presented as a communist with connections to the Soviet Union and Cuba.

That's what the purpose of Oswald's Mexico City trip was all about — to make certain that Oswald connected with Soviet and Cuban officials in their embassies. It was those connections that enabled the plotters to short-circuit the official investigations into the assassination.

We know from eyewitnesses and the forensic evidence that the president was shot from the front in his throat and in his head. The frontal shots were confirmed by the small bullet-sized entry wound in the throat, as Dr. Perry emphasized three times at the press conference that was held immediately after the president had been declared dead, and by the large exit-sized wound in the back of Kennedy's head. The frontal shots were also confirmed by the large number of people who rushed toward the grassy knoll immediately after the shots were fired.

Proof of shots having been fired from the front were essential to the plot. After all, if you're going to frame a person who is supposedly firing from the rear, it ordinarily would not be a good idea to have shots being fired from the front. The frontal shots, therefore, established that Oswald did not act alone. More important, his confederates firing from the front had to be Soviet and Cuban agents given Oswald's recent visits to the Soviet and Cuban embassies in Mexico City, especially since he was said to have met with a KGB officer who worked in the Soviet Union's assassination department.

Yes, the communists had killed America's admired and beloved president as part of their international communist conspiracy to take over the world.

That necessarily meant retaliation, which, in turn, necessarily meant all-out nuclear war, which the United States and the Soviet Union had narrowly avoided just a year before.

In 1963, nothing scared the American people more than the prospect of nuclear war. People were building bomb shelters under and adjacent to their homes. Elementary schools throughout the 1950s were conducting "duck and cover" drills with their students in the event of nuclear war.

The plotters used this deep fear to their advantage. That was the sheer ingenuity of their frontal-shot strategy.

The only way to avert nuclear war was not to retaliate and instead to simply settle for pinning the assassination on Oswald, who was killed only two days after the assassination. Of course, that meant that he could never testify as to who he really was — a government agent who was being framed for a crime he didn't commit, which would explain Oswald's otherwise cryptic statement after his arrest, "Now everyone will know who I am."

The federal bureaucracy and the Warren Commission were pushed into the direction of avoiding nuclear war and pinning the crime on Oswald. That was reflected by the memos that FBI Director Hoover and Deputy Attorney General Katzenbach sent out on the Sunday and Monday after the assassination emphasizing the importance of convincing the American people that Oswald was a lone assassin.

When Earl Warren and Sen. Richard Russell balked at serving on the official body to investigate the president's assassination, President Johnson recited the World War III cover story to them, telling them that they had a moral duty to help prevent nuclear war.

What would Johnson have said if anyone within the federal bureaucracy had asked why the United States shouldn't respond to the communist assassination of America's president? He had the perfect response. He would have said something like, "Those two Kennedy boys were trying to assassinate Castro with their Murder, Inc. in the Caribbean. They were the ones who started this assassination game. Castro and the Soviets just beat them at their own game. I'll be damned before I send this nation into nuclear war over an assassination game started by Jack and Bobby Kennedy."

Having induced the federal bureaucracy to avert nuclear war by pinning the crime solely on Oswald, the plotters still had to convince the American people that Kennedy's assassination had been committed by a "lone-nut" communist, one who was not acting in concert with the supposed international communist conspiracy. That's where the fraudulent autopsy came into play. The task assigned to the military pathologists, who were clearly operating under the control of some malevolent Deep-State force, was to hide any evidence of shots having been fired from the front and to report only shots fired from the rear.

That's why it was imperative to prevent an honest autopsy from being conducted by Dallas County Medical Examiner Dr. Earl Rose, as required by Texas state law. Instead, a team of Secret Service agents, headed by agent Roy Kellerman, forced their way out of Parkland Hospital with Kennedy's body after brandishing guns, initiating force, and issuing a stream of loud profanities warning hospital personnel to stay out of their way.

Operating under orders, Kellerman's team transported the body to Love Field in Dallas, where President Lyndon Johnson was waiting for it. Johnson's responsibility was to transport the body to Maryland and deliver it into the hands of the military.

Why the military? After all, America has always prided itself on being a civilian-run nation, not a military-run nation. Why not employ a team of top-ranked civilian forensic pathologists in Washington, D.C., to conduct the autopsy?

The answer is threefold: One, military pathologists could be counted on to follow orders, especially when national security was at stake; two, the autopsy could be shrouded in military secrecy; and three, matters relating to the autopsy would fall under the criminal jurisdiction of military officials, not civilian law-enforcement officials.

Statements by Marine Sergeant Roger Boyajian, Navy personnel Dennis David and Donald Rebentisch, Gawler's Funeral Home, and Dr. Pierre Finck, establish that the president's body was sneaked into the Bethesda morgue at 6:35 p.m. on the evening of the assassination. That was almost one-and-a-half hours before the official entry time of 8 p.m. The purpose of the secret early introduction of the body into the morgue was to hurriedly and brutally alter the body in such a way that there would be no evidence of shots having been fired from the front during the official autopsy, which began at 8:15 p.m.

To hide the fact that the president had that massive exit-sized wound in the right rear of his head that Dr. Robert McClelland, Dr. Kemp Clark, and numerous other treating physicians and nurses at Parkland had witnessed, the military altered the autopsy photographs showing the back of the president's head so that it looked intact in those images, totally contrary to what was seen in Dallas and even by some witnesses at the Bethesda morgue. The military pathologists then engaged in a cover-up during the weeks following Kennedy's death to hide the fact that Kennedy had also been hit in the throat by a frontal shot.

We saw how the pathologists lied when they stated that there had been only one brain exam following the autopsy on JFK's body. The ARRB staff established that there had actually been two brain exams, the second of which could not possibly have involved the brain of the president and undoubtedly was a brain specimen retrieved from the Bethesda Naval Medical School, where brains were readily available, given that it was a teaching hospital.

Recall also the testimony of Saundra Spencer, the Navy petty officer who had developed post-mortem photographs of President Kennedy on the weekend of the assassination. Having been led to believe that she was working on a classified operation, she had kept her secret for some 30 years. After examining the official autopsy photos showing the back of Kennedy's head to be intact at her ARRB deposition, she implicitly denied the authenticity of those images by unequivocally repeating that the close-up photo she had developed of the back of JFK's head showed a "blown-out chunk" missing from the back of JFK's skull, just as Dr. McClelland and those other Parkland Hospital witnesses had stated some 33 years before.

Into this maelstrom of evil was sucked Abraham Zapruder, a Dallas businessman, father, and amateur home moviemaker who went out that sunny day to film the president he deeply admired. Little did Zapruder know that what he thought would be a pleasant outing to create a positive memory for himself and his children would end up being the worst thing that ever happened to him.

When Zapruder undoubtedly read the December 6, 1963, issue of *LIFE* magazine, he had to have realized that the magazine was lying about the contents of his film. That was the issue in which *LIFE* columnist Paul Mandel falsely asserted that Kennedy had turned toward the Texas School Book Depository when he was shot in the throat. By that time, *LIFE* had full ownership and possession of Zapruder's film, having agreed to pay him the princely sum of $150,000 for his film, which is the equivalent of about $1.3 million dollars today.

Zapruder would have consulted with his wife and his son Henry about the article. Should he publicly disclose Mandel's assertion as a lie? Or should he remain silent about the lie? He chose to remain silent, undoubtedly deeply afraid of what would happen to him if he went public with his accusation.

Meanwhile, the CIA, which has no legal authority to conduct domestic operations, was busy on the weekend of the assassination secretly diverting the camera-original 8mm Zapruder film to the CIA's National Photographic Interpretation Center in Washington, D.C., where a team headed by Dino Brugioni, one of the world's foremost imagery experts, was charged with making enlargements of frames from the film and posting them on briefing boards.

The film was then shipped to the CIA's top-secret photography laboratory known as "Hawkeyeworks," where, according to what Ed Green, the Kodak manager of the research and development facility, told Brugioni, they could "do anything" with film. Given that CIA officials in Washington could watch the 8mm film and make enlargements of frames, there was no reason to send the film to Rochester other than to alter it.

After deleting incriminating frames depicting the extremely wide turn of the president's limousine from Houston Street onto Elm Street, after deleting frames showing exit debris traveling through the air to Kennedy's left rear, after deleting the brief car stop or near-stop, after blacking out the large exit wound in the back of his head, and after altering the head explosion and reducing it to only one frame instead of several frames, a new 16mm, unslit "double 8" film, now masquerading as the camera-original Zapruder film, was taken back to NPIC in Washington, where a brand new team again made frame enlargements from this "sanitized' film, which were later mounted on a completely different set of briefing boards from the ones made the day before.

It is revealing that Brugioni, the number two man at NPIC and the duty officer in charge that weekend, was kept in the dark about the Sunday-night team's activities, presided over by Homer McMahon, who, in turn, was kept in the dark about Brugioni's team.

When Brugioni saw the extant Zapruder film as a motion picture in 2011, he stated that the film he saw on the weekend of the assassination was different from the extant film. He specifically recalled that the head-shot explosion consisted of more than one frame (which is all we see in the film today); that the exit debris from the head explosion went much higher into the air than it does in the extant film; and that the head explosion he recalled was white, not red, as it appears in frame 313 today.

Brugioni also stated that the film he viewed showed brain debris shooting straight upward in a large cloud of mist that surrounded a piece of JFK's head, a phenomenon that does not exist in the extant film. Even though the head explosion he recalls seeing in the film differs from the one his partner, Erwin Schwartz, remembered seeing in the film the weekend of the assassination, neither of these two recalled versions of the head explosion is seen in the extant film today. The Willis family and others in Dealey Plaza recalled a large cloud of red debris exiting the rear of JFK's head and expanding into the air like a halo, and traveling to the rear — a sight that is most definitely not seen in the Zapruder film that exists today.

Altering the Zapruder film was an ingenious strategy. Since the altered film could be used to reinforce the fraudulent autopsy photographs showing the back of Kennedy's head to be intact, it would constitute persuasive corroborative evidence challenging the veracity of anyone who insisted that president had a massive exit-sized hole in the back of his head, such as Dr. McClelland, Dr. Clark, Saundra Spencer, and all the others.

Several months after the assassination, Zapruder was summoned to testify before the Warren Commission. Rather than show Zapruder a copy of his film, the commission's attorney showed him muddy, difficult-to-decipher, black-and-white photographs of frames from the film. Nonetheless, Zapruder undoubtedly noticed that there were frames missing from the film and that frames showing the head wound and head explosion had been deleted and altered.

Nonetheless, Zapruder remained silent, thereby implicitly acknowledging the authenticity of the film. If he later questioned the authenticity of the film, he could be viciously attacked for changing his story, one that he had given under oath.

But publicly questioning the authenticity of his film was not a road that Abraham Zapruder would take. He, along with his wife Lillian and his son Henry, knew that if he accused Mandel of lying, or if he stated that his film had been altered, people would have come after him with a vengeance. They would have denounced him as a communist sympathizer, one who had come from Russia as an official agent of the communists. *LIFE* magazine, under the auspices of CIA acolyte C. D. Jackson, undoubtedly would have stopped making any more yearly payments on the purchase contract for the film, which would have meant that Zapruder would have lost the equivalent of around $900,000 in today's dollars. Right-wingers in Dallas would have done everything to induce people to boycott Zapruder's dress business, with the aim of destroying it completely. Every single anti-Semitic trope would have been trotted out and applied to Zapruder.

Thus, when Abraham Zapruder went out that sunny day in Dallas to film President Kennedy, little did he know that the evil force that was about to carry out one of its patented regime-change operations would end up confronting him with one of the worst choices a human being could ever face: Should Zapruder maintain his integrity and go public with the truth, knowing that he and his family would be destroyed in the process? Or should he instead sacrifice his integrity and live a life based on a lie, which would preserve himself and his family in the process?

Who can blame Abraham Zapruder for the decision he made? How can any of us be certain about what we would do if faced with that same choice?

But there is little doubt that the choice that Abraham Zapruder made is what threw his internal life into turmoil, depression, and consternation. He knew — and he knew that his beloved wife Lillian and his son Henry knew — that he was now living a life based on a lie — and, in the process, remaining silent about the evil that had caused him to live that way.

It was that life of the lie — not Abraham Zapruder's grief over the Kennedy assassination and not the misgivings over having received so much money for his film, as his granddaughter Alexandra asserts in her book *Twenty-Six Seconds* — that is the dark secret that underlies the decades-long Zapruder family taboo against discussing the film.

We have already seen how Alexandra Zapruder declined her father's request to talk about the film after he was diagnosed with terminal cancer.

Another revealing incident occurred during a presentation about her book that Alexandra delivered in 2017 at Southern Methodist University in Dallas. Near the end of the question-and-answer period, Alexandra exclaimed to the moderator, "I can't believe nobody asked about the files — Are you going to ask about the files? I love that nobody asked about the files."

What she was referring to were the assassination-related records that the CIA is still keeping secret from the American people some 58 years after the assassination, on grounds of "national security."

The moderator good-heartedly obliged her: "What do you think about the files?" Everyone laughed. After having invited the question, Alexandra laughingly responded: "I don't think anything about the files."

In this regard, you will recall from chapter 15 that Alexandra castigated New Orleans District Attorney Jim Garrison for his prosecution of Clay Shaw. During the trial, Shaw delivered the following sworn testimony:

Q: Mr. Shaw, have you ever worked for the Central Intelligence Agency?

A: No, I have not.

In the November 1969 issue of *Penthouse,* Shaw followed up with this statement: "I have never had any connection with the CIA."

In November 2021, however, the National Archives released a document that the CIA had kept secret for almost 30 years. The document was a memorandum from J. Kenneth McDonald, Chief, CIA History Staff, and was addressed to the Director of the CIA. The memorandum, which was dated February 10, 1992, stated in part: "These records do reveal, however, that Clay Shaw was a highly paid CIA contract source until 1956."

Can you see why the CIA wants to continue keeping thousands of its assassination-related records secret from the American people? Do you see why they told the ARRB in the 1990s and President Trump in 2017 that the release of that particular record would threaten "national security?" Do you see why some lone-nut theorists in the Kennedy assassination would prefer not to think about what the CIA might still be hiding in the thousands of assassination-related records that it continues to keep secret from the American people?

In my opinion, Alexandra's response — "I don't think about the files" — was consistent with everything we have seen in this book with respect to her deep trust in the national-security state and her deference to its authority as well as with her subconscious fear of acknowledging and confronting the evil that is represented by the CIA, the Pentagon, the vast military-industrial complex, and the rest of the national-security establishment. She could have responded instead: "The CIA has no business continuing to keep any of its JFK-assassination records secret from the American people — especially its records relating to its handling of my grandfather's film on the weekend of the assassination."

In her book, Alexandra recollected how her father and a friend of his would play the guitar together when she was a kid in the '60s. She said that they would sing "Dylan, the Beatles, and all the old folk favorites." I couldn't help but wonder what went through Alexandra's mind when Dylan came out in 2020 with his most recent song, "Murder Most Foul," which is about the Kennedy assassination and which clearly rejects the official lone-nut theory of the assassination, the theory to which Alexandra subscribes. Here are some excerpts from Dylan's song, including his references to the Kennedy autopsy and the Zapruder film:

"Twas a dark day in Dallas, November '63
A day that will live on in infamy
President Kennedy was a-ridin' high.
Good day to be livin' and a good day to die.
Being led to the slaughter like a sacrificial lamb….
Then *they* blew off his head while he was still in the car
Shot down like a dog in broad daylight….
Rub-dub-dub, it's a murder most foul….
They mutilated his body and they took out his brain….
You got me dizzy, Miss Lizzy, you filled me with lead
That *magic bullet* of yours has gone to my head….
Zapruder's film, I've seen that before
Seen it thirty-three times, maybe more
It's vile and *deceitful,* it's cruel and it's mean
Ugliest thing that you have ever seen…." (Emphasis added.)

Young people might ask: What relevance does the Kennedy assassination have today? After all, most, if not all, the people involved in the assassination are dead by now. Take a look at America. A 20-year war in Afghanistan that just recently ended — a war that was entirely based on lies. A continued occupation of Iraq almost 20 years after an invasion that was fraudulently based on non-existent weapons of mass destruction. Continued assassinations in Syria, Yemen, and other parts of the Middle East and Africa.

The "war on terrorism" continues unabated, with interventionists arguing that it's time to shift its main focus inward — toward the American people. The USA PATRIOT Act continues in existence. There are constant infringements on the liberty and privacy of the American people at the hands of the national-security establishment, including the intrusive pat-down searches at the airports.

State-sponsored assassinations have now become public policy. They are carried out on a regular basis, with nary a peep of protest from the mainstream media or from many Americans. The same goes for torture, kidnapping, indefinite detention, denial of due process of law, and kangaroo military tribunals, as every inmate at the Pentagon's and CIA's prison center at Guantanamo Bay in Cuba can attest. There is also America's established policy of imposing deadly and destructive economic sanctions on foreign citizens as a way to coerce them into ousting their regimes and replacing them with pro-U.S. regimes.

Meanwhile, the Pentagon and the CIA continue to do everything they can to incite new crises with their old Cold War enemies Russia and China and, to a certain extent, North Korea. Of course, there is also the 60-year-old vicious economic embargo that, in combination with Cuba's socialist economic system, continues to squeeze the lifeblood out of the Cuban people.

The national-security establishment has effectively become a fourth branch of the federal government — and the most powerful branch, one to which the other three branches — executive, legislative, and judicial — inevitably defer. One could easily make the argument that it is the Pentagon, the CIA, and the NSA that constitute the branch that is actually running the federal government and that the other three branches exist to support the national-security branch. In this regard, I highly recommend a book entitled *National Security and Double Government* by Michael J. Glennon, professor of international law at The Fletcher School of Law and Diplomacy at Tufts University.

If Kennedy had prevailed in his war against the national-security establishment, the Cold War would have been over within his second term, rather than in 1989. In the 1960s, there were still lots of Americans who remembered what it was like to live under a limited-government system, which would have made it likely that Americans would have demanded the restoration of their limited-government republic.

By 1989, most Americans had been raised under the national-security state form of government. Convinced that the Pentagon, the CIA, and the NSA were essential to their safety and well-being, the last thing most Americans were willing to do is dismantle this totalitarian structure, along with the dark-side, evil powers that came with it, including coups and other regime-change operations and eradicating threats to "national security" through state-sponsored assassinations.

Worst of all, the consciences of the American people remain stultified and paralyzed. The best evidence of that phenomenon are those people who come up with innocent rationalizations or explanations for what are obviously nefarious and evil actions of the U.S. national-security establishment.

The Kennedy assassination is as much part of our nation's legacy as a national-security state as the assassinations of Patrice Lumumba and Rene Schneider and the regime-change operations in Iran, Guatemala, Indonesia, Congo, Cuba, Chile, and others that have left countless innocent people dead in their wake. Denial of that legacy gets us nowhere. As M. Scott Peck pointed out in his book *The Road Less Traveled,* "Mental health is dedication to reality at all costs."

What America needs now is a great awakening, one that brings an elevated and strengthened sense of conscience among the American people, along with a passionate commitment to the dismantling of the national-security state and the restoration of a limited-government republic to our land. That would set America on the road toward liberty, peace, prosperity, and harmony with the people of the world.

What better way to honor the memory of President John F. Kennedy, who, because he was committed to peace, had an encounter with evil on November 22, 1963? What better way to honor the memory of Abraham Zapruder, who, through sheer happenstance, had his own encounter with evil on that fateful day?

Appendix A

Recommended Books and Videos

Books

JFK and the Unspeakable by James W. Douglass.

Inside the Assassination Records Review Board: The U.S. Government's Final Attempt to Reconcile the Conflicting Medical Evidence in the Assassination of JFK by Douglas P. Horne.

JFK's War with the National Security Establishment: Why Kennedy Was Assassinated by Douglas Horne.

The Kennedy Autopsy by Jacob Hornberger.

The Kennedy Autopsy 2 by Jacob Hornberger.

Regime Change: The JFK Assassination by Jacob Hornberger.

The CIA, Terrorism, and the Cold War: The Evil of the National Security State by Jacob Hornberger.

CIA & JFK: The Secret Assassination Files by Jefferson Morley.

Morley v. CIA: My Unfinished JFK Investigation by Jefferson Morley.

Best Evidence: Disguise and Deception in the Assassination of John F. Kennedy by David Lifton.

Brothers: The Hidden History of the Kennedy Years by David Talbot.

The Devil's Chessboard: Allen Dulles, the CIA, and the Rise of America's Secret Government by David Talbot.

Mary's Mosaic: The CIA Conspiracy to Murder John F. Kennedy, Mary Pinchot Meyer, and Their Vision for World Peace by Peter Janney.

JFK and Vietnam: Deception, Intrigue, and the Struggle for Power by John M. Newman.

The JFK Assassination by James DiEugenio.

Destiny Betrayed: JFK, Cuba, and the Garrison Case by James DiEugenio.

The War State: The Cold War Origins Of The Military-Industrial Complex And The Power Elite, 1945–1963 by Michael Swanson.

Why the Vietnam War? Nuclear Bombs and Nation Building in Southeast Asia, 1945–1961 by Michael Swanson.

FFF videos (In the multimedia section of fff.org)

"The National Security State and the Kennedy Assassination," an online conference sponsored by The Future of Freedom Foundation.

"The National Security State and JFK," an online conference sponsored by The Future of Freedom Foundation.

"Altered History: Exposing Deceit and Deception in the JFK Assassination Medical Evidence," a multi-part video series by Douglas Horne.

"The JFK Assassination," a multi-part video series by Jacob Hornberger.

"The JFK Assassination," a speech delivered online by Jacob Hornberger.

"CIA & JFK": An Interview with Jefferson Morley.

Other presentations

"The Zapruder Film Mystery," featuring Douglas Horne, on Youtube.com.

"The Zapruder Film Alteration Debate," by Douglas Horne, at Midnight Writers News: https://midnightwriternews.com/mwn-episode-107-douglas-horne-on-the-zapruder-film-alteration-debate.

Oliver Stone's movie *JFK* (1991).

Oliver Stone's two-hour documentary *JFK Revisited: Through the Looking Glass* (2021).

Oliver Stone's four-hour documentary *JFK: Destiny Betrayed* (2022).

Appendix B

CIA Statement to Rockefeller Commission

JFK ACT 01-07-99 RELEASE

CIA HISTORICAL REVIEW PROGRAM
RELEASE IN FULL 1998

CENTRAL INTELLIGENCE AGENCY

OFFICE OF THE DIRECTOR

7 May 1975

75-3975/1

Document Number 1635-1087

FOIA Review on FEB 1978

Robert B. Olsen
Senior Counsel
Commission on CIA Activities
Within the United States

Dear Mr. Olsen:

Attached is an addendum to our comments on the Hoch memorandum. The comments were sent to you on 29 April 1975.

The addendum is keyed to Page 16 of the Hoch memo.

We continue to check on the question raised by Mr. Hoch on his page 24 concerning anti-Castro group meetings in Dallas. We hope to have an answer for you later this week or early next.

Faithfully yours,

E H Knoche

E. H. Knoche
Assistant to the Director

Attachment: a/s

WARNING NOTICE
This document contains information exempted from unauthorized disclosure by the Freedom of Information Act or the Privacy Act (5 USC 552a; 5 USC 552a(a)).

EHKnoche:rrh:5/7/75
Distribution:
Orig - Mr. Olsen w/att (Addendum to Hoch Memo
1 - OGC wo/att forwarded on 29 April 1975)
1 - IG wo/att
1 - Knoche Chrono wo/att
1 - " Comm Correspondence wo/att
2 - Olsen Letter Request File, 4/18/75 w/att
1 - Warren Commission wo/att
1 - ER

CLASSIFICATION REVIEW EO 12065
CONDUCTED ON
DERIVATIVE CL BY
DECL. DOWNGR TO
REVW ON
DERIVED FROM

Memorandum on Investigation

...ts on the Hoch memo-
...is addendum is keyed
...ich the substance with

...the question
...anti-Castro
...our response to
...of 3 May 1975.

~~CONFIDENTIAL~~

Additions to Comments Concerning Paul Hoch's Memorandum on CIA Activities and the Warren Commission Investigation

Attached is an addendum to our comments on the Hoch memorandum. As with our original comments, this addendum is keyed to the page in Mr. Hoch's memorandum on which the substance with which it deals appears.

We are continuing our investigation into the question raised on p. 24 of Mr. Hoch's memorandum concerning anti-Castro group meetings in Dallas. We hope to forward our response to that question to the Commission during the week of 5 May 1975.

~~CONFIDENTIAL~~ E2 IMPDET CL BY 013 [illegible]

CONFIDENTIAL

P. 16

Addendum to comment on Zapruder film:

In late 1963, the Secret Service brought a copy of the Zapruder film to Director McCone and asked to have the film analyzed technically, particularly with regard to anything that could be learned from the film concerning elapsed time between rifle shots. A laboratory at the National Photographic Interpretation Center (NPIC) was made available for the analysis late that same night. The film was analyzed in individual stop frames, and two sets of four briefing boards each were prepared by NPIC. Because the film had been taken in a spring-powered movie camera, it was not possible to determine precise time between shots without access to the camera to time the rate of spring run-down. We assume the Secret Service informed the Warren Commission about anything of value resulting from our technical analysis of the film, but we have no direct knowledge that they did so.

Secret Service representatives were present during the process of analysis and took the film and one set of briefing boards away with them that night. Mr. McCone retained one set of boards. The set was controlled carefully; very few people saw it. It was retired to a CIA records storage facility subsequently. This set has been recalled from storage and can be made available if required.

CONFIDENTIAL

Appendix C

Transcript of ARRB Staff Interview of Homer A. McMahon

(Former CIA/NPIC Employee) conducted on July 14, 1997 at Archives II in College Park, Maryland

Interviewers: Douglas P. Horne and T. Jeremy Gunn

(Transcribed by Douglas Horne in May 2012; the time annotations are only approximations, for they vary a bit whenever the transcriber's MP3 digital audio recording is searched.)

Horne: OK, it's Monday, ah, July the 14th, 1997. My name is Doug Horne, I'm with the ARRB. I'm here with Mr. Homer McMahon, former NPIC employee — National Photo Interpretation Center — and I'm also here with Michelle Combs of the ARRB; and before we begin, I'd like to confirm with you on the record, Mr. McMahon, is it OK — do we have your permission to tape this interview?

McMahon: Yes, my name is Homer McMahon; not NPIC, I was CIA — that was my cover at the time —

Horne: Oh, OK —

McMahon: — and you have my permission to — at that time "NPIC" was classified Top Secret.

Horne: Yes, sir. OK. Thank you very much.

McMahon: OK.

Horne: Ah, we may be joined later — this is for the record — by Mr. Jeremy Gunn, ah, of the Review Board staff, ah, and also by a new [ARRB] employee, Marie Fagnant, who is in the building today also. Ah, could you summarize for us, sir, ah, your professional experience and training in photography, ah, prior to, up to 1963?

McMahon: I started doing photography in 1938.

Horne: OK.

McMahon: I worked one summer at the FBI lab, and I'm not sure of that summer. Ah, my boss was Jimmy Dunlap, and, who later became, left, and went, ah, in business for himself, and I worked for him part-time, at different times. Ah, I was in photography when I was in high school, and I worked as a photographer on the yearbook committee; ah, I used to work at the "Pop Baker" [phonetic spelling], and that was Eastman Kodak photofinishing in Georgetown, also [in] the summers. I was in photography — ah, on the G.I. Bill. I went to the National School of Photography, and I went to the Washington School of Photography; and I took several extension courses at the, ah, USGS [sic, the witness meant "USDA"], ah, Graduate School and the Armed Forces Institute of Pathology at Walter Reed.

Horne: I see.

McMahon: Ah, I took several courses up in Rochester and Binghamton, and, ah, ANSCO in Binghamton and Kodak in Rochester.

Horne: OK.

McMahon: Ah, other than that, I never had a degree in photography; in those days it was strictly, ah, vocational —

Horne: I see.

McMahon: — there was no, ah, you could get, you could get a Master's Degree up there, ah, at PPA — [unclear] work, but I, I never came to [garbled] or worked on that level. I think you also had to donate time, [and make], ah, presen — national presentations. I was a member of the Professional Photographers of America.

Horne: OK.

McMahon: Ah — Oh, I went to college on the G.I. Bill at the end of the Second World War, and — then I went to work for the CIA. Ah, my mentor, ah, Mel Fromm [spelled phonetically], was an old OSS, ah, operative in the Second World War.

Horne: OK.

McMahon: His Dad ran the National School of Photography, and, ah, I spent two years there; ah, he got me a job interview with the CIA. And I went out at B Street, and that was [the] Printing Service[s] Division, and that was Austin Young, and I worked there a year-and-a-half, or two years; and then I went in business for myself for five years; and then I went back for, I think, 10 years.

Horne: Went back to the Agency, or —?

McMahon: Yeah, but I didn't go back to, ah, the Printing Service[s] Division, I went to the Science Division [DD S&T]. And when, ah, when the, ah, Steuart garage closed down — ah, ah, Kennedy's brother Bob got that built, and, and it was a special building that was behind the barrier, you know, it had the barrier walls you couldn't penetrate, and it was in the Navy Yard, and I worked there for, I guess, close to ten years — and that's when I was Chief of the Color Lab [at NPIC] —

Horne: I see.

McMahon: — I was GS-11, Step 7, was my grade, when I worked there.

Horne: What — do you recall what year it was that you returned, ah, to the CIA, and worked for about ten years, what year was that? More or less?

McMahon: Ha — [smiling] — no, I don't have an accurate recollection.

Horne: OK. Ah, it would be, certainly, before 1963?

McMahon: Oh, yes.

Horne: It would be in the '50s, perhaps?

McMahon: Yes.

Horne: OK, OK. When you went back to the CIA the second time, and —were you working in the Steuart, ah, Motors Building, with, ah —

McMahon: No, I didn't work for the Steuart garage. Ah, I'm not gonna mention names of people that I've worked with —

Horne: OK, that's fine.

McMahon: — ah, well wait, I can give you Harry Lieckert [phonetic spelling], 'cause he's retired, but he worked at the Steuart —

Horne: OK.

McMahon: — and I talked to him, and, and, he said, "I'll get you an interview," and, and I went over — or, they came over, I was working for Austin Young on, in Alexandria, right there at, ah, Duke Street, or King Street, I forgot which —

Horne: That's OK.

McMahon: — and he came over and interviewed me, and, and I transferred. I was ah, LB 16 — I was under, ah, GPO [Government Printing Office] scale, I was in Printing Services.

Horne: OK. Let me go off the record here a moment, and introduce you to some people who just arrived.

[Off the record — tape recorder stopped.]

Horne: OK, we're back on the record. Ah, Mr. Jeremy Gunn, Marie Fagnant, and Mr. Steve Tilley [of the National Archives, NARA's daily liaison with the ARRB staff] have joined us. Ah, Mr. McMahon, do you remember when you became Head of the Color Lab [at NPIC]?

McMahon: Oh, when I went over, I was hired for that position. And, I transferred from an LB 19 to a GS-11, Step 7.

Horne: Approximately what year was that? Is it, ah —

McMahon: Late '50s? [Expressing some uncertainty with his tone of voice.]

Horne: OK, late '50s.

[Transcriber's note: the transcriber received a document from the CIA in 2011 — in response to a wide-ranging FOIA request filed in 2009 — that confirmed Homer Albert McMahon had worked for the CIA briefly from September 22, 1952 through March 20, 1953, as a photographer; and that he had recommenced service with CIA on October 30, 1960, and had worked at NPIC from that date until September 11, 1970, as a GS-11 civil servant with the job title of photographer.]

Were you working at the, ah, National Photo Interpretation Center in November 1963?

McMahon: *Yes.*

Horne: OK. Ah — we spoke previously on the telephone on, on June the ninth, when Mr., Mr. Dave Montague and I called you —

McMahon: Yeah.

Horne: — I think you may recall that — and, ah, you mentioned to us during that telephone call that you were involved in analysis and other events involving a home movie of the assassination. Could you tell us how you first heard about this, and who asked you to come into work?

McMahon: OK, it, it, it — I wasn't an analyst — that, that was a technical term for somebody that did photointerpretation, into my branch, and I was a, a phototechnologist. And what I did, I timed, OK, to my best recollection — I was, I worked in the vaulted area behind a barrier, or [that is to say, I worked with] extremely sensitive material; and my classification [sic — the witness meant "security clearance"] allowed me to work on anything and everything if I had a need-to-know — and I won't tell you what those were, but —

Horne: And I won't ask.

McMahon: Eh, ah, we had, it was, it was, a "world beyond" — we had unlimited budget; we had anything we wanted to buy; unlimited money; and it was [a] palace. It was "Lundahl's Palace," and I think they said 90 per cent of the intelligence came from our operation [at NPIC]. And that was, that was, what the analysts and the photointerpreters did. And, and they knew, along with, I — I was in the Science Division now — but, they also accessed and used other information.

Horne: OK.

McMahon (9:55): OK. But the best that I remember, of how I came to work on this project — and, of course, we all heard of, of, you know, that motorcade, where Kennedy got killed, and I think we shut up shop and went home — af — after that. *And it was within the next two days, a chap was introduced to me* — and I was sworn to his secrecy, it had nothing to do with the Agency's secrecy and, *and he was, to the best of my knowledge, introduced as "Bill Smith."*

Horne: "Bill Smith" of — what?

McMahon: Of [the] Secret Service, he was an agent. *And he had, he had gotten a roll of film directly from the person that had photographed it,* who called the Secret Service and told them that he thought he had that on film — and he shot it with a little 'Brownie,' ah, double 8 [camera]. *And he took it, took it to Rochester, and — we had a division up there, I won't go into that* — but they processed the film — it was Ek — it was Kodachrome (I think, I or II, the daylight version, whichever it was), and it was double 8 [film]. And, after he got it processed, they told him there that we were probably the only place that had the equipment that could do what he wanted to, ah, take every frame on there — [chuckling] — of the entire event, and, and make, ah, the best possible quality reproduction.

Horne: When you say, "They told him," who do you mean, ah —?

McMahon (12:04): *Well — ah — heh, heh — well, Eastman Kodak had, had contracts with the U.S. government, and if you want to know, you can go through the CIA, they'll tell you [unclear].* OK, but he, he got the film processed, and he brought it to us, and he, and three other people, ah, timed the film, for the — through observation you could tell where the gunshots actually caused the hits and the slumps. We didn't know anything about any audio — ah, it was just visual. And we timed it and determined, where the, the time between the, ah — physically timed it, with a stopwatch — ah, where the gunshot "hits" hit. And we, we, we, we went from, I think, maybe two frames before the first hit, and then we hit every single frame — through, and we only, *he only counted three hits, possibly four* — ah, couldn't tell, I think, when, when Connally got hit. It was obvious when, when he [JFK] got hit the first time, and then the second time, as his head [was] going off into the angle, up, and —

Horne: Could I, could I break in and ask you a question? Ah, when you say, "he, and three others, timed the film," does this mean you —people viewed it as a motion picture?

McMahon: Yes. We were in a briefing room, ah, with the camera [sic — the witness meant "projector"], and a large screen — ah, you said I could use Ben Hunter's name?

Horne: Yes, sir.

McMahon: OK, Ben Hunter, and I think he was a GS-7, and, and he was working with me as a, as a trainee, ah, at the time, in the Color Lab; and Bill Smith; ah, excuse me, there were three of us, including myself — that's "it."

Horne: That's it. That's —

McMahon: — to the best of my knowledge.

Horne: *So, the total number of people, that you can recall, is yourself, Ben Hunter, and Bill Smith?*

McMahon: *Yes, that's all that was involved, to my knowledge.*

Horne: How were you first notified, ah, to go in — did this happen during the workday, or after hours? How did you first get notified?

McMahon: I haven't the faintest idea.

Horne: Do you recall —

McMahon: — because I didn't, I didn't, I'd been called in so many times, ah —

Horne: For other jobs? Do you recall whether you did this work during the day, or dur —

Jeremy Gunn: [Interrupting] I — I'm sorry — I just want to make sure that we're, we're clear, on the record. When you say that you were called in 'many other times,' was that for other jobs? Or do you mean you were called in many times [unclear] —

McMahon: When "the Goose laid the egg," we went on 12 and 12 — we [worked] split shifts until we worked out the mission. Ah, or, I, I don't think that's important. The, the other work I did had nothing to do with this.

Gunn: Oh, no, that's fine, but —

Horne: That's all we are trying to do, for the record, is to clarify that when you said that statement, were you referring to this particular film, or other jobs?

McMahon: OK, I — this — I had — I had other clearances; ah, but, but none of these clearances that were given to me under the CIA or other clearances that I held for other government agencies, this was under strictly, a — I was told that none of this could be divulged to anyone (that we had it, that we did it), and I know that it was being used for a briefing, but I don't know who they briefed on it. My only guess — [was] that we normally briefed the Joint Chiefs of Staff; the National Reconnaissance Committee; and the President of the United States, from the work that I did. And I didn't do any of the analysis; I just did the color part that was used in the briefing boards and the teleprompters and that kind of work. And it was also distributed under different Top Secret classifications, to the Community, go ahead —

Gunn: I think what — we just — we just wanted to hear on, is when you said that you were called in several times, only, only if you were only called in once, for the film related to the assassination?

McMahon: I wasn't — I only worked on that one, and, and my — I know I worked on it until it was completed, and I think it was probably more than a workday.

Horne (17:52): When we spoke on, ah, June the ninth, sir, ah, *it was your recollection at that time that ah, that you went in after hours, and that you worked basically all night long.*

McMahon: *Yeah.*

Horne: Does that refresh your recollection?

McMahon: Yes. It was not during my normal, I don't think it was during my normal, ah, I don't think I was there — I think I was called in [after hours], but I wasn't told what I was called in for.

Horne: I see.

McMahon: I didn't have the faintest idea what I was going to do.

Horne (18:19): OK. Would you allow me to, ah, test your recollection on something, the firmness of it? *Ah, you, you said a moment ago that you thought this was, ah, within two days of the assassination.* Ah, is there any particular reason why you associate it as being that close to the assassination, any particular other events, or —

McMahon: *I think, I think I was told — that this — to get the film from the individual; take it and get it processed; come back — was, was, a couple of days* — I'm not sure. I'm not — I don't know [if I can] recall that.

Horne: *Do you recall whether this work that you did was before the funeral, or after the funeral, of the President?* [Transcriber's note: President Kennedy was assassinated on Friday, November 22nd, 1963; and his funeral was on Monday, November 25th, 1963.]

McMahon (18:56): *I'm pretty sure it was before.*

Horne: OK

Horne (19:01): Ah, before we get into some details of what you did, ah, how would you best summarize the tasking that, that your Agency received from Mr. Smith? Could you revisit that topic again, try to encapsulate it —

McMahon: Well, OK, I don't, I don't know how it came through channels, to us, I wasn't told that. Ah, what I'm, what I'm reflecting is what I *think* happened. I know it wasn't under any clearances that I held; I do know that it was being done for analysis and a briefing, but I'm not sure who that was for. Ah —

Horne (19:59): And what is it that he [Bill Smith] wanted you to do again, one more time?

McMahon: OK, what he wanted us to do, after we came to the decision, after we had timed it, was to take a frame-by-frame presentation of that complete sequence, and make, ah — [to my] best recollection, 5 by 7 internegs — and I printed two-up, on an 8 x10, Ben Hunter and myself — exposed them, and processed them. Then we had a period of time where you have to wait for the drying, ah, of the material, and then we went back and viewed all of the negatives, that we had them marked and identified as to the sequence, and we made 3 each, ah, color contact prints, and again, went back and processed those, and had to wait for the drying. Ah —

Horne: So the color prints were, were, ah, the same size, then, as the internegative?

McMahon: I'm pretty sure we, we —

Horne: Contact [prints], without an enlarger?

McMahon: — contacted the 8 by 10 negatives that were exposed two-up — and, and then they were cut apart, and identified on the back, and I did not do that, ah, the identification, I don't think I did — but I might have.

Horne: OK.

Gunn: I'm sorry, can I interrupt just a second? I, I apologize. It wasn't clear to me about the negatives and the internegatives — you referred to there being 5 by 7 internegatives, and 8 by 10 negatives, and I didn't know whether those were two entirely separate things, or whether you were referring to the same thing —

McMahon: It — it's called a working turn — you take an 8 by 10 negative, and you print a 5 by 7 going 5 by 8; then you turn it, with the frame; set up the liquid gate; ah, and make the other one; and then put it in a box. So you've finished, say, the first two. Then you move the frame to the third frame — ah, these were — this was precision equipment, that could make a one-stage enlargement, and my best guess is, is 40x, is what [we] made the little image to —

Horne: By that, you mean 40 times the original size —

McMahon: Forty times the original, ah, half-frame, super, double 8, or whatever —

Horne: Just for the sake of the —

McMahon: We had three different — OK, we had what we call a ten-twenty-forty —

Horne: Is that the, is that the enlarging machine?

McMahon: Yeah, that's the enlarging machine. And you set it up — with, this is a coherent light source enlarger — and we set it up with, ah, a specific optical lens; and a specific, ah, condenser; and a, and a, color pack, with CC filters; so that we could expose all 3 layers of the Kodachrome on the negative. That's —

Horne: You mentioned "wet gate" a moment ago —

McMahon: Yeah, it's a liquid gate — it — it, ah, a liquid gate, is — it's a no-no today, because, ah, it was two parts of, ah — 'kay, we made our own liquid, and what the purpose of the liquid was, it has a refraction index to eliminate the, ah, the surfaces of the film, which degrade the image, the front and back surface, and it's called 10-20-40 fluid — and to my knowledge, it, ah, it was two parts, of, ah, goodness, I don't have, I can't, remember it [garbled, unclear] —

Horne: That's all right. Was this applied by hand, or was it full immersion wet gate?

McMahon: Oh no, you had a little injection [port], and what happened, your front lens came down — OK, it was precision equipment, and the excess fluid went out, so it was full gate, almost like a microscope. All right?

Horne: OK.

McMahon: And if you got air bubbles in it, you had to go back to [the] start again and re-inject it, and then bring it back down.

Horne (25:09): All right. May I ask another question? Ah, before we move along, ah, you mentioned double 8 film a couple of times.

McMahon: Yes.

Horne: Do you recall, ah, the condition of this movie when you saw it, was — had it been slit or was it unslit?

McMahon: I think it was *unslit* — the reason I said that, now we might have slit it, but before we used it — but they were — I thought they were told that they didn't want to slit the film. And I don't — I, I don't think we slit it — I think we used it unslit in a 16 mm projector.

Horne: That was going to be my next question — how did you project it? Do you think it was —

McMahon: I think it was unslit. *This was the original film;* it had been — I think they ran dupes of it, but we actually worked from the, the, the, ah, acquisition material, of the original film.

Horne: Ah, is this something you observed yourself, ah, or something you were told by Mr. Smith, or, or both; or how did you — how do you come to your conclusion today that you had the original film?

McMahon (26:38): All right, I think it was a combination of everything you said, along with, ah, the quality of the film.

Normally, when you dupe it, you, ah, you, you loose a lot of resolution. And, when we made them, you could actu — Kodachrome is, is, a, an additive process; it's black and white film, with filters that give you color separation negatives; and then you use the azo [spelled phonetically] dyes, after you flash them, and redevelop them selectively, onto the original film. And it has a yellow coupler; a magenta coupler; and a cyan coupler — that give you the, the 3 subtractive primary colors that give you the illusion of the, the image and color. And there is very little, ah, dye, ah, that changes [unclear] or, or — it was excellent imagery. Now I don't know whether that still exists or not, ah, but I'm pretty sure that's what, what I used.

Horne: OK. One more follow-up on the first part of the interview, and then we'll move along.

McMahon: All right.

Horne (28:23): *How certain are you that Mr. Smith said he went down to pick up the film from the person who took it, and then took it to Rochester? Are you —*

McMahon: *I know he took it to Rochester.* I'm not certain other than I think he said that — that it — that he got it from the original person himself, but I'm not positive. *I, I am positive that he said that he took it to Rochester — hand-carried it, got it processed, and then they guided him back to us to do the —*

Horne: So —

McMahon: Rochester wasn't set up to do what we were set up to do.

Horne: In the sense that you had the big enlarger and they did not? Is that what —

McMahon: We had a complete "world beyond" facility —

Horne: OK.

McMahon: — OK, a, a multi-billion dollar photo lab —

Horne: OK.

McMahon: — that Kennedy's brother got built for us in what — three months, I think. We moved out of the Steuart, right in.

Horne: Did, did, did your — did the NPIC relocate, was it after the Missile Crisis, ah, after the Cuban Missile Crisis in October of '62 that you moved?

McMahon: When was, when was Kennedy inaug — inaugurated?

Horne: Ah, January '61.

McMahon: '61. It was shortly after that.

Horne: OK. Ah, do you remember the approximate number of internegatives that you made?

McMahon: It was before the Cuban Crisis, because I did a lot — look, I'm not going to talk about that. Now, what was the other question?

Horne: Do you remember the approximate number of, ah, frames on the original film of which you made internegatives?

McMahon: The best recollection [I have] is forty (40).

Horne: OK — and —

McMahon: Might have been twenty (20). Between twenty and forty.

Horne: Between twenty and forty, OK. And, which person in the room decided which frames? Who decided which frames would —

McMahon: We all did.

Horne: It was a joint thing?

McMahon: Yeah.

Horne: OK. This — was this subsequent to viewing it as a motion picture? After that?

McMahon: Well after — hindsight, is you know [in] retrospect, ah, Smith said that he wished he'd done the whole damn roll.

Horne: Wow. When did he say that?

McMahon: After we'd finished [chuckling].

Horne: Oh, saying — during the same event? OK. Ah, after you viewed this as a motion picture, did you — how did you — did you lay it out on a light table and use a loupe? What did you do for further study, before — I'm trying to, ah, ask you to recall the process —

McMahon: OK, after it was viewed — and I'm not sure whether we used the dupe to view it with, or whether we used the acquisition — we might have used a dupe roll to view it —

Horne: For — OK — for the projection?

McMahon: For the projection, I'm not sure, my recollection isn't good; I know that, that he had dupes made of it.

Horne: OK.

McMahon: Ah, and yes, we could use loupes and we could visually look at that, but when, when you put it into the type of equipment we had, you can actually physically see it on the, on the vacuum board, where the film goes —

Horne: I see. That would have been superior to any loupe viewing.

McMahon: Yes, yes.

Horne: Did you gentlemen —

McMahon: And, and we also used a, a 10x magnifier to grain focus the image, each image, before we exposed it on the interneg. So we actually were getting the acquisition, [the] grain of the acquisition material, in sharp focus. 'Cause you couldn't see the image at that [point] — 10 x 40 is 400 —

Horne: So you were focusing on the actual grain?

McMahon: On the actual — well, it's not grain, see, it — the — Kodachrome — the grain is in the negative, and you develop three black and white negatives, and then you selectively expose them with [sic] red, green, and blue light, and develop the complimentary additive primary color, which is yellow, magenta, and cyan couplers. So when these are all developed on this one tri-pack of film, you have, you have a positive dye image. The negative had the grain; the positive had a reciprocal dye image, which would have been a very much finer grain of silver, that — OK, the, the chemical reaction is to, ah, to replace the fine-grain silver positive image with dye, and then you bleach out the silver, and you're left with just the dye image; so, it's not technically grain, it's, it's, ah, perception of what used to be grain.

Horne: OK, thank you for that technical explanation. I — is this process which you have described, was this proprietary to Kodak?

McMahon: Yes —

Horne: OK.

McMahon: — they had a proprietary — well, no; at, at that time they'd passed, ah, a law that they had to relinquish, ah, the processing of Kodachrome, and there were two or three other people, I — one branch of Kodak went out and opened another company — so it, it was *not* proprietary.

Horne (34:58): *Did, at, at any time, ah, during this work, ah, was the motion picture copied as a motion picture?*

McMahon: *No,* not with — not, not in our operation.

Horne: *So you only made internegatives and color prints, is that correct?*

McMahon: [Witness nodded affirmatively]

Horne: And the size of the prints, again? As you best recall?

McMahon: I'm pretty sure they were 5 by 7, to my, the best of — if, if they're the same ones that I made [chuckling].

[**Transcriber's note:** The Witness was aware that a set of briefing boards had been deposited with the Archives, and that he would be examining them later in the interview.]

Horne: OK, when the — after the prints were made, I presume they had to dry; and what happened next, who were they given to?

McMahon (35:33): Ah — now, the, the mounting on the briefing boards, and the, the photointerpretation, so to speak — I was not involved in, OK —

Horne: OK.

McMahon: — and, I think I went home. Heh, but Smith probably went to another — it's not even a vaulted area, it's a finishing room upstairs.

Horne: Ah, did you and Mr. Hunter stop work at about the same time, or do you recall?

McMahon: Well, he might have stayed on and helped, but, ah, there was another chap that probably was involved in that work, and it probably was done by the other chap, not — and I'm sure Bill Smith. Now, I think you mentioned that, that, ah, Ben Hunter said he didn't recall Bill Smith as the name of the, ah, the agent that brought the film in?

Horne: He, ah, he did not independently recall that name.

McMahon: I remember 'Snuffy' Smith, he was a, a Senator from Texas. And I think I asked the guy — 'cause I met him when I was overseas — and, I asked him, "Are you any relation?"

Horne: I see.

McMahon: 'Cause I knew he had, he had been in Texas where he got the film.

Horne: So you remember asking him this question —

McMahon: Yeah, I, I remember that, and he said, "No."

Horne: OK, that's interesting.

Horne (37:13): Ah, you just mentioned another chap who may have been involved with briefing boards and photoanalysis —

McMahon: — and I can't recall his name —

Horne: — can't recall his name —

McMahon: — even if I could, I couldn't tell you, because he was young. [Transcriber's note: the witness meant that because this person was a young employee in November of 1963, he might still be "current" or active, in 1997 at the time of the interview, and for that reason he would not divulge his name, even if he remembered it. The CIA culture is very protective of the names of its employees, particularly if they are operating under cover.]

Horne: Let me ask you this question about names: Ah, do you recall anyone named "Sands," S-A-N-D-S, at this event? [Transcriber's note: McMahon's partner at the event, Ben Hunter, independently recalled to the ARRB staff that CAPT Sands, USN, let them into the building.]

McMahon: Nope, [I have] absolutely no recollection of that.

Horne: If I was to call this person "Captain Sands," would that help any?

McMahon: OK, we might have had an intermediate — a Naval officer that brought the chap in — someone had to bring him in, because they wouldn't have had clearance. Ah, to get behind the barrier, it was, was pretty tough to do, without either Presidential, or, or, above Top Secret —

Horne: I see —

McMahon: — and you're — I had a CIA badge; that would get me past the guard. And to get behind the barrier, I had to have another special badge; ah, and that had to be picked up and turned in, when I went in. And then we were in a vaulted area that had a crypto code that you had to run to get in the door; so it was, it was virtually not penetrable.

Horne: OK.

McMahon: And then after you got in the door, you had to have a procedure to disarm the vaulted area or security would be [chuckling] —

Horne: Extensive security.

McMahon: Yes.

Horne: It's good to hear that. Ah, do you recall whether a, a Captain Sands was on the staff at, at NPIC? Was he —

McMahon: Even if I am [sic], I couldn't talk about that. We, we did have security officers — it was a geo-military operation, and I shouldn't probably tell you that.

Horne: I should explain to you the reason why we're asking you this. Ah, Ben Hunter independently recalled that a Captain Sands brought in the film, and he could not remember anyone being with him. Subsequently, he remembered there might have been a Secret Service fellow, but he remembered a Captain Sands; but he was unclear of, of what the person's job —

McMahon: OK, most of the geo-military that were there were, were under cover, and I can't, I can't, mention any of the names.

Horne: OK.

McMahon: All right.

Horne (40:01): Did you create, or do you recall anyone else creating, any records or notes during your work?

McMahon: I think, ah, Hunter and I did the only records of the work, and I think it was on, a, either a yellow, or a ah, a ah — [chuckling] add something to this —

Horne: You, you just put your hand on a yellow legal pad —

McMahon: Yeah, it was on a legal type pad, unless it was recorded on — we made our own, ah, marks on some of the — to keep the — but I did not put any classification or any[thing] of that nature — I didn't put any control, no classification or control on any of the documents. Normally that's required before you could leave the vault; it has to be controlled with a Top Secret cover sheet. I did not do that. Now, after the briefing board is made from the material, then that classification precedes the classification of, in the [unclear] cover sheets. We made briefing boards, teleprompters, and view graphs, as — for dissemination to the Intelligence Community.

Horne: For other types of work — ah, routine — but for this job you, you recall that you may have made notes on a yellow legal pad —

McMahon (41:35): Now, I 'm sure that this did — I'm sure that this did not go to the Intelligence Community — it was not part of the CIA — it was not — this was [done on] a, a "need-to know" basis, and it was used by whoever brought it in [chuckling] for, for either the Warren Commission, or to brief somebody else.

Horne: Kay.

McMahon: And it wasn't for history, I think it was, to — I don't even know what it was, I think we [unclear] exercise [unclear].

Horne (42:08): Before we move along, and before I show you the notes that the Archives has — ah, let, let me revisit with you, ah, *what exactly did Mr. Smith say in regard to secrecy or non-disclosure, ah, regarding this event, can you tell me that story again?*

McMahon: *I know that, that my immediate supervisor was not allowed in the room* — that it was so sensitive, and he had all the tickets — and he was not allowed in the room. It was strictly on a "need-to-know" [basis], do the job, and get it out, and no one knew about it, to my knowledge. No record —

Gunn: [Interrupting] Just — just so the record's clear, when you say "all the tickets," you mean all the security clearances that he had? He had a lot of security clearances?

McMahon: He had clearance, ah, equal to or [the] same as I had, but he was not allowed — it was not, it was not the CIA, or — a — I held other clearances: Atomic Energy, ah, National Security Agency, and, and it was not under any of these.

Gunn: Was there any other compartment, or was it just with a name, such as, ah —

McMahon: I — There was no code name on it that I know of, and if there was, I couldn't tell you anyway [chuckling].

Horne (43:48): Did, did Mr. Smith ever say to you, ah, "This is classified at a certain level" —

McMahon: *Yes.* He said it is definitely classified on a "need-to know;" and he didn't give me anything other than it was — that I was sworn to secrecy, and I had — I don't know whether I had to sign the document, I don't recall that. But I do know that it could not be divulged.

Horne: Did he give you a level of classification, like Confidential or Secret —

McMahon: I have no — no, it did not have — *he said it was above Top Secret* —

Horne: OK —

McMahon: OK, ah, that meant that it had to have a code name. Now, I don't know what turned up on the briefing boards, I never saw 'em.

Horne (44:28): Before we, ah, examine the notes that the Archives has, ah, Jeremy, did you want to ask some follow-on questions?

Gunn: Ah, yes. Ah, this goes back to something you said, ah, early on in the interview, where, ah, a couple of things, where you said, as I recall, ah: "He had — he took three hits, possibly four." And it wasn't clear to me whether the "he" was Kennedy, or included Connally. Did, did you reach a conclusion as to the number of hits that you thought President Kennedy had [unclear — several words too indistinct to be made out]?

McMahon (45:13): *Ah, my guess was 6 or 8, but the, the consensus of opinion was 2 or 3.*

Gunn: *Hits on Kennedy?*

McMahon: *Yeah.* Connally, they said it hit Kennedy and then went into Connally — ricocheted.

Horne: Did they say that that night? Or is this —

McMahon: That, that, that was the — we, we were just trying to, to get where all the shots of action — and covered frames from both ends of it. And, I la — I know that later, they found some sound audiotapes, and that they deduct — they said they, they can get, like voice prints on sounds, and they can tell how many super [sic] — separate weapons were fired, because of the Doppler — ah, front and back — and from directions it came from. And it showed up on a police, ah — tape that was recorded — one, one of the motorcyclists had a, had it on. I don't know.

Gunn (46:25): *Ah, how was it that you and others came to reach the observations of the number of hits?* Was that while the film was rolling, or was that frame-by-frame analysis?

McMahon (46:38): *Well, the, the person who brought the film in, had already seen it; and he knew where — he had already reviewed it.* And he already had pre-knowledge, before we had it, so maybe we were swayed to go along with his, ah, ah, first impression. I don't know.

Gunn (47:01): Did he say anyth — could you just sort of recount the events as they occurred, in terms of what — ah, this is Bill Smith?

McMahon: Yeah.

Gunn: OK, what Bill Smith said about what he already knew about the film and what it showed?

McMahon (47:17): It — you didn't — you, you didn't — after it was processed, at Eastman Kodak; *and it wasn't in — it was not in the Kod[ak] factory — it was at "Hawkeyeworks."*

Horne: *Pardon me?*

McMahon (47:30): *There, there was another Top Secret lab —*

[End of Side One of audiotape; Mr. McMahon was cut off in mid-sentence. Side Two of audiotape commences below.]

Horne (00:03): We're back on the record — we turned the tape over.

McMahon: OK, I was just selected to do the one job that I did, that I covered, and, and, I, I really don't think I should talk about what happened before, because I don't have — it, it's hearsay information, I have no [personal] knowledge of it.

Gunn: Just so it's clear, that — the only things that we want to ask any questions about relate to the film of the assassination —

McMahon: Yes.

Gunn: — that's, that's all that we, we are asking about. But it's important for us to be able to get as much information as we can about the processing and the analysis of the film of the assassination. So, a — any other work we are not asking about, but this is something where we want to try and collect as much as we can. And to the extent that Bill Smith told you something about the film, that's very important for us to, to be able to know and document, and what happened, so if you could just tell us what he, what he said had happened —

McMahon (01:03): OK, to the best of my recollection, he said that he was contacted, through his organization, of a film — a person called up and said they had it, and, and they felt — that, they thought they had [it] — and they felt that they didn't want us to give it to anyone or to sell it or make a profit on it — they wanted it to go to, ah, the Secret Service and let them have that. And he gave the original film — the person who did the photography — to the Secret Service. And, I don't think anyone else knew about it until much later. All right.

Gunn: All right, let me, let me try [a] question there. You're acquainted with the Zapruder — what film is called the Zapruder film — is this the Zapruder film, or is this a different film?

McMahon: I haven't seen it for 35 years. Ah — I never heard "Dal Kruder" at the time — I heard that much, much later.

Gunn: Zap — you mean Zapruder? Ah, did you say, "Dal Kruder?"

Horne: [Addressing Jeremy Gunn] He did. [Then, addressing the witness] Ah, the, the name of the gentleman who took the historically most famous film is "Abraham Zapruder."

McMahon: "Abraham Zapruder" — I never heard that, or if I did, I don't remember it.

Gunn (2:54): But, but right now, you're not certain whether the film that you processed, or that you were involved in, ah, working with, was the Zapruder film?

McMahon (3:03): Well, I'm told it was the only coverage they had of it, that that was "it." No one else had photographed it. Now, I don't know whether anyone else had, or whether this is the original, or — historic film.

Gunn (3:18): OK, and, ah, *what did, ah, Mr. Smith say had happened to the film prior to the time that he brought it, in terms of processing, where it had been, and how it had been processed.*

McMahon (3:33): OK, because of expedite and the, the expedite part, is, is in — they wanted to find out what happened, and they had, they had film, that was generously turned into them by a very patriotic person, and [they were] told that he would give it to them, because they — it might help in the investigation. That — this is what, what he was told — *what I was told* — and that it was of the utmost urgency. So he hand-carried it through; *and flew to Rochester; and got it processed at the — the processing division there, and they were made aware that he was coming.* Ah, and did it immediately for him, and I also think they made duplications of that, which I was told, and then he came back [to Washington D.C.], because they told him they couldn't do what he wanted to get done, and that NPIC could do it. And it fell in our laps, and we did it.

Gunn (4:55): What — when you said, "They couldn't get done what needed to be done," did you mean the enlargements, or was there some other —?

McMahon: They, they didn't have a, a laboratory that, that could do the quality of work that he wanted. He wanted maximum sharpness, the most "seeability" that, that he could get of the imagery, and that we were set up to do: and we were well beyond the state-of-the-art in, in the quality that was turned out.

Gunn: For the film of the, the assassination, was it your understanding that anything more had been done to it other than developing the original film and making some prints of the original film?

McMahon: The prints, the prints were duplications of the original —

Gunn: Film.

McMahon: Yeah.

Gunn: Had anything else been done to the film, besides —

McMahon: No, no one else had gotten it — to my knowledge.

Horne (5:52): *Was it your understanding that Mr. Smith had come directly to Washington from Rochester?*

McMahon: *Yeah — mmm-hmmm, yes. He'd gotten off the airplane and came from National Airport directly to, to our building.*

Gunn (6:06): Just so we're, we're clear on something — it was our understanding that the film had been processed by Kodak; ah, *when you said it was done in Rochester, it — was that an inference that you drew, when they said it had been processed by Kodak, or did the — did he mention Rochester?*

McMahon: *Ah, you're, you're getting on classified grounds here, ah, that I can't answer that question. I know, but I can't talk to you about that. There was another Top Secret lab, that the government — you —*

Gunn: Ah, if you're uncomfortable talking about it, we, we can stop that here, so that — that's fine. But this is something that would — that is important for us to be able to do, so we can go, ah, back to the Agency, and talk to them, so [unclear] —

McMahon: No, you can do that back through the Agency, and I know that hasn't been downgraded, to, to — public domain. [Transcriber's note: McMahon was referring here to the code-name "Hawkeyeworks," for the Top Secret lab at Rochester.]

Gunn: Ah —

Horne (7:12): I think there's a way to rephrase the question, so that it's ah, not a classified — so that you don't perceive a classified intent. I, I think the way to rephrase the question might be, *did*

Mr. Smith say, ah, "This was done at Kodak?" or did he say, "This was developed at Rochester?"

McMahon: *Again, again, I know where it was done; I know who did it. And I'm not going to answer [chuckling] —*

Horne: *Is there any chance that, ah, where it was done was at a Kodak lab in Dallas?* That's another way of raising this question.

McMahon: *To my knowledge, no —*

McMahon (8:08): When you're in bed with the Yellow God [Transcriber's note: the primary color in the Kodak logo is yellow] — we had their top scientists and photochemists and optical people working in the 'world beyond;' we had their people — *I shouldn't even talk about it, I'm sorry. And there was a definite link, on the national level, where we had "the best there was" working with us.*

Gunn (9:01): *Would it be fair to say that there was, ah, another facility —*

McMahon: *Yes.*

Gunn: — *where [it was] your understanding that this was processed —*

McMahon: *Yes.*

Gunn: — *and that that facility was mentioned to you by name, so that you knew —*

McMahon: *Yes.*

Gunn: — *where it was —*

McMahon: *Yes.*

Gunn: [Is] That fair [garbled] to say —

McMahon: Yes.

Gunn: OK, but in terms of the name of it we don't need that, but just — there, but, there was reference made to a particular place —

McMahon: But, I don't know if there was any downgrading [of the classification level of that facility's code name, "Hawkeyeworks"]. "National Photographic Interpretation Center" was Top Secret

— you could not say it. You could say "NPIC," and that was Secret.

Horne: I see. That's —

McMahon: And my cover was that "I worked for the CIA" — I did not work for NPIC. And the military that worked there, worked for the military — whether it was Navy, Army, Air Force, or whatever — they did not work for [unclear].

Horne (9:55): I, I'd like to ask a follow-on, if I can, on ah, on the opinions in the room while you were discussing the, the hits, the shots that hit the people in the limousine — ah, the Governor and the President. Did Mr. Smith tell you the directions the shots came from, or did you people try to determine that on your own during your study of the film?

McMahon (10:38): OK, let, let me not answer that question, and take a little detour. I'm an Army brat; my Dad was in the First and Second World War[s]; and he was, ah, an officer, and when I was four years old I learned how to do tricks, and I was one of the greatest trick-shot artists. When I was 16, I used to fire at Peary [spelled phonetically], Camp Peary, in Ohio. Now, and I fired in the NRA National Championships — I was always in, ah — now, I'm talking about target-shooting, not, not tricks. I was what they call a sight-shooter; I could hit without aiming. In other words, if — I was a trick-shot artist — and my Dad would hold a dime between his fingers, and at 50-foot I could shoot, shoot it out with a little trick gun. And, [he could] throw three balls up into the air, golf balls, and I could pump and shoot three of them before they hit the ground. In other words, I — I used — had a rifle range in my own basement, and, and, I would shoot every day, and I became — it was, it was, like driving a car; after you've done it so long you — your reflexes — you do it automatically. I could shoot without looking at what I was — OK, I didn't close one eye and shoot through a sight. I could actually shoot and hit what I wanted to hit, and I think that I could really see the bullets hitting the object; I could see the trajectory of the path of the bullet[s]. And I could compensate for that if I missed; it was a feedback mechanism. And, I was extremely good at what I did; in fact, I used to make money in the, in the money matches, ah, in the, the larger rifles — and I could make as much as four and five hundred dollars in prize money, firing. So, I was a professional, ah, shooter. And yes, I can look at pictures, and, and tell you where the shots came from, and how many there were, and, and where they came — *possibly* where they came from — up, down, right, left. Now, this is [in]tuition, and, and I don't know how to explain, ah, how I know that.

Gunn (13:18): *So, what was it that you observed on the film of the assassination?*

Horne: Your opinion.

McMahon: *About eight (8) shots.*

Gunn: *And where did they come from?*

McMahon: *Three different directions, at least.*

Gunn: Do you remember where — what the directions were?

McMahon: No; but if you have the film — you can plot vectors. Because you, you can go out — I'm a photogrammatrist, as well [chuckling] — [you] go out — with a — OK, there's a way to do it, believe me.

Gunn: Were you ever asked to do any of that kind of analysis on the —

McMahon: *No, no.*

Gunn: Did you say this at the time that you were looking at the film with the others?

McMahon: I wasn't a photogrammatrist at that time [chuckling].

Gunn: No, I understand, but if — when — when you —

McMahon: I later, I later worked for Photoscience. This was a photogrammetry [job] — I was a, a, a [sic] aerial photographer, and I, I did aerial photography for, ah, whatever you want to call it, for mapping, for first, second, [and] third order, ah, survey; and I did that for about twelve years.

McMahon (14:38): And — now, I was a shooter, and that's the only reason I can tell you what I saw, and thought I saw; and it wasn't stereo-vision, it was just intuition. *No, I did not agree with the analysis at the time that I was doing the work;* but that — I didn't have to, because I wasn't a photogrammatrist [chuckling], I wasn't, I wasn't asked to do that.

Horne (15:12): *Do you remember what Mr. Smith's analysis was, or what his —*

McMahon (15:22): *He thought there were three shots.*

Horne: OK. *Do you remember what direction he opined?*

McMahon (15:28): *Well, he went with the standard, ah, concept that Oswald was the shooter* out of the second story. Now, you've got psychological files on Oswald — ah, you've got tons of it [unclear, garbled] figure out.

Gunn (15:53): Were there — there was a selection made of the photographs to be enlarged, or frames to be enlarged —

McMahon: I didn't make any selection, I just went sequential for that one group. Everything was from sequential, nothing was left out.

Gunn: Does that mean from the time that you first identified there was having been a shot until the motorcade left, or [unclear] —

McMahon: Up, up to what they thought there were three shots.

Gunn: Doug, approximately how many frames are there between, ah, let's say, between the, the sign and the head shot?

Horne: Right. Well, ah, the limous — the limousine occupants disappear behind the sign at about frame 190, and ah, the final head shot, according to the Warren Commission, is frame 313, so that's quite a few frames —

Gunn: That's, that's more than a hundred —

Horne: Yes.

Gunn: — frames, so then, the question that I have is —

McMahon: Ah —

Gunn: — is how many frames were actually made —

McMahon (17:07): Maybe then for each of what they thought were the three shots, we went before and after. I'm not real clear on that. But I know that, that we covered three shots, but I thought that — OK, I thought that they were sequential, one frame after the other, when I did it. And again, I'm only talking about 40 shots that I was involved in making —

Gunn: Forty frames.

Horne: Forty frames.

McMahon (17:32): — so that it might have been that it was before each hit that they thought was detectable, but I thought that there were others in there, and that — that's another opinion, that's all.

Horne: Did they ask you —

McMahon: *No* [unclear] —

Horne: — for your opinion?

McMahon: Well, I couldn't convince anyone.

Horne: Did you try?

McMahon: Yes.

Horne: You did express your opinion —

McMahon (17:54): *Oh yes, I expressed my opinion — but you know, it, it, it was pre-conceived. That's the way I felt about — it was pre-conceived, so you don't fight City Hall. I wasn't there to fight 'em, I was there to do the work.*

Gunn: What do you mean pre-conceived, that the, that the Secret Service agent already had —

McMahon: Yes.

Gunn: — a notion in mind, and that he was just — wanted others to agree with that?

McMahon: Mmm-hmmm. And, I, I didn't care; I had no, you know, you know, no vested interest in, in what was happening.

Gunn (18:30): Ah, one time, ah, in, in the course of the discussion, you were talking about the viewing of the film, [and] if I recall correctly, you said — referred to the people who were in the room "and the camera" — and I just wondered if you meant motion picture —

McMahon: Motion picture camera —

Gunn: — [garbled].

McMahon: — and I'm sure it was a —

Gunn: Projector.

McMahon: [Correcting himself] Projector.

Gunn: A projector. Was there a camera, or just a projector?

McMahon: It was a projector. And we had the, ah, still-frame filters that we could put in and stop it [without damaging or burning individual frames]. We could run it forward and backw — it was a unique one, it was not a cheap one.

Horne: But it was, ah, was it [a] 16 mm projector?

McMahon: OK, now, I seem to recall it as being a 16 mm — that, that — but again, that — we had every kind of, ah, projector. It was in a briefing room, we went up to one of our briefing rooms. And they have all that equipment up there.

Gunn (19:31): When, when, when you say "double 8 film," I assume that you are referring to the kind of film where there would be one series of images that goes down one side, and another series of images that comes up the other side. Is that —

McMahon: Correct, absolutely —

Gunn: — now, when that's — if that were projected as a 16 mm film, you would be seeing two series of action, one in reverse, and one going forward, with one upside down. Do you have a recollection of whether that happened?

McMahon (19:57): *I, I think that happened from the original film, when I put it on the optical precision enlarger.* OK — because a — but we would center, you can center that film in the liquid gate — the frame — right in the center of it, [and] then you don't see it.

Gunn (20:22): That was — that was my next question — I had assumed that when you made the, the negatives, you were focusing just on the, on the single frames that would be in the assassination sequence. Do you have any recollection now as to anything that was in the other part of the, the double 8 picture, the part that is not in the assassination sequence?

McMahon: Ah, I have senile dementia; I, I can't remember, really — anything. Most of, of my reflections are, are, are what I have recalled and remembered after the fact. In other words, I did it once, and then I recalled it, and remembered it. I don't know how the mind works, but I do know that I — that I'm not — OK, I'm a recovering drug addict and alcoholic. Do you know what a "wet brain" is? You're looking at one. I damn near died, and I'm not a competent witness, because I don't have good recall — absolutely not — absolute recall.

Gunn (21:41): With, with regard to the other events that you talked about, ah, what, what is your sense of how accurate your memory is of that?

McMahon: I just told you, I don't, I don't have a full deck. Ah [chuckling], I don't know how, how accurate I am, I am presenting anything here. So, this is not — at the time I did it, I was not — I was not impaired, but I later became impaired. So, whether you're talking to a reliable witness or not is up to you to decide [chuckling].

Horne (22:29): Shall we move on to the notes? OK, ah, I'm going to go off the record just temporarily here, while I break out, ah, some notes that the Archives has.

[Tape recorder turned off temporarily.]

Horne (22:39): OK, we're back on the record. And from Record Group 233, Flat 90A, at the Archives, I have pulled out, ah, document ID number 1993.07.22.08:41:07:620600, titled "Analysis of Zapruder Film." Ah, the document date on the RIF [Record Identification Form] is 5-22-1975; and I'm now going to hand these, ah, notes to Mr. McMahon and let him read them and tell us whether he's seen them before. Please take your time.

McMahon (24:35): [Witness examines documents for a considerable period of time — a total of five pages, with one page a half-sheet, having writing on both sides.] *Some of the writing is mine;* I don't know whose this is.

Horne: And by "this" — ah, this page here, sir?

McMahon: I don't know whose that is.

Horne: OK, the page that we're not sure about is the page with 3 shot scenarios — ah, one, one [shot scenario] is labeled: "LIFE magazine," and then the [other] two [are labeled] "other possibilities," OK.

McMahon: *This is my writing.*

Horne: OK, the one that Mr. McMahon has identified as his writing is on the back side of a half-page, and the back side reads: "shoot internegatives, one-and-a-half hours; process and dry internegatives, two hours; print test, one hour; make three prints," [it] looks like, the 'each' sign [that is, the symbol "@" follows the phrase "make three prints," and precedes the time duration of] "one hour; process and dry prints, one-and-a-half hours;" for a total of "seven hours."

McMahon: Yeah.

Horne: Below that, there are some — *that's in pencil* [meaning the time duration for the creation of internegatives and prints discussed above] — below that there are some *blue ink,* ah, long divisions and additions.

McMahon: *This is my writing.*

Horne: And those [the arithmetic calculations in blue ink] are also your writing?

McMahon: *Yeah.*

Horne: Also the pencil?

McMahon: *Yes.*

Horne: OK, could you explain what that — well, what are the long divisions and additions, do you recall what those are?

McMahon: [Sighing] Idiot marks — I don't know what they — it's my writing, I think.

Horne: OK.

McMahon: No, wait — wait a minute — I think it's my — it's either mine or Ben's.

Horne: OK.

McMahon: And, have you got Ben's handwriting?

Horne: I, I can show you one section on these notes that he recalled was his handwriting, ah, if you'd like, and then I can ask you that —

McMahon: This — this looks like Ben's handwriting, here.

Horne: OK, and now you are looking at the other side of the half-sheet —

McMahon: This looks like my writing here —

Horne: — OK, the other side of the half-sheet, which is a description of the four (4) briefing board panels, and when you said it looked like Ben's writing you were pointing at the, the pencil: "Panel I, Panel II, Panel III, Panel IV." [Transcriber's note: these are column headers on the short half-sheet; and below each column header there are two sub-columns, listing print numbers, and corresponding frame numbers, for the prints mounted on each briefing board panel.]

McMahon: Yeah.

Horne: Ben identified for us, right below that, ah, the printing: "print #" and "frame #" — these, these two marks here are the only two that he thought were his writing, right here, in [pointing] — which are underneath the column labeled "Panel I."

McMahon (27:01): Mmm-hmmm. This is in — this looks like Ben's writing, to what I…[now, suddenly focusing on the bottom of the half-sheet] *this looks like my writing.*

Horne: And your writing, ah, would be, ah, at the bottom of the half page, where we're, we're talking about frame numbers and time between shots. [Transcriber's note: the writing referred to here is found at the bottom of the front of the half-sheet, the side containing the content descriptions for the four briefing board panels.]

McMahon: This is — yeah — and, I'm not sure about this — this looks like mine, and this looks like mine.

Horne: OK, so the, ah —

McMahon: Ah —

Horne (27:33): *— just for the record, the descriptions of how long it took to make internegatives and prints are Mr. McMahon's writing.*

McMahon (27:54): *This is not mine.*

Horne: OK, Mr. McMahon is now looking at the page, ah, [wherein] the top half says, "at 18 frames per second;" the bottom half [reads] "at 16 frames per second;" and he has just said that —

McMahon: *This is not mine.*

Horne: — that is not his writing.

McMahon: OK, *and, this is not my writing* — and now, that might have been Ben Hunter's writing.

Horne: This next page that is not Mr. McMahon's writing is a page which, in the upper right-hand corner, reads: "Questions from the 8 mm film — how do they know exact frames of first and second shot?" Question —

McMahon: OK, we didn't know — we were told what they thought they were; and this is what we were told they thought they were; and this is what we concluded they were; and this is what we set the photography team [unclear]. Ah [that's the] best I can do for ya.

Gunn (28:57): Do you remember when you prepared the notes that we just examined?

McMahon: Yeah, we were in a briefing room, ah, in building 213 in the Navy Yard. And, it was — we were viewing it there because of the equipment.

Gunn: So they — these were made on the day then that you — [were] processing —

McMahon: Yes, this is when we — these are fairly accurate timing shots — tim — the way that, that it, that we timed it. The 16 frames per second — I, I don't know whether I agree on the 18 — it *might* have been 18 frames per second. *This might have been a further analysis.*

Gunn: Do you know whether somebody else was preparing other notes that you don't recognize, at that time, or were they made later [unclear]?

McMahon: Ah, they, they conform to my best recollection of, of what we wrote on, that's all I know. I don't know why I remembered that.

Horne: By that you mean the yellow, legal-sized paper?

McMahon: Yeah.

Horne (30:66): OK, we would like to show you, ah, four (4) briefing board panels which have survived, and ask you if you recognize the prints. [Pause] Let me go off the record while we figure out how to unload the briefing board panels.

[Off the record briefly while removing the four briefing board panels from the box]

Horne (30:45): OK, we're back on the record, and from the same Flat, 90A, ah, we're looking at the RIF [Record Identification Form], which reads as follows: document ID number 1993.07.21.15:48:04:930600. This is titled, quote, "Briefing Panels Containing Zapruder Photos of Kennedy's Assassination," end quote. The date on this RIF document is 11-23-1963. I'm, I'm handing, ah, Mr., Mr. McMahon Panel I of IV for his examination.

McMahon (31:34): *They've been trimmed out, but that's what we shot.*

Horne: OK, and you say they've been trimmed?

McMahon: Yes.

Horne: But you do recognize these as prints that you made?

McMahon: They've also deteriorated.

Horne: Yes, sir.

McMahon: To the best of my knowledge [unclear].

Horne: We'll, we'll show you each of the four panels [and] ask you if you recognize — the same question for each. This is labeled Panel II.

McMahon: Yup.

Horne: OK, you also recognize these, for the record, as photographs that you — prints that you made?

McMahon: [Witness nodded in the affirmative]

Horne: You're nodding your head [in the affirmative] —

McMahon: Yeah.

Horne: If at any time, you see prints that do not look like prints that you made, please say so. This is Panel III.

McMahon (32:39): There's something missing. I don't know — they — tell me — I don't know, I —

Horne: This is, ah, the final panel, Panel IV.

McMahon (33:03): *Yeah — I did all this.*

Horne: OK, now that you've seen all four panels, ah, do you feel like this represents all of the views that you created, *or do you still feel there is something missing?*

McMahon: *No — there's some missing.*

Horne: OK, as a matter of interest, I might point out that, ah, in the working notes, on the page labeled, ah, "Briefing Panel," it lists 28 different prints — a total of 28. And earlier, you had said that, that somewhere between 20 and 40 —

McMahon: Yes.

Horne: *— and your opinion now is that you still think some that you made are not present?*

McMahon: *Yes. I — yes, I think there's some missing.*

Horne: I know it's a long time ago —

McMahon: No, I'm not [chuckling] —

Horne: Do you recall, do you recall the image content that might be missing, what it might have showed?

McMahon: You mentioned, they went behind the sign and then came out again? I don't think they had all of that sequence there.

Horne: Here's Panel II —

McMahon: Then there was one of the FBI agent jumping up — not the FBI, the bodyguard — jumping up on the back; and then there was one where his head fell down in her lap — that [I] don't see here.

Horne: When you say "his head," you mean the President?

McMahon: The President's head — after the — the one that you showed, the last briefing board that you showed, not this one.

Horne: Yes.

McMahon (34:34): But again, that might have been not used.

Horne: Here's, here's the last one, Panel IV, and the last print on the board shows, ah, Secret Service agent Clint Hill, on the rear of the limousine. It's the only frame that shows him —

McMahon: Yeah, I, I think there ultimately were two agents on the back of the limousine, but that was a — you know, the barn door was — no sense in closing it at that point. Maybe that was their —

Horne: Let's look at Panel I and II. Panel I shows the limousine half behind this road sign — there, there are several road sign shots — and at the end of Panel I the car is coming out from behind the road sign. Does this sequence look like it represents —

McMahon: Yes, that looks —

Horne: OK.

McMahon: —*fairly entire, but I think there were more before the road sign.*

Horne: Before, OK — this frame here, ah, the frame —

McMahon: Maybe they determined that —

Horne: This first frame on Panel I, although the frame is not numbered on the panel, in the working notes it's labeled as frame 188. *Is it your recollection that there may have been other frames prior to 188?*

McMahon: *Yeah — where, where there was some action of some sort.*

Horne (36:17): I see. I'd, I'd like to clarify, ah, for the record — I, I think we've covered it already but just for the sake of those who listen to this tape later — *did you ever see these actual briefing boards* —

McMahon: *No.*

Horne: — the night [of your activity at NPIC]?

McMahon (36:37): *I saw the pictures, the actual pictures; I made the pictures; and I made three (3) each of everything.*

Horne: OK, and did you give them to Mr. Smith when you were finished, or do you recall?

McMahon: Ah, I know that, that Ben Hunter, and if it *was* Smith, whoever it was [chuckling], ah, took them, and had the briefing boards made upstairs, and I might have gone up, but then I didn't stay to, ah, to see the finished product. 'Cause it — they had to take [and] make what they call 'headliners' and text, and, and they might have put classifications on them — I think there was a classification [at] the head [unclear], I'm not positive of that, but —

Horne (37:38): *Do you — in relation to the discussions that were held that night by the workers — by yourself, and Mr. Smith, and Mr. Hunter — do you have any, ah, opinion on what these triangles might mean on the briefing board[s]?* On Panel I there's a red triangle, ah, on the first row; and on the second row there's a blue triangle; there's a blue triangle [on] the second row in Panel II — [Transcriber's note: the small colored triangles, placed between prints on the various briefing boards, seem suggestive of someone's idea of when shots may have struck occupants of the limousine during the assassination; but if so, they seem inconsistent with the three-hit scenario endorsed by "Bill Smith," who couriered the film from "Hawkeyeworks," in Rochester, to NPIC, in Washington, D.C. There are a total of six colored triangles placed on the four briefing board panels, with two triangles *appearing together* at the frame depicting the head explosion.]

McMahon: *I haven't the faintest idea.*

Horne: OK. Do you recall what happened to the internegatives?

McMahon (38:35): *Yeah.* They were given — all of the information, including the scraps, were given to Bill Smith [chuckling].

Horne: I understand.

McMahon: Everything that we did, including scraps, waste, ah, test sheets, was all given back, and nothing, no part of it, was saved.

We didn't even put, put it in classified trash. We, we gave the trash back.

Horne: I see. OK, is there anything about this event that, that we have not, ah, covered yet that, that we should cover? Anything that comes to mind — we've been discussing it now and — for a while — ah, there may be something important that you feel should be covered that we have not asked you about.

McMahon (39:41): Yeah — you know what opinions are. Opinions — everybody has an opinion. And, and yes, I do have — I'm very opinionated, and I have a lot of opinions. And we all have opinions. And I'd just as soon not — I was trying to reflect, this, this was for history, of, of — and I don't want to interject, ah, anything into this that shouldn't be. In other words, I'm trying to be as open and honest at, at telling you what I can remember, and I don't have good remembrance anyway. It's ah — I'm almost 70 years old, maybe; or I'm almost 80 years old; [or] I'm almost 90 years old, I don't know. And, so, that was the best of my knowledge.

Horne (40:55): OK, well, I want to thank you very much for your time, and — I'm sorry, Michelle, before I close, is there anything you would like to ask? You've been taking notes here today —

Combs: I just have one very quick question: Who called you in?

McMahon: *I was not contacted.*

Combs: Were you already in the building? When you all started? Did you come in [unclear]?

McMahon: OK, ah, I think that I was — OK, when I'm contacted, it — from home, it, it, it's by a security officer —

Combs: By the Duty Officer?

McMahon: The Duty Officer, 'cause I probably had to open the lab, turn on the electricity — tricity — and I know it was, it was an all-night affair —

Combs: Do you think the Duty Officer called you at home?

McMahon: I'm pretty sure it would be recorded somewhere in, in the security [records]; and the opening of the vault would be recorded — if they kept those records. Ah —

Combs: OK.

Horne: OK, OK.

McMahon (42:17): These have deteriorated rather badly. Ah, there's dye — tremendous dye loss. You could see the features in the faces, and everything else, much clearer, when they were originally, when I originally made them; so that there's been a tremendous loss of image and quality. Ah, you've lost at least 60% of the, the, ah, the magenta, ah, resin-core coupler; and about 80% of the yellow resin-core; and maybe just 10% of the cyan. So ah, they were — a lot of information is not there. Ah, that's, that was a problem with the old resin-core couplers. They were not stable, even with, ah, proper dye buffing; buffing solutions couldn't stabilize the dyes for 35 years.

Horne: I see.

McMahon: But —

Horne: Well, I thank you very much for sharing your time and your recollections and your opinions with us. And, ah, there have been many things about these notes that were actually, ah, either not understood, or I think misunderstood by many people, including myself. This has been very helpful for the record, thank you very much.

McMahon: OK.

[Off the record — tape recorder turned off briefly]

Horne (44:18): We're back on the record, this is Doug Horne with Mr. McMahon. I, I just found one more, ah, photographic print — it's separate from the briefing boards. Ah, it looks to me like it's 8 by 10, or very close to 8 by 10 — it's bigger than the photos on the briefing boards. It's ah, document ID number 1993.07.22.08:33:27:250600, dated 11-23-63. It's an 8 by 10 color print of a frame from the Zapruder film in-between the road sign and the head shot; and on the back, there's a color crayon marking, "80x" — I'd like to ask Mr. McMahon to explain what this is.

McMahon (44:53): This was made from the 40x internegative, and it was a 2x enlargement, done on a, ah, ah DeVier [spelled phonetically], not a precision enlargement. And it, it, ah, it shows — I'm not sure of the sequence, where it is — but it was made to show what the enlargement would look like, compar — the contact print was of a better quality, because we didn't have a 2x briefing board enlarger set up to do it. We had to do it on a, on a, on a cheaper, Italian DeVier [spelled phonetically] enlarger. If we'd put it on our briefing board enlarger with the liquid gate, we, we, we could have gotten equal quality to resolution and sharpness. But it wasn't available for some reason, so we couldn't use that piece of equipment; and we had to use a lesser, and, they would rather go — it was big enough, and they'd rather go with the sharpness, ah, and the resolution, so it was elected, there was too much loss —

Horne: Too much loss with reproducing the image in the manner it is in this one print?

McMahon: Well, it was, it was, it was not a liquid gate; it was a 2x, ah, conventional enlarger.

Horne: OK —

McMahon: And it —

Horne: — from the internegative?

McMahon: From the original, the, the, ah, the 40x interneg.

Horne: Right.

McMahon: So we elected not to go that way.

Horne: OK, so this would have been a test, made, ah —

McMahon: That was —

Horne: — prior to the prints on the briefing boards, perhaps?

McMahon: Well, we made a contact print, and we made a 2x enlargement —

Horne: I see, I see.

McMahon: — and the contact print was far better in quality, than this.

Horne: OK.

McMahon: But it wouldn't have been if we'd-a-had one of the briefing board enlargers, to make the 2x —

Horne: I see. But you didn't —

McMahon: It was — for some reason it was down, for the copying.

Horne: So this "80x" on the back, [it] looks like colored pencil, is that your writing?

McMahon: Yes, that's my writing.

Horne: OK, there's a, there's a number in the corner, a blue number, it's either a nine (9); or a six (6), upside down; I think it's a nine (9) — looks like a nine (9) — do you recognize that number?

[End of tape — and of interview]

§

About the Author

Jacob Hornberger is the founder and president of The Future of Freedom Foundation, a non-profit educational foundation whose mission is to present the principled case for the libertarian philosophy. Jacob grew up in Laredo, Texas, and received his B.A. degree in economics from Virginia Military Institute and his law degree from the University of Texas. After 12 years as a trial attorney in Texas, he left the practice of law to become program director at The Foundation for Economic Education in Irvington-on-Hudson, New York. Jacob founded FFF in 1989.

Jacob is the author of five books on the Kennedy assassination: *The Kennedy Autopsy; The Kennedy Autopsy 2; Regime Change: The JFK Assassination; The CIA, Terrorism, and the Cold War: The Evil of the National Security State;* and *An Encounter with Evil: The Abraham Zapruder Story*. He also wrote the foreword to *CIA & JFK: The Secret Assassination Files,* by Jefferson Morley, also published by FFF. He is the author of countless articles on the JFK assassination, all of which are posted on FFF 's website.

Jacob's video series entitled "The JFK Assassination" is found in the multimedia section of FFF's website (fff.org). Videos of his presentations on the JFK assassination at FFF's two conferences on the

JFK administration and the JFK assassination can also be found in the multimedia section of FFF's website (fff.org).

Jacob is also a contributor to the following books published by FFF: *The Dangers of Socialized Medicine,* edited by Jacob Hornberger and Richard Ebeling; *The Case for Free Trade and Open Immigration,* edited by Jacob Hornberger and Richard Ebeling; and *The Failure of America's Foreign Wars,* edited by Richard Ebeling and Jacob Hornberger.

He is also the author of a booklet published by FFF entitled *Economic Liberty and the Constitution.*

Jacob wrote the foreword to the following three books published by FFF, all of which were authored by Sheldon Richman: *Separating School & State: How to Liberate America's Families; Your Money or Your Life: Why We Must Abolish the Income Tax;* and *Tethered Citizens; Time to Repeal the Welfare State.*

About The Future of Freedom Foundation

The Future of Freedom Foundation (fff.org) is a non-profit educational foundation whose mission is to present the principled case for the libertarian philosophy. Founded in 1989, FFF fulfills its mission through articles, books, conferences, speeches, and lectures.

FFF has published eight books related to the Kennedy assassination:

— *The Kennedy Autopsy; The Kennedy Autopsy 2; Regime Change: The JFK Assassination; The CIA, Terrorism, and the Cold War: The Evil of the National Security State;* and *An Encounter with Evil: The Abraham Zapruder Story,* all of which were authored by FFF president Jacob Hornberger.

— *JFK's War with the National-Security Establishment: Why Kennedy Was Assassinated,* by Douglas Horne.

— *CIA & JFK: The Secret Assassination Files* and *Morley v. CIA: My Unfinished JFK Investigation,* both of which were authored by Jefferson Morley.

In 2021, FFF hosted an online conference entitled "The National Security State and the Kennedy Assassination," which featured Douglas Horne, Dr. David Mantik, James DiEugenio, Jefferson Morley, John Newman, Dr. Michael Chesser, Dr. Gary Aguilar, Michael Swanson, and Jacob Hornberger. Videos of those presentations can be found in the multimedia section of FFF's website (fff.org).

In 2017, FFF hosted a conference entitled "The National Security State and JFK," which featured Oliver Stone, Jeffrey Sachs, Michael J. Glennon, Stephen Kinzer, Douglas Horne, Michael Swanson, Peter Janney, Jefferson Morley, Jim DiEugenio, Ron Paul, and Jacob Hornberger. Videos of those presentations can be found in the multimedia section of FFF's website (fff.org).

In 2014, FFF published a five-part video series by Douglas Horne entitled "Altered History: Exposing Deceit and Deception in the JFK Assassination Medical Evidence." It can be found in the multimedia section of FFF's website.

For more than 20 years, FFF has published its *FFF Daily,* a daily libertarian commentary page sent to subscribers free of charge. It consists of original articles, Jacob Hornberger's daily blog, and links to libertarian articles in the mainstream press and on the Internet.

Since January 1990, FFF has published its monthly journal *Future of Freedom.* It consists of timeless essays advancing libertarian principles within the context of the burning issues of the day. The subscription price is $25 a year or $15 for the email version.

As a non-profit foundation, The Future of Freedom Foundation relies on donations from our supporters. To become a supporter and help FFF to advance the principled case for individual liberty, free markets, and limited government, please visit the support page of FFF's website (fff.org).

Acknowledgements

Thanks to Mike Swanson for taking the time to read my manuscript and for giving me so many helpful suggestions that improved the quality of my book.

This book would not have been the same without the editorial assistance of Doug Horne. Special thanks to you, Doug, for taking so much time to carefully read my manuscript, note my mistakes, give me your invaluable editorial suggestions, and explain complex issues to me. Thanks also for contributing chapter 17 to the book and for securing the kind permission of Thom Whitehead and Sydney Wilkinson to include the partial transcript of Thom's interview of Paul Rutan, Jr., and Garrett Smith in that chapter. The transcript served to greatly reinforce points I made in my book. Thanks also to Thom Whitehead and Sydney Wilkinson for giving me permission to include it.

"The truth that makes men free is for the most part
the truth which men prefer not to hear."

— Herbert Agar,
A Time for Greatness (1942)

Printed in Great Britain
by Amazon

23386834R00219